The Boys on Cherry Street

*From the Crazy Innocence of College
to the Loss of Innocence in Vietnam*

Ron Boehm

RBoehm Publishing
Houston, Texas
2015

Copyright 2015 © by Ron Boehm

RBoehm Publishing
10104 Spring Place Drive
Houston, TX 77070

Library of Congress # — 2007012345

978-0-9908205-0-5 — Perfect Bound
978-0-9908205-1-2 — MOBI ebook
978-0-9908205-2-9 — ePub ebook

www.BoysOnCherryStreet.com

Production Team
Rita Mills — Project Manager
www.bookconnectiononline.com
Faye Walker — Editing
Martin Vives — Cover Design

Printed in the United States of America

Dedication

*This book is dedicated
to my friends from college
who contributed to such a wonderful time
in my life, to my friends in the military
who served in Vietnam, and to all
the young men of the Vietnam War Era
who answered their country's call.
God bless you all.*

Table of Contents

Acknowledgement and Special Thanks

Pat Reith — My lifelong friend and college roommate for his good memory and great stories about our college life. His storytelling and inspiration is part of the reason I wrote this book.

Malcolm Bech, Tiger Favret and Corky Barris — My buddies for being the subject of many of those college stories.

Col. Jack Rippy — My Marine Corps buddy from flight school, squadron mate in Vietnam and California and source of many of these stories and for his help in editing this book.

Rick Spitz — My friend from A6A training squadron, roommate in Vietnam and lifelong friend who is the subject of many of these stories.

Fred Bonati — My friend from USMC The Basic School, roommate in Vietnam, buddy in California and source of many of these stories.

Dave Anderson, Tom Broderick, Dan DeBlanc, David Noyes and Phil Vannoy — My Marine Corps friends for letting me use some of their stories of Vietnam.

Mike Sommers for his organizing of our Basic School reunions that brought back many of these memories and for his help in editing this book.

Ron Boehm

Foreword

There are many great books about war, the courage, heroics and sacrifice that those who fought in the wars experienced and demonstrated. In this book, it is not my intention to make light of war or the terrible results of war, the tragic deaths and the awful wounds, both external and internal that those who participated in it carry for the rest of their lives. War changes you forever.

But this book starts with the care-free innocence and craziness of my college days and then to the loss of that innocence in going to war as a young Marine pilot in Vietnam. This book, although it has stories about heroes and heroic actions, is mainly about the many comic occurrences and sense of humor that men in combat were able to show in some of the most difficult of situations. I believe it was that very sense of humor that was a coping mechanism used by many of us to deal with those stressful times.

The title of the book The Boys on Cherry Street came from one of the off-campus houses that my roommates and I lived in while attending college in Hammond, Louisiana. We shared a duplex on Cherry Street with another group of friends and did a lot of crazy and outrageous things together. But The Boys on Cherry Street is really symbolic of the young men of the Vietnam war era, my college roommates, my friends from the neighborhood, my classmates in high school and college, and my Marine buddies who flew and fought in Vietnam.

In writing this book, I wanted to share some of the funny and outrageous stories that I experienced in that most wonderful time in my life that made for such good sea stories in barrooms and at parties.

Regarding the authenticity and accuracy of my stories, I make the same disclaimer as Dave Marshall made, a Marine A-4 pilot flying out of Chu Li with MAG 12 in his article, "Chi Li 'War Stories,'" in which he quotes another Marine, Anthony Swofford, author of Jarhead who, when asked whether his book was fact or fiction, responded, "I don't know. It's what I remember."

Ron Boehm

———————

The Boys on Cherry Street

CHAPTER 1

College

College

In June of 1961, a boyfriend of my big sister Maggie came to pick me up from my home in the Lakeview neighborhood of New Orleans to take me for a visit to a small college in southeast Louisiana. He was a star baseball player there, and I had just graduated from Holy Cross High School in New Orleans at which I was a very average baseball player. However, my whole life had revolved around baseball and I just wanted to continue doing what I loved. I was a little guy, five feet, six inches, 135 pounds, with a lot of hustle and drive. That was the start of one of the greatest and most fun times in my life.

In looking back, I remember that one day in my senior year of high school I had determined I was going to college. My family was blue collar, my dad and uncles worked on the railroad, and no one from my family had ever been to college. I recall telling my dad that I was going to college, and he said, "That's great, but how do you intend to pay for it?" since I was one of nine children and the son of a railroad worker who had completed only the eighth grade.

I said, "I don't know just yet, but I'll figure it out."

It didn't dawn on me that I might not be able to do it. When you are young, you just don't know about limitations. I ended up working that summer and saving all that I could, going to politicians and asking for grants to get enough money for the first semester. Now that I look back on it, I don't think that the politicians actually gave me grants but just wrote me checks out of their own pockets.

My second semester, having made a good grade average, I applied for a National Defense Loan. At this small college at that time, the tuition, books rental, room and meal ticket was only about four hundred dollars, if I remember right.

So on that day I drove with my sister's friend, Frank Misuraca, to Southeastern Louisiana College in Hammond, Louisiana, to check it out. I didn't know anybody going there other than Frank and on the way he told me all about the school and the baseball team. He told me about the championships they had won and I don't remember if he told me much about the academics. I didn't know much about college, other than I was going to go to one and this one had a baseball team that I had a chance to play on.

When we got there, I was impressed; it was like a big high school. I had gone to an all-boy's Catholic high school and my graduation class had only about 120 students. This small college had a total enrollment of about thirty-seven hundred at that time. It was in the country surrounded by pine trees, and a railroad track went right through the middle of town and on both sides of the track was a street with shops, restaurants, the train station with a diner called the Beanery and bars. I loved the small town atmosphere and I immediately felt at home.

Most of my friends from New Orleans who were going to college were going to go to Louisiana State University, but they had parents who were going to pay for it. As it turned out, I had a bunch of friends who went to SLC and most of them paid for their own education or paid for a large part of it.

I remember my first day standing in line for registration. I was standing next to another guy from New Orleans who was to become my roommate, my teammate and a very good friend. His name was Corky Barras, and he was one of the funniest people I have ever met. We spent a lot of time sitting on the bench together for the first two years and he was also one of the premier bench jockeys in the conference. Some of the crap he, Pete Freeman, and Joe Thomas would come up with drove the opposing teams nuts and me into hysterics.

Coach Pat Kennelly once told Corky that he had coached a lot of teams, but "You guys are the toughest bench jockeys on the other team that I've ever seen. Corky, you could give the Pope the red ass."

Years later, when I was talking to my friend Bubby Winters who was a pitcher on that team, he recalled one time not being able to pitch to Corky, who was the catcher, because every time he looked at Corky's grinning face through his catcher's mask Bubby would start laughing to the point he couldn't pitch. The coach had to come out to the mound to calm him down.

Getting back to registration day, Corky and another soon-to-be-friend, Tom Bruno, who was also from New Orleans, asked me what I was going to major in.

I said, "Major, what do you mean?"

They said, "You know, your main subject."

I had never heard of that term before and obviously had never considered it, so I said, trying not to sound dumb, "I'm not sure. What are you guys going to major in?"

"Man, B.A., Business Administration is the thing, that's what we are signing up for."

"Yeah, I was leaning that way too," I said. "So I guess I'll go with you guys."

Then they said, "What courses do you have scheduled?"

"Well, whatever you guys have will be OK for me."

I never had that kind of stuff in high school; they just told you where to go. So here I was signing up for a curriculum that I didn't have the slightest idea about. But business is what we were all going to do sooner or later, so why not.

Here I was "in college," the first of my family to do so and I felt excited in anticipating a new adventure and a new life. However, I also had felt like that before and many times thereafter, like I was over my head and not ready for this. Later, when flying in the Marine Corps, we pilots had a term for it, "behind the power curve," which meant that you were about to crash. I have always had this thing about pushing myself past my level of comfort and not knowing how I was going to handle a particular circumstance or accomplish what I was about to do. But I would end up doing it someway, somehow.

When I was in kindergarten and supposed to go to school with my older brother and sister, I'd get impatient and take off on my bike, crossing a boulevard and going about a mile by myself. My younger sisters, on the other hand, would have to be taken to school two blocks away by my mother. My taking off all by myself scared my mother to death, but I thought it was OK; I knew my way.

When I was in Little League, my dad took me the first day; then after that I rode my bike to practices and to games. And when I was about twelve years old I had a paper route. I hated Sunday mornings, because we had to get up at 5:00 AM and ride our bikes in the dark to throw our papers and finish up just after daybreak.

I remember a friend of mine Freddie Rapp and I would hunt for little turtles in the City Park, and then sell them for twenty-five cents to a pet store. One summer we made about forty dollars, big money for two twelve year olds. We also got caught by the police several times. When they caught us, they would confiscate our fishing nets, put our bikes in the trunk and take us to our homes. Thank God my dad wasn't home, because I'd be in big trouble.

However, my mom, who was one of the sweetest and shyest people in the world, would be too embarrassed to come to the door, so she would send one of my sisters to meet the police. She would cover for me with my dad, who didn't put up with any crap. My mom's idea of discipline was to threaten us with a floppy terrycloth slipper that she would wave back and forth like she was going to spank us with it, but she never did. What a beautiful person she was. Marine DI she was not. My sisters would complain about my getting off so easy much of the time and she would remind them, "Ronnie made 'A's in religion." You can imagine how well that went over with my siblings.

So I was again on my own, signing up for college and not knowing what I was really doing, just going with the flow and figuring it out as I went along.

I loved college from the very first day. I was on my own, paying for college by myself and not having to answer to anyone but myself. I don't remember ever asking for much advice from my parents because they didn't know much about college either. I just made up my mind what I wanted to do regarding college and did it. To my mom's credit I thought she just trusted in me. However, it could have been that being a mom of nine children, she didn't have much time to think about it. To my dad's credit, he just expected I would handle it, because he was that kind of a person himself. He was to me the epitome of self-reliance, confidence and strength. Of course, no one would have mistaken him for a psychologist either. It was his way. Period. He was a very confident and self-reliant man, but he never really shared his inner feelings with his children.

The first day of classes was great; however, I was a little bit lost. I thought it was neat that you didn't attend classes all day, going from one class to the next like in high school. You could hang out in the student union and meet people, play cards, or study until your next class then go have a beer afterwards. The prime spot or bar was the Brown Door, and since in Louisiana you could drink at eighteen years old in those days, that was definitely on my list of places to go. One thing that was very different was the fact that there were girls in my classes. I had gone to an all-boys Catholic high school and having girls in class for the first time since grade school was a bit distracting at first, but nice.

There was an excitement in the air and in me. It was all great, that is until test and term papers came around. But even test time was a whole new thing. The guys I hung out with in Business Administration would get together and study, or later on, spend most of their time "looking for the help." Which meant they heard that someone had stolen the test or had last semester's test. It really amazed me, because that went on for five years. If they would have spent that much time studying instead of looking for the test or trying to break into the teacher's office, they would have all been on the dean's list. Let me clarify that, the dean's academic excellence list. A lot of us were on the dean's list, but that was more like the "most wanted list." Actually, several of the guys were very smart and made straight "As."

One of my roommates, Ronnie Ratelat, had a great memory and just picked up everything in class. Hell, I never could focus long enough in most classes to pay that close of attention. If there was Ritalin back in those days I would have been a candidate. It was either that or I was too busy taking notes to listen and grasp what was being said by the instructor. Ronnie would start studying, get bored and go have a few beers. We would find him passed out with a book on his chest, and the next day he'd ace the test. I'd study for hours and get "Bs" and "Cs" and now and then an "A."

Three of our gang were straight "A" students; the rest of us were pretty good students. We mostly lived together from the second year on for the whole four or five years. Most of us were paying our own way through school or paying part of our way, so even though we had a ball, we made sure we made passing grades.

None of us had much money, but we could always find enough for beer or partying. Where there is a will there is a way.

I don't want to get ahead of myself, so let me get back to the beginning of my college career. It was September of 1961 at Southeastern Louisiana College in Hammond, Louisiana. I got acclimated to college life pretty fast. I was living in the one of the freshmen dorms and my roommate and I were at opposite ends of the spectrum. He was quiet, studious, smart, and very different from the people that I hung out with. But then, the people from New Orleans were a little different from the rest of the state anyway. We had a Brooklyn kind of accent with a southern drawl, the people in southwest Louisiana had a Cajun French accent and the rest of the state had a southern accent like Mississippi or Arkansas.

New Orleans was the biggest city in the state, with Baton Rouge, the capital, second biggest, and the rest of the towns were really big or small. But off course, Baton Rouge had LSU and the best looking girls in the state.

Anyway, back to my roommate: we were not on the same wavelength, and I hung out with the other guys in our suite. Four rooms all shared a bathroom in the center. To my pleasant surprise, Corky and Tom were my suitemates. Through them I met Danny Gleason, Billy Jewett, Jimmy Ames, Ronnie and a bunch of other guys from public schools in New Orleans. Their public school education was different from my catholic school education. But I knew most of them from the neighborhood or going to the same places in

New Orleans. That was the beginning of our group. We had a great deal in common, being from the same area in New Orleans, putting ourselves through college and barely making ends meet. We were out to have a great time whenever we could, had very creative minds when it came to having fun and last of all, we were going to stay in school.

Corky became one of my best friends and we were both going out for the baseball team. Tom, Jimmy and Ronnie were very smart and Tom was a wiz in accounting. I didn't have a clue about anything having to do with accounting, so I was always asking Tom for help. I hated accounting and changed my major to Industrial Technology the second semester mainly because of accounting and typing.

In typing class I was doing about thirty words a minute and the girl next to me was doing about two hundred it seemed. I was cursing more than I was typing. My baseball hands with my fingers shaped into slight claw-like digits just didn't want to move fast enough over the typewriter keys, hence my frustration.

The rest of my first semester went along pretty good. I made OK grades and met some great people. Going to class with girls took a bit of getting used to because I found myself looking at them more than the professor. And after class there were all kinds of neat things to do: night beach parties down on the river, football games, drinking and partying at the Brown Door. Like I said, the Brown Door was the main hang-out bar for the college kids in Hammond. You could go there at night and party or during lunch time and bet the horses running at Fairgrounds in New Orleans, or just catch a few beers and a roast beef po-boy after classes.

The real partying for football was going to the games at LSU. My friend Danny Smith was there and would set me up with a date for the football games. The parting started about 4:00 PM on Saturday after everybody got out of classes and the game got started at 7:30 Saturday night. The party continued after the football game until the girls had to be back in their dorms at midnight. On one occasion my date got a little too drunk and missed curfew by a bit.

The doors were closed so we drove to the back of the dorm, stood on the roof of my friend's car and stuffed her through her dorm window with the help of her roommate.

—•◦•—

Tiger Favret

Tiger Favret was my friend from Holy Cross High School. He was a year older than I, and his brother Bob and I were classmates in high school. Tiger had been to several colleges and finally ended up at Southeastern with the rest of us. Bob went to LSU.

One time we were partying before and after the game, drinking Bob's roommate's homemade blackberry wine. I got a little carried away and dove off the second floor balcony into the swimming pool while in my jockey shorts. I was lucky I didn't break my neck because I scraped the bottom of the pool. When I came up from the bottom, the student monitor, who was an all American football player at LSU grabbed me and pulled me out of the pool. I think I shoved him or something else that really pissed him off. So as he was about to hammer the hell out my little five foot six body, my good big friend (six three, 230 pounds) Tiger Favret came up. Tiger happened to know the guy and saved my ass. For that matter, Tiger saved me a number of times while we were in college. If you are a little guy, it always helps to have a big friend. And I introduced him to his wife Linda Haney. Actually, I had a crush on her from the first time I met her, but when Tiger showed an interest in her, I just kept it to myself.

Tiger was my real buddy in college and we had some great times together. If you had ever met him you never forgot him. Seemed like everybody knew Tiger and Tiger knew everybody. It didn't matter where we went, somebody would always know Tiger.

He was a piece of work. His given name was Lionel. I guess it was a cat thing, Lion-el, Tiger. He was already balding in college and looked about thirty-five; however, at fifty-five, he still looked the same. He was big and smart, from a well-off family, very confident and cocky. He also had the record, I think, for the most number of colleges attended. I think it was like four or five. Tiger could also drink more than anybody I knew. And me being half his size, I'd get hammered trying to keep up with him.

I rode back and forth to college, from New Orleans to Hammond, about an hour's drive just about every weekend with Tiger in his Chevy Corvair. Towards the end of the week I'd be broke and borrow five dollars from Tiger, then pay him back the next Sunday, and then just borrow it again at the end of the week. This went on week after week until finally Tiger said, "Ronnie, keep the five dollars."

We used to go to this dirt road bar down the street from the Brown Door called Toulouse. Believe me it had no commonality with the famous artist. It had sawdust on the floor, a back room where the local farmers and college students played a card game called "Bourre" or "Booray." Booray was a south Louisiana card game like spades and poker combined where you tried to take the most tricks in a hand and thereby win the pot or avoid taking no tricks and match the pot. It's a killer: you could be winning all night and then in one hand you would have to match the pot and get wiped out.

Emmett the bartender was a character also and a little naïve. Some of the guys would take advantage of him.

Tiger and I were drinking Jack Daniel's black straight out of the bottle like the cowboys did. We were feeling our oats and he said that I could have the first punch to see if I could knock him off the bar stool, so I hit him hard, as hard as a guy five six and 135 pounds could, but I barely moved him.

Then he said, "OK, now it's my turn." Oh shit! I thought, this isn't good, but if you are going to play cowboys, then you've got to man up. So he hit me—hard—and knocked me off the stool.

I got up and said, "OK, it's my turn." Well after about three times, I knew that I couldn't knock him off and that soon I wasn't going to be able to get up.

As we were walking out side by side, he put his arm around my shoulders and he knew that pissed me off. You know like, "Come here little buddy." I don't remember exactly how it happened, but a confrontation ensued and I hit him with one of those sidewalk chalkboard signs. Well, that pissed him off and he chased me all over. I ran down the street to the Brown Door and saw Linda, his future wife, and hid under her table. He came in looking for me and said that if he found me he was going to kick my little ass all over the place. I took that threat very seriously and stayed under the table until he left.

Linda was a very nice and pretty girl who had a very nice and pretty Corvette. Tiger and I borrowed it one time and drove it up to Baton Rouge to party with our buddies and his brother Bob at LSU. By the time we had finished partying and started back to Hammond forty miles down the road, the weather had gotten very foggy, to the point that we couldn't see the edge to the road even though we were only driving about ten miles per hour. So I got out and sat on the right front fender and guided Tiger with hand signals following the edge of the highway all the way back to Hammond. It kind of goes with the saying that God protects drunks and idiots I guess.

Tiger had a neat car also. It was a 1961 Corvair, the car Ralph Nader made famous in his 1965 book Unsafe at any Speed. It had an air-cooled flat six-cylinder rear engine and a trunk in the front. We would put a case of beer in the front trunk and ice them down for the beach parties at the bridge on the Tickfaw River. It was like a giant ice cooler. We would cruise to Baton Rouge, New Orleans or on our way back to school with a beer and a long slender Marsh & Wheeling cigar. It was all so cool. I really loved Tiger; he was great and I knew if I was with him nobody was going to kick my ass too bad.

I looked up to him and admired his confidence. He had natural leadership qualities, which in my mind, were only rivaled by my other older and good friend Malcolm Bech.

Malcolm Bech

Malcolm was a few years older than I was, from the same neighborhood in New Orleans and had gone to school with my older brother and sister. He was a legend to us younger guys. We had heard stories of his fighting prowess and that he had never been beaten in a fight. He wasn't mean and didn't look to start fights—that would describe his little brother Bruce. Bruce was one fighting son of a gun. He was a nice guy until you messed with him. I think the only one that could beat Bruce was Malcolm, but Mal wouldn't mess with Bruce because as Mal said, "If you beat Bruce, you have to keep fighting him until he finally beats you." He never gave up and when Bruce got mad he would try to kill you.

Malcolm was almost what we called a "professional student." He had been in college there for a long time. But that was because he was working his way through school. He was also tall, great looking and a very good athlete. He probably could have been a great college wide receiver, but Mal didn't take any shit from anybody and that included the football coach who he didn't have any respect for. He had gone to SLC on a track scholarship and was a championship javelin thrower. He had held the javelin record for this division level school until Terry Bradshaw of Louisiana Tech broke it several years later.

Mal didn't date much, but when he did, it was the best looking girl on campus. He later married the school's beauty queen, Jenna Hebert, had a bunch of kids, two of whom played football for LSU, and one for the New Orleans Saints.

I had great respect for Malcolm. I was proud to have him as a friend and we are still good friends. He also had that special leadership quality. Later, when I became a Marine Officer, I understood what those qualities were all about. We became roommates later in my second year and he was part of our gang or band of "merry men."

At one time, Mal and his friend Big George lived in a tent on a friend's farm. Malcolm drove a Triumph Tiger motorcycle to class which I thought was very cool. He didn't go in for too much silliness, unless we got him drunk which wasn't often. Another roommate of mine, Pat Reith was an instigator and would egg Malcolm on to do mischief. Pat would tell me that Malcolm was an Indian, and if we got him drunk he would go crazy and do wild things. I told Pat, that if that was so, we had better not get him drunk. But Pat said that it was more fun that way. I think Mal liked our craziness and enjoyed laughing at us, but I don't think he was an Indian.

Malcolm Bech

Living Off Campus on Magnolia Street

As I mentioned, my first year I lived in the men's freshmen dorm and in the Stadium Athletic Dorm. The second year, I moved off campus to a house on Magnolia Street with Pat Rieth who I had known since first grade and Malcolm Bech who I knew from the neighborhood in New Orleans. It was then that I met our other roommates: Ronnie Radelat, otherwise known as "Rattle-trap"; Jerry LeBlanc, "Seagull"; and Ricky Davidson, "Ricky, Dicky

Doo," all from the New Orleans area. There were two other guys who were like our roommates, because they hung out with us and ate with us often. They were Hans Neilsen, "Fingers," and Jimmy DeMoss, "Demis." We would pretty much stay together for the rest of our time at SLC, with the exception of Ricky Davidson, who thought rightfully that we were too crazy and moved out.

Jerry LeBlanc "Seagull"

Jerry LeBlanc, "Seagull" or just "The Gull" got his name while on Spring Break in Panama City, Florida. He was drunk, passed out, lying on the beach, all wet when Malcolm saw him and said he looked like a dead seagull that had washed up on the sand. The name stuck.

The group trekked to Florida for Spring Break in Pat's 1957 green airport limousine. It had eight doors and a big luggage rack on the roof. They had just cruised into town with a keg of beer on the roof when the cops stopped them. By the time my teammate Lamar and I got there after we finished our baseball game, they had already left to go back home. They went before the judge who asked each one how much money they had and fined each one accordingly leaving them just enough to get home.

In Hammond we lived in a two story four-plex house about a block from campus which was next to another four-plex that had some equally crazy guys living in it. Sam and Everett were our next door neighbors and between us we had some crazy parties held in the area between our houses and in the houses. This is when the insanity started at our rented house on Magnolia Street.

In our house, all of the guys were hunters. We all had shot guns, rifles and even bows and arrows. Our freezer always had some type of wild game in it such as ducks, fish, squirrels, quails, rabbits or some other game. We tried to arrange our class schedules during duck hunting season the best we could so as not to interfere with morning or evening hunting down in the Manchac swamp. Manchac was a big swamp on the west side of Lake Pontchartrain in between New Orleans and Hammond.

It was a great duck hunting area: teals in the early season, mallards and wood ducks in the winter.

We also hunted down below New Orleans towards the mouth of the Mississippi River where the river branches off into several gulf outlets. On some of our duck hunting trips down the river we would shine nutria at night, shoot them and sell them at the dock the next day for about one dollar apiece. This would pay for our hunting trip.

The nutria looks like a big rat or small beaver with webbed hind feet and big orange beaver like teeth. They are aquatic animals that eat vegetation and were introduced into Louisiana when they escaped from a fur farm in Louisiana in the 1930s. They multiplied greatly and became a nuisance, destroying vegetation and eroding levees. A couple of the guys found a nutria nest and got two baby nutrias from it. They were so small that both of them could fit in your shirt pocket. One of the tiny babies fell off the bar in Venice, Louisiana, and died; however, the other one was brought back to our house and became our pet. He grew into about a twelve pound rodent. We named him Moogins and he looked like a brown beaver with big webbed hind feet, big orange cutting teeth and a rat's tail. Dogs wouldn't even mess with him. He was a great pet and would climb up in the bed with Pat and sleep under his arm. One problem was we couldn't house break him, and he left nutria droppings all over the house. We would feed him heads of lettuce, which he would eat sitting on his hind quarters. He'd pull off one leaf at a time and rotate it in his little hands and eat the leaf around the edge in a circular fashion. He would also sit on your foot and pull on your pants leg, show those big orange teeth and beg for food, while making his little nutria sounds.

Each one of us would take turns taking Moogins to our homes back in New Orleans whenever we all left for the weekend. I took him home to my parent's house one weekend in a box while he was still little. My sisters were frightened of him and my dad was not too pleased with having a rat in the house.

One time, we decided that we would leave him in the off-campus house up at school while we all went home. We left him three heads of lettuce to eat; nutrias got their water from the vegetation they ate, and locked him in the bathroom. When we got back we found that he had eaten all the lettuce, eaten through the bathroom door, through the bedroom door and the kitchen door leading outside. To our dismay, we also learned that our elderly landlady had gone in the house to check on us and almost had a heart attack when she saw a twelve pound rat-looking creature run across the room.

Moogins died when he fell off the up-stairs balcony at one of our parties and he burst a gut hitting the ground. Poor Moogins, he was about fifteen pounds when he died.

On one of our early morning duck hunting trips in the Manchac swamp, we set out before sunrise in a couple groups of two in pirogues (a small flat bottom skiff-like boat pointed at both ends seating one or two people, common in south Louisiana) to a couple of different ponds. I was paired up with Ricky and we went as far as we could in the boat then waded through the swamp in the dark night to the pond. I went to one end and Ricky went further down to the other site.

I have to give you a little background on Ricky. He had poor eyesight, wore thick eyeglasses and I don't think he had a lot of hunting experience. So there we were just before dawn in our hunting positions waiting for the sunrise and the ducks to start flying. All of a sudden I heard three shotgun blasts ring out "bang! bang! bang!" and someone shouted, "You son-of-a-bitch, you shot my decoys!" Evidently, Ricky didn't want to wait for the sun to rise or to do the sporting thing of shooting the ducks in flight. He saw all these ducks on the pond and opened up on them. I think he sank a couple of them, much to the displeasure of the others hunters who had set out their decoys to attract ducks, not near-sighted hunters.

Friday Keg Parties

Alot of times we would have a keg of beer on a Friday afternoon after classes got over. Sam and Everett were our co-hosts usually. We would bring down chairs to the common area between the houses and have our party. One time Everett shouted up to Sam, who also lived on the second floor, to bring down something to sit on. All of a sudden the window opened and a couch came tumbling out the upstairs window. These parties got nuts and led to some crazy things, including a naked run down to and around the girl's dormitory. Shoes were allowed.

As I said, all the guys had guns in the house, and Jerry had his "long-tong" ten-gauge shotgun. I don't remember the circumstances leading up to the event, but I'm sure drinking was involved. It ended up with someone shooting out Sam and Everett's window and they then returned the favor by storming our house, kicking open our door and shooting up the ceiling in our house while wearing cowboy boots, gun belts, hats, jockey shorts and nothing else.

Another time we wrapped Jerry up in a blanket and threw him through their window. We had broken out and replaced the windows so many times that we had written on most of the window sills the dimensions for easier replacement.

Another time someone noticed a squirrel up in the tree next to our house and we shot it out of the window. As I said, wild game was part of our diet and food budget. One of our neighbors heard the shot and called the cops on us. When they showed up we had hidden the gun and they wanted to search the house. We told them that they could have at it, but we were in the process of eating dinner and sat at the table and ate our dinner. They looked around a bit and left.

It was probably the people who lived behind us who called the cops on us with whom we had some differences from time to time. One of the parties was a crawfish party that had started outside but moved inside. We had the keg of beer and a wash tub full of crawfish in the living room. It was before there was much air conditioning and most of the old homes had window fans. Well, as we were eating the crawfish and discarding the shells, someone decided to get rid of the shells by throwing them out through the window fan. We all followed suit and the next day the side of the neighbor's white house was covered with red crawfish shells and the yellow fat. It was not a pretty sight. It looked awful. We got in trouble for that also, and that might have been the final straw, because we got thrown out of the house on Magnolia Street by our landlady. She was quite justified in evicting us.

Dave Thomas

Another one of our zany cast of characters was a tall lanky guy from the New Orleans area named Dave Thomas. Dave was truly a funny guy and would do anything to make people laugh. He would go to the cafeteria at lunch or dinner time when it was busy as hell and in the act of opening the door, he would kick the bottom of the door and then grab his head like he had hit his head on the door. Of course everybody in the place would turn to look and he would stumble into the cafeteria holding his forehead and everybody who didn't know Dave would think, "What a clumsy ass." As I said, Dave would do anything for a laugh.

But my favorite Dave Thomas memory was when we had a double date to the Saenger Theater in downtown New Orleans. Back then, if you wanted to make it a special date to the movies you would go downtown to one of big theaters, the Loews or the Saenger, not to a local neighborhood movie. The Saenger was really nice; it looked more like an opera house then a movie theater. It had statues on the walls, elaborate architectural designs and thick carpet on the lobby floors and on the stairs. So there we were with our two dates and me wanting to impress mine since it was our first date together. As we walked out of the upstairs lobby and started down the stairs Dave trips, grabs for the banister, rolls down a few stairs, bounces up holding his elbow and knee with a look on his face like "How did that happen." I had just told him five minutes before not to do any dumb Dave stuff that night. The girls were all concerned and saying, "Dave, are you OK?" He was acting all embarrassed and mildly sore, and I knew he had just pulled another Dave stunt. He did many more, but those were the ones that come to mind.

Our Magnolia Street apartment was also where I had my first sexual experience in college other than in the back seat of a car. There was an older lady, about thirty or so (I know, but I was just nineteen at the time) who lived below us in the house. She took a fancy to me and taught me a lot. When you are a nineteen-year old guy a thirty-year old woman was fantasy land. In the middle of the night, she would knock on the ceiling, which was a sign she wanted me to come down for "fun and games." Man, it got so I was spending a lot of time down in her apartment and both my grade average and my baseball batting average went down.

My roommates were jealous and Ronnie wanted me to let him pretend that he was me, go down there in the dark and get some of that. He said that if she left the lights off, which she usually did, she wouldn't know the difference. I wasn't about to ruin a good thing, even if my grades and batting average had to suffer.

Ron Boehm

Cherry Street and Alac's Place

When we got kicked out of Magnolia Street, we split up for the rest of the semester. I moved in with Corky, Tom, Danny, Billy and Jimmy in their place on Cherry Street. Pat, Ronnie, Jerry and Malcolm went somewhere else for the rest of the semester. Then the next semester we got back together; Pat, Ronnie, Seagull and I moved out into the country in one of three houses that farmers Sam and Kelly Alac had moved to their land outside of town.

When we moved to Alacs' place in my third year of college, we lived in the middle house of the three. The Alacs had bought the three houses that were in the right-of-way of the new highway 55 being constructed and had moved them onto their land just outside of Hammond. The brothers spoke with a broken English Cajun accent; I don't know what their native origin was but it seems they had come to Hammond from Simmesport, Louisiana, up the Mississippi River from Baton Rouge. Alac told us that his daughter was a telephone "mopa-rater in Simpoot."

To the left side of us were some guys who were into parachuting. A couple of times we saw them jump out of a plane and parachute into the back yard which was a field. I swear one time I saw this guy parachute into the back yard with his school books under his arm. But you know how your memories play tricks on you after all that time. We didn't have much contact with them and just kind of waved to them as we saw each other.

On the other side of us lived two English majors, Frank and Phillip. They were OK guys, but very different from our group and we messed with them quite often it seemed. Phillip was thought to be a pyromaniac who was kicked out of the dorm for setting the trash cans on fire. Frank was a smart guy and mild-mannered.

One time they had dates over at their house for dinner and we came up with the bright idea of launching an Indian attack on their house. We got our bows and arrows out, wrapped rags around the arrow heads, dipped them into kerosene, got into Hans' Karmann Ghia and DeMoss' convertible and drove around their house like the Indians did to the wagon trains. We had head bands with feathers and war paint all the while giving the ol' Indian war whoop. As we drove by the front of the house we shot several flaming arrows into their front door. We were jumping up and down shouting our war whoop when Frank and Phillip came running out. Frank was pulling the flaming arrows out of the door and Phillip was in a trance-like state, rocking side to side looking at the fire, telling Frank to let it burn. Frank pulled them out and stepped on the flames and said some choice words to us. What a bunch of assholes we were.

Another time at our Friday evening beer time, we were shooting Seagull's 10 gauge "long-tong" shotgun at the fast moving chimney swifts as they darted about catching insects. Frank and Phillip were tossing a football back and forth and just as Frank threw the football to Phillip, Seagull shouted "Pull" and Ronnie shot the football out of the air. It came down like a dead duck with a bunch of pellet holes in it. Who said guns and alcohol don't mix.

Well that really pissed Frank and Phillip off and they got back at us over the weekend when we went home to New Orleans by throwing a brick through our window. I guess we deserved it. Window replacement was a common activity with us.

The evening time beer and shotgun thing continued on, especially at our Friday evening keg parties. We would all take turns trying to shoot the chimney swifts, which were very hard to hit. Drinking didn't help your accuracy any, that's for sure. When we got tired of that, we came up with a new idea involving the bow and arrows. We would all stand in a tight group with the bow shooter in the center; he would shoot a hunting arrow straight up into the air. We would all watch as the arrow went out of sight and wait for it to reach its apex and come back into sight heading downward. As soon as we saw the arrow we would run like hell away from the falling

Ron Boehm

arrow. It was kind of like Russian roulette or maybe Indian roulette would be a better fit.

Most of the time the arrows would go off course or be blown off course and land away from us or in the roof of one of the houses. At one point the roof looked like a porcupine with all the arrows sticking up. That didn't make the landlord very happy. He told us, "What's a matter with you boys, you shoota arrows in my roof, you breaka my door? You boys from New Orleans are crazy."

Someone, maybe it was DeMoss, got a baby yellow chick for Easter and he became our next pet. We called him Peep, because that is what he did, peeped all the time. We kept him in a box mainly, but once we had put him in the dirty clothes bin as a convenient enclosure. But to his misfortune, we forgot about him and someone threw some dirty clothes on top of him and he suffocated.

We were saddened by this and felt that we had to do something for Peep, so we decided to have a funeral for him. We didn't have a church service and a procession of cars, but rather we had a military type service with armed guards and pallbearers. The armed guards all had shot guns or rifles, someone may have had a bow and arrow, followed the two pallbearers who held a pillowcase by the corners on which they carried Peep all the while stepping to Rufus Thomas' song "Walking the Dog" being played on the record player.

The ceremony's culmination was a twenty-one gun salute aimed at Frank and Phillip's roof. Of course, we followed that with an Irish wake that included more drinking. Peep would have been proud if he could have seen his funeral, himself buried with military honors.

It seemed like guns were a big part of our activities and we used to sit on the couch in our living room and shoot at mice in our kitchen with our 22 rifle. It wasn't exactly big game hunting, but it kept the mice population down.

We also had a naked run (tennis shoes permitted) down to the highway and back. I have no idea who came up with these crazy ideas, but they just seemed to come up in the middle of drinking and with general agreement that they were good ideas at the time.

During one of the keg events we were all partying and talking when we heard Ratelat shout from up on the roof. We looked up and there he was totally naked on top of the roof waving his arms and dancing around. That was not a pretty sight.

The landlord told us with his heavy accent, "You boys from New Orleans, you'll must be smoking the stuff that make you crazy; you breaka my refigarator, you shoot arrows in my roof, you shoota my mule" (Jerry shot at the mule with a BB gun) "and you got Sleepin Jesus drunk. You boys got to go."

Sleeping Jesus was this old black man who did odd jobs for the landlord and would clean up around the rent houses. One time he came by to clean up Saturday morning after one of our parties and we had some beer left in the keg, so we told him that he could have it. He hadn't had any alcohol to drink in years and got drunk to the point the landlord found him passed out at our house. I have no idea where he got the name "Sleeping Jesus."

So ended our stay at the house in the country; I still feel bad to this day because we were not good tenants and caused damage with all our drunken parties. From there we moved back to Cherry Street next to Corky's crew. This is where the book's title came from. It was where this crazy group from New Orleans got together.

Corky's parents owned a drug store in Metairie, Louisiana which was a part of greater New Orleans. We would drop off Corky there and he would invite us in. When his mother wasn't around he'd open up a big jar of barbiturates and tell us to grab a hand full to "study with" back at school.

The house on Cherry Street was very convenient, in walking distance to the bars downtown and about five minutes from school. It was a duplex with their crew on one side and our crew on the other.

Gas Balloons

It was there that we came up with idea of gas balloons. I don't know who came up with the idea, but one of my pyrotechnically inclined buddies thought it would be a brilliant idea to fill balloons with natural gas send them aloft and ignite them with dynamite fuse. We developed a method of making the balloons out of the polyurethane bags that clothes came in from the cleaners. We would tape the top closed and fill them with natural gas from the gas line when we disconnected the bathroom heater. We would then tape the bottom closed and attach dynamite fuse to it, light the fuse and send it aloft. You could light up an entire city block when it ignited. Wow! It was an awesome spectacle. But it only ignited about fifty percent of the time. You had to burn through the plastic bag and get an oxygen and gas mixture to get ignition.

We had some interesting adventures with the gas balloons. Once we made a small test balloon and it went off in the house and made a nasty burn spot in the ceiling. Another time we let one go in front of our house and the wind took it into a big oak tree; it burnt the tree down and the fire department was called to put out the fire. We told them that a power line caused it. They mentioned that it was a telephone line and not a power line.

Another time we sent a big balloon aloft, it went off and made a huge fire in the sky. Someone told us that people called the police department and reported a UFO.

But our greatest balloon feat had to be at our homecoming game that year. We made a big balloon and two small test ones. The big balloon was as big around as your circled arms and about three feet high. We decorated it with green and gold crepe paper for our school's colors. Hans, who we called "Fingers" for short, and I were chosen for the job of taking the balloons to the football game and getting them to float right down the middle of the field at half time and ignite.

We were chosen for the job because we were the only ones who didn't have dates for the game. We loaded the two balloons in to Hans' Volkswagen Karmann Ghia and headed to the football stadium. Damn, we were such dumb-asses; if the balloons had gone off in that car, there wouldn't be a trace of us left.

We had the two small test balloons to check the wind direction and speed to find the right spot to launch them so that they would track down the middle of the football field. We timed the test balloons' flight to determine how long it would take to reach the middle of the field and then cut the dynamite fuse to the proper length. If I remember right, dynamite fuse burnt at a rate of three feet per minute. To get a better chance of ignition, we also taped match heads at the end of the fuse and cut the fuse end on a slant to get a longer spit of fire.

We launched the first test balloon but it was way off, the wind taking it way off course. So we moved to a new spot behind the administration building which was directly north of the football field. We then sent the second one aloft and this time the test balloon went straight to the end zone. We timed it to when it made its way to about the thirty yard line and cut the fuse for the big one. We lit the fuse and let it go. It floated right to the end zone and down the middle of the football field with the green and gold crepe paper ribbons waving in the breeze and everyone watching it and saying, "What the hell is that?" The fuse burned down to the balloon at about the thirty yard line, but to our disappointment, and probably in everyone's best interest, it didn't ignite. The fuse just made a hole in the plastic bag and fell to the ground.

Wow, the whole stadium was watching it. Man, that would have been legendary; people would still be talking about it if it had gone off. People were talking about it over the campus as it was. Had it gone off, we probably would have been kicked out of school and maybe had jail time.

Hammond, Louisiana, was a small town surrounded by farms. In those days, you could go to the local hardware store and buy dynamite to blow up tree stumps, which we did. We blew up trees, fish in the river and any other thing we could find. The trees were just for fun, the fish we ate. I had a case of dynamite stored under my bed for a whole semester when we lived on Chestnut Street. Years later, Pat told me that he found some of the dynamite caps in his garage. Intelligence and doing dumb things are not always mutually exclusive of each other.

Hammond was also the strawberry capital of Louisiana and you could buy strawberries directly from the farmers. You could just pay the farmer and go pick your own berries during season, but you could also buy strawberry wine all year round. You would see the bottles of wine sitting on a fence post with a For Sale sign; not great wine but inexpensive. And as you know, in college, inexpensive was good.

The strawberries used to be protected from touching the ground by pine needles or straw placed around the plants, hence the name strawberries. This was also pine tree country so the straw was plentiful. At the time I went to school there the straw had been replaced with black plastic.

Years later Malcolm ran into Dean Harper, the Dean of Men when we attended SLC and asked him if we were a real pain in the ass. Surprisingly, he told Malcolm that the hardest thing for him to do when he would confront us on Monday morning after a wild weekend was to keep a straight face. He had to look stern, but he was amazed and looked forward to find out what new crap we had come up with. And we did come up with a lot of crazy stuff.

Chestnut Street

From Cherry Street for the next semester we moved to a house on Chestnut Street. It was a three bedroom house with a screened front porch. Corky, Danny, Tom, Jimmy, Billy and

Corky's brother Junior moved in next door. Man, that was a fun year. We did some outrageous stuff.

This is also when Leg moved in with us. Leg's real name was Richie Cerise, but we called him Leg because he had an artificial leg. He had a stump below the knee that he would put a sock like cover on and slip the stump into the fiberglass lower leg and foot. He lost his leg when he was about ten years old trying to jump onto a moving train back in New Orleans. He slipped as he was trying to get on the train and the train's wheel ran over his toes and cut them off. Gangrene set in and they had to cut his foot off. That didn't stop the infection so they cut off his leg below the knee. The doctors told him that if that didn't work they would have to take off his whole leg.

It didn't bother him that we called him Leg, because he had it most of his life and he was one of the gang. To the contrary, he didn't like it when people were too overly sensitive around him about his leg. He just thought of himself as more or less normal, so we treated him as more or less normal and were insensitive to him about his leg to the point that we screwed with him about it.

I remember when I first met him. It was the night before school started and I got to the house late that evening. Tiger Favret and I got sidetracked on the way to school and ending up covering some bars before he dropped me off at our new house on Chestnut Street. Pat and I had the front bedroom and Ronnie and Leg had the middle bedroom. The lights were off as I was making my way to the bathroom when I stumbled over something sticking out from under the one of the beds. I looked down, let out a startled, "Oh shit," and jumped about a foot off the ground. I had tripped over a leg sticking out from the bed. Pat then said, "Oh that's Leg's leg," and told me the story.

Leg was another New Orleans guy from the Lakeview neighborhood and Warren Easton High School like a bunch of the other guys. Ronnie, Malcolm, Tom, Jimmy and Danny were also from Warren Easton. They were mostly B.A. or Accounting majors and mostly all were in the KDT fraternity, the wildest fraternity on campus.

We were always messing with Leg. One time we painted his artificial leg with red stripes like a barber's pole. Then another time we put it in the freezer and when Richie pulled it out of the freezer it was covered with ice. That really pissed him off, because he had to go to school on his crutches. But that wasn't the worst thing we did to him; we cut some hair off our own arms and glued it to his prosthesis. We told him that it was to make it more like a real leg. That didn't make him very happy either.

One of the funniest things to happen regarding Leg was when Malcolm had left his motorcycle at the house and Pat cranked it up to take it for a ride. Well, Leg wanted to go with him on the back of bike. As they were riding around, Pat rounded a corner close to the curb, Leg's artificial leg's foot slipped off the foot peg, hit the curb and knocked his leg off. So Leg was screaming, "Pat, stop, stop!" Pat asked him why, and he said, "I lost my leg." So they had to go back and find his leg lying in the street.

However, the funniest thing that happened with Leg was when we were "crawfishing" in the Manchac swamp. We all had hip boots on and were wading in knee deep water with a soft mud bottom making our way back to the car. Pat and I were carrying the sack of crawfish and crawfish nets. Ronnie and Leg were following us. It was a tough going for Leg because he kept on getting his boot stuck in the mud for which Ronnie would berate him for slowing us down.

Ronnie had a foul mouth and little patience. Then Leg got his leg really stuck to the point that he couldn't pull it out of the mud and called for Ronnie to help him get it unstuck. Ronnie said, "Leg, you're a pain in the ass," but went back to help him.

So here was the scene: Ronnie was behind Leg with his arms around Leg's chest and both of them trying to extract Leg's stuck boot out of the swamp mud. Ronnie said to Leg, "On three pull."

"One, two, three, pull!"

Then all of a sudden they were both sitting in the swamp water up to their chests with Leg's artificial leg clad in a torn hip boot sticking out of the swamp like a cypress knee.

Ronnie shouted at Leg, "Leg you crippled mother------."

At that sight, Pat and I sat down in the swamp and laughed our asses off.

———•—•——

The Old Swamp Hermit

There was an old hermit that lived in a shack built on stilts in the swamp that had a long wooden walkway leading back to the road which we used as a base of operations for hunting. The shack was owned by a friend and hunting buddy, Freddie Kursh. The hermit had a mean-ass dog and somebody asked him what kind of dog it was. He replied, "Part spitz and part bitin' son-of-a-bitch." We agreed and gave the dog a wide berth. He also told us about catching frogs on the highway after a heavy rain.

Anyway, Leg was a great sport and a good roommate. He actually didn't mind too much the crap that we gave him, it made him feel like he was just one of us, which he was. He and Ratelat argued like they were a married couple. Jerry "Seagull" and Malcolm were our other roommates.

We had a small arsenal in our house: shotguns, rifles, bows and arrows, and blow guns. As I mentioned earlier, we even had a case of dynamite that we kept under my bed to throw in the river and get fish or to blow up trees for the fun of it.

In New Orleans, most of us were Catholic, and back then you ate fish on Friday. We tried to be good boys and eat fish on Friday, but we probably lost a few heavenly points by blowing up the fish in the river to eat. Pole fishing just took too long.

In this refined fishing technique, we would station several guys downstream to catch the fish as they floated to the surface while a couple of guys upstream lit the dynamite and tossed it in the river. The concussion knocked out the fish and they floated up to be picked up by us. Fish for dinner. But it was just fun to see the dyna-mite explode in the river.

———•••••———

Blow Guns

Someone found some aluminum aircraft tubing and we decided to make blow guns out of them. We took a piece of coat hanger about six inches long, sharpened one end and put a foam stop-per on the other end for the dart. We made the stopper out of the insulation that went around air conditioning pipes. The blow guns were about six feet long and pretty damn accurate. We painted a red bull's eye on the wood weather boards on the front of the house on Chestnut Street and would stand across the street about forty feet away and put a number of darts in the target. We nailed a few squirrels with them also. It was a good diversion from all the intense studying that we did. (Tongue in cheek.)

A good afternoon would be drinking beer and blowing darts at the target on our house. About forty years later I went to Ham-mond and toured the neighborhood and the houses that we lived in and you could still see the small holes in the weather boards on the house made by the darts.

Jimmy DeMoss who we called "Demis" was our pyrotech-nics guru and I think it was he who took the lowly blow gun to an-other level by putting a dynamite cap on the end of the dart to make it an explosive projectile. We tested it by shooting it at Corky's and the boys' house next door.

To our surprise, it went off on contact, blew a hole in the weather board on the side of the house and the sheet rock of the inside wall. Everybody inside came running out shouting, "What the f_____ is going on!" We were all amazed and laughing at our new weapon or toy. I think it was Junior Barras who was studying close to the explosion when the hole was blown next to where he was sitting.

How we ever made it through college without killing ourselves or somebody else is amazing. God must have been looking out after us, 'cause we sure the hell were not doing a good job of looking after ourselves.

Much later when I was talking to someone about having been in combat in Vietnam they said, "Man, you are lucky to come back in one piece."

And I replied, "Well, I never got hit in Vietnam, but I got shot in the balls in college."

No wonder I liked dropping bombs from an airplane, it was just a continuation of sorts of what we did in college. We also made pipe bombs in high school and blew them up out in the woods and once on the same 17th Street Canal levee that failed during Hurricane Katrina and flooded our Lakeview neighborhood in New Orleans. Our blowing a hole in the levee had nothing to do with it failing years later during the hurricane. I just wanted to make that clear.

This was before there was a terrorist threat and we were just having fun, not trying to hurt anyone.

Since we never had much money, we had to supplement our diet with other food sources that we shot, caught, trapped or whatever other method we might have used. We even shot a squirrel out of the tree with the blow gun.

At any one time we might have frogs, doves, ducks, squirrel, quail and even alligator in our freezer.

Ron Boehm

The Help

All the guys in the house next door were BA or Accounting majors including my two roommates Ronnie and Leg. As I had mentioned they were all in the same fraternity, KDT, which was mostly made up of New Orleans guys. It was a crazy scene whenever test time came around. These guys spent most of their time looking for "the help," which was the answers to the test. "The help" might be last semester's test, yesterday's test answers or a copy of the test that someone stole from the professor's office.

A couple of the guys, I won't mention names, actually broke into the professor's office the night before the test and got copies of the test. Man, that is ballsy.

Whenever you saw a whole bunch of cars at somebody's house, you knew that they either had "the help" or there was a gang bang going on.

Homecoming

Homecomings were some pretty interesting times to say the least. Everybody got up for homecoming and many people got dates for the game, but I think I only had one home-coming date in all my five years. I think it was my junior year and it was quite memorable. I got shot with a BB gun and had to go to the hospital to have the BB removed.

After the homecoming parade I got to keep the papier-mâ-ché lion's head from the Industrial Tech Department's float, which

I had helped make. It was a pretty good likeness of a lion's head. So I brought it home and put it on a table in the corner of our living room. After the football game most of the gang was at our place drinking Gipsy Rose wine out of a gallon jug. We had found some old 78 rpm records in an old house and proceeded to have a skeet shooting contest in the living room using a Benjamin Pump air rifle. We would pass the gun and the wine bottle around, someone would shout "pull!" and another guy would sail a record across the room and the guy with the gun would fire the BB gun at the record.

Of course this was very safe, because we were all trained professionals. Well, things were getting a little crazy and someone shot my lion's head with an arrow. It pissed me off, seeing my lion with an arrow sticking in his eye. Then Casey Kilian decided to shot the lion's head with the air rifle. I had a rotisserie rod in my hand and just instinctively shoved it in front of the lion's head and said to Casey, "Don't shoot it." But he did exactly that and the BB ricocheted off the rod and hit me in the groin area. It stung and I admonished Casey that he could have hit me in the eye and went to my bedroom to check it out.

When I looked down I saw that there was a spot of blood and a hole in my khaki pants. I dropped my pants and immediately saw that I was shot in the scrotum and with more careful examination I felt the BB in my scrotum. Thank God that it did not hit me in the testicle, but I yelled to my roommate Pat that Casey had shot me in the balls. Well, I got sober real fast and told them to take me to the hospital emergency room.

The emergency room in the little town of Hammond, at 2:00 AM on Saturday night was nothing like New Orleans where there would be five gunshot wound victims and twenty other bleeding cases. There in Hammond we had to ring the bell for help and a young candy striper about seventeen years old came to see what we needed.

She said, "What's wrong?"

My other roommate Ronnie answered in an intoxicated voice, "My roommate's been shot in the balls."

The young girl almost fainted when she heard that. I was now in grave pain. The nurse's aid ran to get the doctor and this

Ron Boehm

guy must have wanted to be a comedian or something because he thought it was rather humorous. I, on the other hand, didn't see any humor in it at all.

I was put on the cold metal table with my privates exposed while my friends, still drunk, were having wheel chair races down the deserted halls of the hospital.

The Doc said, "I have been a surgeon for fifteen years and this is a first for me; it's like one of those western movies. Nurse, get me a pan of hot water and give him a bullet to bite on."

I didn't find it in the least bit funny and my balls were hurting like hell.

Then the Doc came out with some big ass needle, and I asked, "What are you going to do with that?"

And he said, "Got to deaden it, son."

"Holy shit Doc, that in itself will kill me."

Anyway, he deadened it and made a slight incision and squeezed the BB out and gave it to me. I kept it for years and finally lost it.

When my mother heard the story, she wanted me to go to our family doctor to have him look at it and maybe get x-rays taken. I said, "Mom, we don't want to x-ray that area of my body. That's not a good idea. You could have a grandchild with two heads or something."

The next day my balls were swollen up big time and one half of my scrotum was pink while the other half bruised deep purple. I had a difficult time walking because they were so sore and swollen to about twice their normal size. I kind of dragged one leg, like Chester in Gun Smoke, so as not to touch them while I was walking.

There was this fat girl at school that we called "Bright Light" who really liked me and when she heard what had happened she was all concerned and came up to me to see how I was doing. She wasn't very bright, but was real sweet. I never knew her real name. But she asked how I was and I said I was OK.

Then she said, "No, I mean, how are you really doing?"

I said, "Oh, I'm OK, they put it in a cast, but it's as hard as a rock."

I couldn't help putting a little humor in it.

There was a bunch of girls whose real names I never knew, just the names we gave them; actually I think Pat and Calvin gave them most of their names. There was Tons of Fun, a fat girl, Bright Light, who wasn't very bright, The Manchac Maiden, I guess because she was from the Bayou Manchac area, One Sock, because she was doing some guy with one sock on when a couple of the other guys were watching, and Tic Toc. Tic Toc was a handicapped girl who was short, round and whose legs didn't work very well, so that when she walked she waddled from side to side. You know "tic toc, tic toc" like a clock. I think that was another one of Pat's names. One time years later when we were telling stories he said, "Did you hear that Tic Toc died?" I said, "No." And he said "Yeah, her time ran out."

Parties were always happening, mostly on Friday evenings, but we didn't have very many quality girls come to our parties. I guess that was because of our reputation. One of the parties got crazy and the cops were sent to our house. Man, people were scattering all over, running out the back door, Reith and a girl were under the house hiding; it was crazy. This may have been the second or third time we had been visited by the cops.

For Christmas that year we had a Christmas pine tree we cut down in the woods and decorated it with rubbers and firecracker chasers, the kind that you would light on the ground and they would run all over whistling.

Spring Break was coming up and we were trying to find ways to get some money to go to Panama Beach, Florida. We usually went to Our Lady of the Lake Hospital in Baton Rouge and sold our blood for extra money, but that was only about twenty-five dollars, so we needed other sources for money. Someone mentioned that if we could capture the "alligator in the lake at Zemurray Lodge" we could sell him to the Reptile Jungle and get money to pay for our trip.

The Reptile Jungle was a tourist attraction on the side of the highway that afforded people not from the area, for the price of admission, a chance to see snakes, turtles, alligators and other creatures of the swamps. Zemurray Lodge was a big estate that belonged to a rich lady who died and left it in her will to be made into a park. It had a big old house with a bunch of beautiful azalea bushes and a big lake surrounded by dense woods. The lake was off limits for fishing, but we would sneak in there anyway and fish. But the neat thing was that in that lake was a big old alligator; a big alligator that could be captured and sold to the Reptile Jungle for Spring Break cash.

I think this was another one of Reith's ideas along with his co-conspirator, Calvin.

We decided to begin making plans to catch the alligator. Now, just the fact that we decided that this was a good idea had to mean that we were under the influence of alcohol or that we were crazy or both. Pat and Mal were biology majors and suggested that we might shoot the alligator with a dart that had some kind of sedative to knock it out. We could then tie it up and carry it off. This was an eight foot plus alligator we were talking about.

But anyway, it was Pat and Malcolm's job, since they were biology majors, to find some kind of sedative from the biology lab and then we had to find a dart and method of delivery. We saw on those wild animal television shows how they sedated the animals with darts and then captured them. But Pat said that alligators had such a primitive neurological system that it might not work and they didn't think that SLC's biology lab had sedatives or darts. So that didn't work out and we had to come up with a new plan.

So one night while drinking at the Brown Door, we decided that we would get into Zemurray Lake the back way through the dense woods and reconnoiter the situation and the alligator. The team was made up of Pat, Calvin, Demis and myself. We managed to get through the woods to the lake with cuts and bruises from the trees and underbrush.

DeMoss and I climbed up in a tree to spot the gator, and we could see him floating in the moonlight out in the middle of the lake. We devised a game plan whereby we would carry a two-man yellow life raft, a ten foot pole with a wire noose on it and a bunch of rope. The plan was for Pat and Calvin to stealthily paddle up to the sleeping alligator floating on the moonlit lake, place the noose around his snout and then pull him to shore where we would then tie him up and carry him out strapped under a pole. Kind of like you would see in a cartoon. Damn, here was a bunch of geniuses!

Some time later Pat and Calvin went to get the gator. They were in a two-man yellow rubber raft with a long pole and a long rope paddling towards the alligator. As they got to within about twenty feet of the beast, he gave a big splash with his mighty tail and submerged. But with that mighty switch of his tail, the plan changed from capture to retreat. Man, it looked like that rubber raft had a motor on it going full throttle in reverse. They were paddling so fast in reverse that they left a wake glittering in the moonlit water. Another brilliant plan gone to waste.

After that, we had no further plans for that alligator. However, we did shoot another alligator. We skinned it, cut it up, and ate it. But it was big, old, and tough. It was like trying to eat cotton with a fish or frog flavor. You would just chew and chew and chew on it, but you never could swallow it. I don't think there was a farmer's pond within twenty miles that we hadn't tried to fish. DeMoss and Reith had them all spotted out.

One of the alligators that we shot—well, Pat shot—came out of the pond of a prominent oil company owner and years later Pat's nephew was talking to the owner's grandson who mentioned that his grandfather used to have an alligator in his pond and Pat's kid said, "Yeah, my uncle Pat shot him."

Pat's picture with the gator

Ron Boehm

Summer Jobs

I was one of nine children and my folks couldn't afford to send me to college, so I worked in the summer to send myself to college and support myself. I did this by working summer jobs, saving as much as I could and borrowing the rest from The National Defense Student Loan Program.

I worked one summer as a marble setter's apprentice, putting in tiles, marble stiles in restrooms, fascia on buildings and marble floors and altars in churches. Another summer I spent on the oil rigs in the Gulf of Mexico as a "roust-about," and yet another summer at a chemical plant on the Mississippi River across from New Orleans.

The chemical plant job was a good job. I got the job from my neighbor across the street, Mr. Diaz, who was the plant manager. I, in turn, got my buddy Joe Henry hired since he got me the job with the marble company the previous year. The neat thing about this job was that the plant made 192 proof pure alcohol that was mixed with some other ingredients and then sold to companies like Listerine™ for mouth wash and stuff like that.

The plant was very regulated by the government. You had to get a government inspector to unlock the lock on a valve before it could be opened when pure alcohol was involved.

Product like molasses used to make alcohol would come in via railroad tank car and alcohol pure or denatured would go out via tank car. It was my and Joe's job to unload the tank cars, clean them and fill them up.

Joe and I would have to clean out the railroad tank cars by getting down into them with a big air hose to dry out any moisture. In the middle of summer, it was not very comfortable inside of a tank car with a temperature of about 110 degrees. However, the other part of the job was to fill the cars with 192 proof alcohol. In the process, we would have to run sample bottles from the tank cars to the lab so that they could be tested for purity and moisture content. We would sit on top of the tank car and lower the bottles down by a string with a noose around the neck of the bottle, bring up a full bottle, put a cap on it and take it to the lab.

When we went to the lab to get a sample bottle, we would sneak out with a second bottle for us. By the end of summer Joe and I both had a gallon of 192 proof alcohol to take back to college. Proof is twice percent, so that was ninety-six percent alcohol. Man, talk about a party-maker; that was awesome. Our punch made with our special ingredient was intoxicating, to say the least.

President Kennedy

The tragic thing that happened in my third year was when President Kennedy was killed, November 22, 1963. Everyone remembers where they were when they got the word that the President was shot. I was walking across campus coming from class when someone came running by and shouted that the President had been shot. I ran to the dorm and we all gathered around the TV in the lobby to watch the event unfold.

President Kennedy was my first vote for president and it seemed everyone including me was devastated by his death. When Walter Cronkite reported that the President was dead, my eyes filled with tears. I couldn't believe that this could happen in our country. But then after that Martin Luther King and Bobby Kennedy were also assassinated.

Ron Boehm

Sonny Costa

Another one of the wonderful characters of my college experience was Sonny Costa. Sonny was a big strong and tough guy, who wrestled in high school. We had both attended Holy Cross High School in New Orleans.

A traveling carnival had come to Hammond with an assortment of rides, games and side shows. They also had a muzzled baboon that the show promoters offered to anyone in the audience who would wrestle the baboon in a caged ring for the opportunity to win fifty dollars if you could stay in the ring with the baboon for a certain amount of time.

That was a lot of money back in our college days. The baboon's manager would also take side bets on baboon or the challenger. We talked Sonny into wrestling the baboon and we all bet on him since he was a former wrestler and bigger than the baboon.

The much anticipated event started with Sonny entering the cage with the baboon, who was on the opposite side of the cage, but before Sonny could even get into a position to defend himself the baboon sprung from clear across the cage straight at Sonny's throat. It scared the shit out of him and he responded by grabbing the baboon and throwing him against the cage wall, which put a big hurt on the animal who crumpled to the floor in a state of half-consciousness. The manger called a foul and disqualified Sonny and wouldn't pay him the fifty dollars, at which time Sonny threatened to do the same to the manager if he didn't pay him. I don't remember much after that, but I think we had to leave the scene.

East Mary Street

The next year, which was my senior year or my final year, we moved into a house on East Mary Street. Our place was a nice old wood house, had a front porch and sat off the ground on two foot brick piers. It was about a block from a nice little park and about fifteen or so blocks from school.

One of the things I remember about our stay there was that at dinner time we would watch Amos and Andy reruns on television. That was some good stuff. The Kingfish and Andy kept us laughing throughout dinner. In one episode Andy was looking to beat the hell out of the Kingfish for some scam or other crap that the Kingfish had done to Andy. Kingfish was talking to J. Calhoun the lawyer about the legal ramifications of someone beating the hell out of someone else and Calhoun said that it depended upon who is the "beator" and who is the "beatee."

It was a shame they were pulled off the air. I guess it wasn't politically correct, but I didn't see much difference between Amos and Andy and the later show, The Jeffersons.

Frogs on the Highway

One day while we were sitting on the porch having a beer and watching it rain someone said, "Hey, remember what the old hermit said about the first heavy rain after a long drought?"

This old hermit guy that lived in the Manchac swamp where we hunted told us that if we wanted to get some bull frogs we should come out on the old Hammond highway that runs through the swamp at night after the "first heavy rain" following a long drought. He said that we could just pick frogs up off the road then. "Yeah!" we said. "Let's go get some frogs." We could taste those frog legs already.

Boy, when we got there, there were frogs everywhere on the highway. Some had already been run over and squished on the road. The technique was to stop the car in front of the frogs with the head-lights on the frogs, get out with a big oyster sack and walk around to the back of the frogs, being careful not to break the beam of the car's headlights. The frogs were mesmerized by the headlights, and we would just pick them up and throw them into the sack. But as we would put one frog into the sack, another would jump out.

In no time we had a sack full of big bullfrogs in the car and a couple of them got out and were jumping all around in the car. It was a crazy scene with a car full of guys and frogs jumping all around as we tried to catch them and return them to the sack. We would catch one, put it back in the sack and another would jump out. We were all laughing our asses off and having a good time. Man, we ate frog legs for weeks after that.

This was the year that I had "the hots" for this tall girl named Cara. She was about five feet ten inches or so and I was only five six. She was a great-looking girl and was amazed that a short guy like me was interested in a tall girl like her. That was the first tall girl that I dated, but there were many more to follow. I love tall women. I remember one tall girl asking me if I was intimidated by the height difference and I replied, "Look, if I walk into a bar or restaurant with some tall good-looking girl and everybody turns to look at us, do you think they are thinking, 'Look at that poor little guy with that tall good-looking woman?'"

Anyway, Cara and I had a few dates, but I had this fantasy of making love to her in my Renault Dalphine, which was a very small car in both length and width. I figured that I could open both back doors, having her head sticking out one side and her feet sticking out the other side. Girls were pretty straight-laced back then, this being before the advent of the Pill. So a lot of guys talked a good game, but to make it to home plate with girls back then, you usually had to be going steady or engaged in some cases. So my fantasy remained just that, a fantasy.

——•••——

Renault Dalphine

With regards to my Renault Dauphine, we had some interesting times with it. It was sky blue with four doors and a piston on the top of the floor gear shift and I had paid three hundred dollars for it.

One time I walked out the front door of our house to go to class in the morning and to my surprise my car, the Renault, was up on the front porch about three feet off the ground. I had to run the three miles to school in order to make it to my class on time. When I got back home after classes, all my roommates were laughing their asses off at such a great prank.

I still can't believe that Pat, Seagull and DeMoss were able to lift the car onto the porch. Pat was the biggest guy and he was only about five feet eight. Jerry and Jimmy were little guys like me.

Another time we were driving in the mud during a rain storm on what was the road base being built for the new highway. We were turning circles in the mud, knocking over construction barrels and just having a great time. The Renault had this big wrap-around front bumper to protect it.

We were actually on our way to "the Cowboys' house." The Cowboys were a group of guys from East Jefferson parish who were into cowboy stuff like horses and rodeo. That group included Dan DeBlanc, Farrell Fresh, Calvin Serpas and Don Dufore. Dan was a rodeo bull rider and ended up being a pilot in the Marine Corp like me while Farrell stayed with the rodeo circuit and ended up being a champion rodeo rider winning a number of titles.

Ron Boehm

Dan and I crossed paths in OCS and a couple of times in Vietnam. Don Dufore had gone to Holy Cross High School with me. Farrell was a small tough as hell guy who was a bronc rider in the rodeos with Dan.

The guys that we hung around with were for the most part from New Orleans and the surrounding area. We had the Lakeview guys who mainly went to Warren Eastern High and the Jefferson Parish guys that went to East Jefferson High.

Well anyway, back to the story; it was dark and raining like hell and I was driving like crazy all the while looking for the road to the cowboys' house when Pat shouted out "turn here." I turned, but to our surprise we turned onto a railroad track not the road. So there we were riding down the tracks going bump, bump, bump, bump! I think it screwed up my wheel alignment big time and we put a big dent in my fender. But like always, it was fun. Alcohol was probably involved again.

A block down the street on East Mary Street were two sisters, Patsy and Missy Noonan. Missy was one of the campus queens and was as nice as she was pretty.

I was closer to Patsy than I was to Missy and sometimes I would walk down to their place and visit. Patsy and I would go down to this park about a block away and sit on the swings and visit. It was very nice and so were they.

Baseball

Four of my five years at SLC I played on the baseball team and lettered in two of those four years. Our team won the Gulf States Conference baseball championship title four of those five years. It was great times and I loved playing baseball. It was my main focus, more perhaps than college itself.

In my freshman year I was doing great, having a ball and getting good grades, but the main thing on my mind was baseball. My life had revolved around baseball ever since I was eight years old. I couldn't wait until the following semester and the start of baseball season. I must admit that I was nervous about going out and making the team. I was just an average high school ballplayer and not very big, but I couldn't imagine not playing ball.

The first semester ended and I had passed all my subjects. And now it was the second semester and baseball tryouts were on. I was small, fast and played with a great amount of enthusiasm. Corky and I were both sweating making the team. He was a catcher and I played second base. We made the first two cuts and now it was the big "do or die day," the final cut. We got called into the coach's office and we were both tight as a drum. I was trying to prepare myself for the words, "Sorry, but we can't use you."

Coach Pat Kenelly called me into his office and I stood in front of his desk. Coach Pat was a very tall man, about six foot five, and very tough looking. He was also a football coach. For years I thought he was seven foot tall, which is another story I'll tell later. So anyway, there I was standing in front of this big stern looking coach who had my life in his hands. He was sitting behind his desk stuffing chewing tobacco in his mouth with his size fifteen shoes resting on the desk. I could barely see over his feet.

I said, "Yes sir, did you want to see me, Coach?"

I thought that he was going to say, "Thank you for coming out, but we didn't have a spot on the team for you." I had never ever been cut from a team before.

Coach Pat with a stern face said, "Little Man," (he always called me Little Man and never Ronnie, which was something I was very proud of), "I think you can help us with your glove and I like the way you hustle, but hell son, I'm gonna have to go the high school to find you a uniform."

That was my first taste of his wonderful and funny dry wit. He would say some things in tense situations that would tear you up. But I had made the team and life was very good.

Once I had made the team, Coach Pat got me into the athletic dorm which was part of the football stadium. That was my second semester and it helped me out financially. Coach didn't have but a few scholarships to work with and he would give out part scholarships to help the guys who needed it. I was putting myself through school without any help from home, so it was a big advantage.

It was great living with a bunch of jocks in the stadium dorm. There were free haircuts in the bathroom area, as we would give each other haircuts. From our dorm room we could open a window and climb out on the student union building's roof and sunbathe. That was great plus the dorm was right in the middle of campus. I stayed there for that semester and then in my second year I moved off campus with the crew that I would be with for the rest of my time at Southeastern.

One time we were playing in a close game and all three of our very good outfielders had made errors by letting balls go through their legs. One guy, Jimmy Ruddick, was a left hander both throwing and hitting and the other guy, Billy Ladner, was a right hander but batted left handed. When they came off the field into the dugout, coach said, "Ruddick, you look like a monkey trying to f--- a football out there, and Ladner, you look like a right handed Ruddick."

On the bench I would usually sit next to Corky at the end. We warmed a lot of bench that first year, and he was as funny as Coach Pat, but without that dry wit. Corky was a great bench jockey also and just flat funny with his comments and riding the other teams.

Corky, Pete Freeman and Joe Thomas were the great bench jockeys on our team and they would ride the other teams unmercifully. The other teams would say, "Hey man, what did we do to you?" And they would get on them even more. Coach Pat told Corky that he had coached a bunch of teams before, but none of them could compare with those guys for riding the other teams. Coach Pat told Corky one time that "he could give the Pope the red ass."

My good friend Henry "Bubby" Winters, a pitcher, was warming up on the mound before the start of a game, throwing to

Corky and every time he would look at Corky through his catcher's mask he started laughing to the point that he couldn't throw the baseball.

Coach came out and asked, "What's the matter?"

Bubby said, "Coach, I can't look at Corky behind that mask: he has a silly grin on his face and it breaks me up."

Coach looked at Corky and told Bubby, "Yeah, I see what you mean, but you are out here to throw the ball."

Years later, Henry and I met up in Houston, Texas, for the first time since college and we became best of friends and hung out together drinking and partying in the local bars. One time I told Henry that Coach Pat was the only seven-foot tall man I had ever met.

Henry said, "Ronnie, I'm six foot two and Coach Pat can't be more than six four, six five at the most."

I said that I would bet him five dollars that coach was seven foot.

So Henry said, "Let's call him and see who wins the bet."

Of course, we were in a bar drinking at the time so it didn't enter our minds that it was 10 PM and Coach Pat, who would be in his seventies, would be in bed at the time.

Henry called information for Hammond, Louisiana, and got Coach's phone number and we called him, the first time we had talked to him in twenty years or so.

When Coach Pat answered, Henry could hear his wife saying in the background, "Pat, who is calling at this hour?"

Henry said, "Coach, it's Bubby Winters and Ronnie Boehm" (Bubby was what we all called Henry in high school and college).

He was happy to hear from us and Henry told him that we had a five dollar bet that I said he was seven-foot tall, but Henry said that he thought that coach was no more than six five.

Coach said, "Bubby, put The Little Man's money in your pocket, 'cause everybody looks seven-foot tall to him."

Later on I was in my fifties and playing in a men's senior baseball league in Houston and had hit my first home run in my whole life.

I told Henry, and he said, "Let's call Coach Pat and tell him."
Same scenario, we were in a bar drinking and called Coach.

He answered the phone and Henry said, "Coach, you won't believe what Ronnie did."

Coach Pat said, "Don't tell me the Little Man went deep?"

Henry said, "Yes sir, he hit his first home run ever."

Coach said, "It only took him fifty years; I guess miracles never cease."

We had some real characters on those SLC teams. It was a small school and Coach Pat had very few scholarships to work with, so he gave them mostly to the pitchers and as I said before, he would split them up to help the guys who needed the money the most. If he had a good prospect with questionable academic skills, he would bring him in for the second semester in time for baseball and that way they couldn't flunk-out and become ineligible before that baseball season was over. So it was with this one pitcher named Lou Poternostro from Istrouma High School in Baton Rouge.

On that team we had four guys from that same Istrouma High School team that was the 1961 Louisiana High School AAA State Championship runner-up team from Baton Rouge, and three guys from the Championship Jesuit High School team from New Orleans.

One day a professor called Coach Pat to tell him that one of his baseball players had only been to his class one time in the whole semester and that he wondered what happened to him. It was Lou, who was never going to be mistaken for a Rhodes' Scholar. When coach asked Lou why he had not been to class, he told him he was claustrophobic and classes made him nervous. Lou was a good pitcher and a truly funny character and as you might suspect, he lasted only just one season.

Another character was Jim Reynolds, an outfielder and the son of the famous New York Yankee Hall of Fame pitcher, Alley Reynolds. He was also a hot-head with rabbit ears and could torque off in an instant. Once we were playing at LSU and the fans really got on him. They were calling him "Alley's offspring" and that really pissed him off. In about the fifth inning or so he lost it and ran in from centerfield all the way up to the wall behind home plate and shot the whole stands "the bird" with both hands along with some choice words.

Well, that really got them going. It was in that same game I had started at second base for the first time and made three errors. I'd get to the ball, but would field the ball with stiff hands. I had a couple of hits in the game and stole a base. But after the game, Coach Pat told me, "It looks like you might help the team with your bat, but hell son, I've got to get those stiff wrists out of the infield." Hence, I was now an outfielder and a bunch of the guys began calling me "SW," short for stiff wrists.

Both of my roommates in the athletic dorm were tall guys who loved to screw around with me. Lamar Lebeau, our first baseman, was about six two and the best hitter on the team in both hitting average and home runs. Roy Baker was about six four, a tall lanky guy who played on the basketball team and was a pitcher on the baseball team.

One time I came home drunk and passed out on my bed. I was wearing shorts at the time, so they decided to use barber's clippers on me and put a racing stripe up the side of my hairy legs. Then another time, just for the hell of it, they rolled me up in one of those thin striped mattresses that came off the bunk beds, taped it around and rolled me down a flight of stairs.

They were really good friends, but just liked to screw with me every now and again. But to get back at them, I put hot analgesic balm, a heating rub, in their jock straps. It worked well on muscles providing heat to the area applied. You can imagine how it felt in a jock strap. Well, that really pissed them off and they dumped me in the clothes bin in the locker room.

I loved playing baseball in college and I had a great deal of fun doing it. I had my share of screw-ups, too. We were playing at Spring Hill College in Mobile, Alabama, and the students there would sit on this four foot high brick wall along the first base line. I got a walk and was on first base taking a lead off base when I looked back at first. What I saw was a coed sitting on the fence with her legs open and that got my attention. It also got the pitcher's attention, because he picked me off, another base-running jewel on my part. Coach also had some choice words for me.

The next day we went to the golf course in the morning, since our game was later that day and four of us, Corky, Ernie Knoblock, Pete Freeman and I teed it up. None of us had played golf very much and were not very accurate with our shots. Ernie could hit a baseball a mile and so too with the golf ball.

There were these two priests playing in front of us; Spring Hill was a Catholic Jesuit College, and we hit into them about three or four times. Each time, knowing proper course etiquette, we would shout "fore!" I guess on that last time we should have shouted "Sixteen!" As we came up to the next green, the priest said, "You boys play through so we can hit into you little bit." They probably thought if these guys play baseball the way they play golf, our team should have no problem.

Another time we were playing at home against a team that was ranked just below us in the standings and I was starting in left field. I never paid much attention to the score and had to always ask the center fielder Earl Barron what the score was. There was a high pop up hit towards me just out of the infield over third base. As I came charging in to make the catch I had to run hard then come almost to a quick stop under the baseball, and when you do that you started running on your heels and that makes the ball look like it's jumping up and down. The ball just tipped my glove, hit me in the forehead and then bounced about twenty feet away. I was looking all around and couldn't find it. The third baseman retrieved it and made the play and as I was looking around, the trainer, Doc Morgan, came out and, being concerned about my having been hit in the head, asked me what the score was. "Hell Doc, I don't know." Then he asked me what inning it was. I never paid any attention to that detail either, and told him I didn't know that either, so he thought I was knocked out on my feet and took me out of the game.

The next day we were playing the second game of a three game series and I didn't get to start. I was mad because I had blown the play yesterday and thought that that was the reason I was on the bench. About the sixth inning, coach told me to get out in left field. Man, I was thrilled. I picked up my glove and took off running from the dugout towards the outfield. Just as I got twenty feet from the dugout, several guys called to me from the dugout and when I turned around about five batting helmets came sailing out the dugout with the chorus, "Take this, you might need it."

I had a girlfriend named Patsy who loved to see me play ball, but she didn't know much about baseball or the terms very well. She would say things like, "Are you all playing a double feature today?" And, "I love to see you with your little semi-circular legs (I had bowed legs) when you get off first base to run and then slip into second base. You look so cute." Cute? I was a major threat to steal second base. Oh, well, I guess that would come under the eyes of the beholder heading.

Our starting catcher in my first year on the team was Roy Branhurst, who was a very good catcher, hit very well, had a great arm and ended up playing some pro ball. Roy also had a speech impediment and talked with a sort of lisp. One time during practice he was warming up a pitcher, and while in a crouched position behind home plate this big ass dog runs onto the field, runs up to Roy and pounces on him, knocking him down. So there is this big dog standing over Roy who is lying on his back and the dog is licking him on the face while Roy is saying in his impeded speech, "Det dis ton of a bitch off me." And we were all laughing our asses off on the side; it was pretty funny.

I was fairly fast back then and a pretty good base runner. I had stolen a bunch of bases; however, one time I got a little careless and got picked off at third base. I dove back to the base but came up about six inches short and was tagged out. The out ended the inning and a rally. As I lay there, I could hear the thundering of Coach Pat's big footsteps coming out of the dugout towards me. He got next to me, then he got down on his hands and knees and shouted in my face, "If you ever run on my bases again, it will be a cold day in hell." So I sat way down on the other end of the bench for the next few games.

Ron Boehm

Another time he said that I must have glass in my stomach in order to see because I have my head so far up my ass.

Me stealing second base

Our right fielder in my first and second year was John Fred Gourrier from Baton Rouge who was about six four or five, played on the basketball team, and was the fastest guy on the team. John Fred was also famous, at least around Louisiana, as a singer who made hit record called "Judy in Disguise." He was a very nice guy. After him, our right fielder was Ernie Knoblock who, along with my roommate Lamar, was one of the two best hitters on the team. He had a lot of power and very quick wrist.

He and Lamar, our first baseman, were in the top of our conference in home runs and runs batted in. Ernie loved to screw around with me during the games when I was playing second base by throwing knuckle balls to me from the outfield with men on base. The ball would come dancing all over the place to me and I'd have a moment of panic trying to catch it while worrying about missing it and letting a run score. He thought it was very amusing. He also had the best arm on the team, other than the pitches, and could throw a rocket from right field to any bag with good accuracy. He made some very impressive throw-outs from the outfield.

Our team, as I guess it was with most teams, had a cast of some real characters and odd balls. We had one slight-framed and not very tall pitcher who had a very large member if you know what I mean. He was too embarrassed to get dressed in the locker room, because he didn't want anybody to see and laugh at him. Hell, the rest of us, if we had that kind of equipment, would be bragging and flashing that thing all around and being real proud. My roommate "The Gull" had the same kind of physical attributes, slight of frame, maybe five six, and big in the equipment area. One time, we bet these other guys that our guy Seagull had the biggest piece of equipment and they of course said that their guy had the biggest one. So we got together, put up some money and had an official measuring. Both guys pulled out their equipment and laid it on the table and we measured each guy. Seagull won "hands down" or dick down to be more precise. I don't know if that is the right descriptive terminology to describe it, but you get the idea.

In my junior year, Coach Pat was replaced by Coach Tommy Bell and Coach Pat went back to coaching just football. Coach Bell liked me and my playing time increased.

My junior year on the team was the only year of my four years that we didn't win the conference championship, but that was a pretty good run and a lot of fun.

Pictured from left to right:—first row—Ronnie Boehm, Gary McKenzie, Bill Nestler, Anthony Liuzza, Eddie Schmidt, David Wilcox, Danny Dufrecha, David Godchaux; middle row—John Thomas, Paul Durro, Jack Vaughn, Danny Douglas, Bobby Cotton, Corky Barras, Earl Barron, Stan Cheatham, Joe Thomas; back row—Bernard "Slick" Oubre, Dennis Crowe, Jessie Daigle, Jim Felder, Henry "Bubby" Winters, Johnny Winters, Ernie Knoblock, Lamar Labauve, Wayne Brasher, Pete Freeman, and coach Tommy Bell.

SLC Baseball Team

Ron Boehm

The End of College

Recruited into the Navy, then the USMC

About mid-way through my final year in 1966, I was contemplating what I was going to do when I got out of college. I didn't like the idea of just getting a job and staying in New Orleans and then there was the draft to think about. I guess I was looking for a little adventure in my life.

My military adventure all started when I saw the Navy recruiters driving onto campus in their white convertible with "FLY NAVY" written on the side in big letters. I thought to myself, "If you were a Navy pilot then you would have to carry a big stick to keep all the women off of you, 'cause you would be so cool." So I decided to go check it out.

I talked to this Navy Lieutenant about the Navy and flying and told him that I had never been flying even though I was in the Civil Air Patrol for a brief period when I was about fourteen years old. I was a senior in college and had never even been on a plane before.

He asked me if I would like to go flying with him the next day. I said, "Hell yeah, I would." So he said to meet him at the Hammond Airport at such and such a time and he would give me a ride. I was so excited that I barely slept that night; I couldn't wait for the next day.

The next day, I showed up at the airport a little early and very excited. The Lieutenant greeted me and asked if I was ready to go flying and I confirmed that I was. He gave a briefing on what we were to do; pre-flight, emergency stuff and communications between us, how to get in and out of the aircraft and so forth and so on.

As I walked up to the plane, my heart was racing. This wasn't some civilian aircraft.; This was a Navy T-34 training aircraft with a slide back canopy and the U.S. star insignia painted on the side. He showed me how to climb up on the wing and then get into the back seat. When I slid into the seat and he began to fasten my seat belt, hook up my mike and put on my head set, I was just in heaven. He climbed into the front seat, got strapped in and did his cockpit pre-flight. When he clicked the mike and asked if I could hear him and was I all set, I thought to myself, "Wow, I'm really going to fly; this is great."

He started the engine, contacted the tower, received taxi instructions and we began to taxi to the end of the runway. We held short on the runway, did a run up and got our takeoff clearance. It just kept on getting better every moment. When we taxied onto the runway and lined up looking down the centerline, I knew that this is what I wanted to do—fly airplanes.

He gave it the power and we began to roll, then we began to lift off the ground, my first time to fly. I watched as we climbed and the ground began to drop away. It was wonderful. We were off of the runway, then climbing above the trees and then coming up to the clouds. "Man," I thought, "this is awesome."

We leveled off at some altitude, maybe three or four thousand feet, and he did some banks with right and left turns, or as he said, "port and starboard." Even that sounded really neat.

Then he asked if I wanted to take the controls.

"Yes, Sir," I replied, trying to hide my excitement.

He said, "You've got it," and I shook the stick indicating that I had the control of the aircraft as he had told me to do.

Then told me how to bank and get on the rudder pedals. He told me I was doing great and asked how I liked it so far.

I said, "Yes, Sir. I love it."

He then said, "Well now we are going to see if you are really meant to be a pilot."

He took back control of the aircraft, pulled the plane up into a climb and the beginnings of a loop. At the top of the loop, I was looking at the earth upside down under the top of my head with my feet bracing against the sky.

I said, "Sign me up Sir, this is what I want to do."

He said, "Roger that."

Ron Boehm

I took the flight test which was a two part test and passed it. I did well in one section but barely passed the second section which was the math part. I would always tighten up whenever I took a timed math test and that is what I did on this test also.

So I signed up with the Navy for pilot training and started going through all the application processes and security investigations. The recruiting officer said that all looked great and that I would probably leave for training shortly after my graduation in May, 1966.

Well, about one month before graduation, I got a letter from the Department of the Navy which said that they had changed the test criteria and that I now did not qualify because I didn't have a passing grade on the second part of the test. They said that I would have to retake the test.

I retook the test and passed both sections with no problem this time, but I was told that I had to go through the entire application process all over again which took about six months.

About the same time, I got a letter from the Draft Board saying that I was to be drafted into the Army. So I went to see the Navy Recruiting Officer to find out what he could do for me in this situation. He said that he couldn't do anything for me, that I had to go through the process again and that I would not be draft exempt while I did. So then I asked what else could I do? He then said that I could go talk to the Marines. I said, "The Marines? You have got to be crazy to go into the Marines." And he said, "No, but it helps."

I didn't even know that the Marines flew airplanes. The recruiter said that they flew the same airplanes that the Navy did and that you went you through the same training with the Navy in Pensacola, Florida. You would in fact become a Naval Aviator, but a Marine pilot.

So I went to talk to the Marine recruiters down at the Federal Building on Canal Street in New Orleans. Well, once you go into a Marine recruiting office, you rarely leave without being signed up for the Marine Corps. They were great recruiters.

The recruiters that I met with were Captain Fanning who was a helicopter pilot and a Major that was an infantry officer. They said that I would make a great Marine officer and pilot, "Just sign here." So I said that I would and that I couldn't wait to go the OCS (Officer Candidate School) and Flight School.

They then said that if I were to be a real Marine officer I needed to go to TBS or The Basic School at Quantico, Virginia which was on the same base as OCS. I asked what TBS was and why I should go. They informed me that OCS just qualified you to be a Marine officer, but that TBS was where you learned how to be a Marine officer and then I would get to go to flight school.

I argued that I just wanted to go in on a Flight School contract and go to Pensacola like a couple of my friends were doing after OCS. At that time you could go to OCS and go straight to Pensacola for flight school on an aviation contract, but it turned out that now every Marine Officer went through The Basic School.

Captain Fanning and the Major insisted that I go through TBS and they talked me into it. This is where, in retrospect, I can see God's plan working for me. When I was running up and down the hills in the snow in Quantico in January and practicing to be an infantry officer, I was cursing the recruiters and my stupidity for letting them talk me into this when my friends were already flying in Pensacola.

But it was just because of this at the end of TBS that I was selected to be one of the very first Marines to go through Air Force Flight School and that I was guaranteed jets. It turned out that all of the Marines going to Pensacola except for a very few at the top of the class who got jets were to get helicopters. I am sure that I would have gotten helicopters if I had gone to Pensacola. Not that being a helicopter pilot was a bad thing; they were the guys with the big balls, but I loved jets and it worked out great for me.

There was a saying going around about helicopter pilots— well actually there are a lot of sayings about helicopter pilots. One was "If your wings are moving faster than your fuselage, then that very fact means you are in an unsafe condition."

Another one was "Having helicopter time on your flight record is like having VD on your health record." My apologies to my buddies Steve Benckenstein, Tom Broderick and Dan DeBlanc. Hell, if you were a chopper pilot in Vietnam and hadn't been shot up or shot down you couldn't even get into the conversation. All those guys were heroes: just ask a Marine grunt who was extracted from a battlefield or medivaced when wounded.

So I signed up to be a Marine Officer; it was the best decision I ever made in my life, for it shaped who I am and for the rest of my life being a Marine was the proudest thing I've ever done. I graduated from Southeastern Louisiana College in May of 1966, but my Marine Corps OCS class was not to start until January of 1967. After graduation, I needed a job until I would leave for the Corps.

Waiting to Go into the Marine Corps

While waiting to go into the Marine Corps I continued to play baseball that summer along with my SLC teammate buddy Corky Barras and some other guys I knew from the New Orleans area. The team leader and coach was Jack Fleming, who ran the operations for his dad's asphalt company. When Jack heard that I needed a temporary job until I left for the Marine Corps, he offered me a job with Fleming Asphalt Company.

My job was to drive a steam roller, or asphalt roller to be more correct, a tractor and do other odd jobs with the asphalt crew. The crew was made up of a foreman, three or four black laborers and myself. It could get quite amusing at times. One of the crew was a short guy like myself, about five six, named Frank, and another guy who was big and strong about six three who was built like a tight end by the name of Melp.

Frank spoke with a very thick black New Orleans accent and I sometimes had to get one of the other guys to interpret for me.

One day I asked Frank why they called the big guy Melp, because that wasn't the name on his paycheck. Frank said to ask Melp where he lived, so I did and Melp said that he "lived up there on Melpa—aaa Melpa—aaa up dere around Magazine Street." Melp couldn't pronounce the street in New Orleans named Melpomene Avenue so everybody just called him Melp.

It was a living comedy working with these guys. Another time we were just starting to clear a lot overgrown with weeds and trees in order to construct a parking lot. I told Frank and Melp to go out and walk the lot to make sure there wasn't anything hidden in the weeds that we didn't want the bulldozer to destroy such as a fire plug or a gas line or something like that.

Melp said to me, "Aaa Mister Ronnie, I can'ts go out there in that lot 'caus' they got snakes in there."

I said, "Melp, if there are any snakes out there they won't hurt you and they are more afraid of you then you are of them."

He said, "No sir, trust me I'm more afraid of them then they is of me."

Frank nodded in agreement.

Then Melp said, "They got rattle snakes and 'bow construc-tors' out there."

I then told him, laughing, that there are no rattle snakes or boa constrictors in New Orleans other than in the Audubon Park Zoo.

He said, "Yes sir, they do and that the 'bow constructor' is that big mean snake that hangs from a tree and when you walks by wraps around you, licks you slick and swallows you whole."

So I sent two other guys into the lot. I couldn't argue with reasoning like that.

Those guys were a constant source of amusement, but there was another guy that was the funniest of them all. He had the ability to make up words that fit perfectly to what he was trying to say, but just were not to be found in the dictionary. One time I was working on the asphalt roller that seemed to break down every other day. I got so frustrated that I hit the roller with a big monkey wrench and cursed

Ron Boehm

it by saying, "They should have shit-canned this damn thing ten years ago." And this guy says," "Yeah, that do look pretty ageable alright."

The summer and the months leading up to my leaving for the Marine Corps passed pretty fast, plus I met my sweetheart and future wife, Eileen, at a club down in the French Quarter. She was a pretty blonde and eighteen years old. I was twenty-three at the time.

———•———

CHAPTER 2

USMC Training, OCS. TBS.

Officer Candidate School

I got my orders from the Marine Corps to report to Officer Candidate School (OCS) in Quantico, Virginia, in the first week of January in 1967. I had an airline ticket to Washington, D.C. That was the first time that I would fly on a commercial airliner and I was excited and quite nervous about my new adventure.

I arrived at the airport in D.C. and thought there would be someone to meet me and take me to Quantico, but to my surprise there was no one there. Instead I saw some other guys milling around and found out that they were there for OCS also. Someone said that we were to get on a train to Quantico, so I followed the crowd and boarded the train. As we pulled out of the station I noticed that it was snowing; that was the second time that I had ever seen snow. The first time was in 1961 in New Orleans, but it was just about an inch thick. This was real snow and it was really coming down. I thought it was great at the time, but I would not like it so much later on when we were running and training in it.

The train arrived in Quantico and as we got off, the Hell began. Drill Sergeants began to shout at us telling us to get into a formation.

"Hurry, hurry, get in line, get your spacing."

A Drill Instructor came up to me and asked to see my orders and when I handed them to him, he glanced briefly at them and threw them in the air, scattering them in the breeze and onto the snow. He screamed at me to pick them up and get in formation. Next thing I knew, we were marched to the barber shop and got all our hair cut off. Then we were marched to the supply center to get our green utilities uniform.

Everything after that was kind of a blur, but I remember getting to our barracks and as we entered I saw bunk beds lined up on both sides of this long room which had a wooden floor and foot lockers in front of the bunk beds. It was pretty stark, but it would be our home for the next ten weeks.

Our lives would not be our own for some time to come. Our every move, every minute would be controlled and planned. The Marine Corps had, at that time, 192 years of turning young men into Marines and nothing they did was not for a reason and part of a plan.

Our days included waking up at 5:30 AM, getting into the showers, getting dressed in the uniform of the day and off to the chow hall. Then it was classroom time, Physical Training and then to "The Grinder," an asphalt area for learning to drill. The real ball-buster was the forced march in the snow and ice up and down the hills, through the woods on trails with names like the Hill Trail and the South Bank trail.

It was hours of pure agony and gut check time. They pushed us to the breaking point and if you fell behind, stumbled or couldn't continue for a while, you would get a chit from the Platoon Sergeant or the Platoon Commander. The chits would say things like you showed a "Lack of courage," "Lack of fortitude," "Lack of desire," or something of that sort. I thought, "Damn, I wouldn't have fallen behind if I hadn't fallen five times in the snow." Here I was running up and down hills in the snow which was the first time I had seen hills and the second time I had ever seen snow. And then I was getting dressed down by Lieutenant Van Dam our Platoon Commander for showing lack of courage. I would do everything I could not to let that happen again.

The march was supposed to be a march, but would end up being a run to catch up with the guys in front of you in what was called an accordion effect. It was the means by which they tested your character, stamina and mental toughness.

One time, as we were running up and down the hills in the snow on the South Bank trail, I began cramping up. Just in back of

Ron Boehm

me was a tall buddy of mine and as my leg cramped up and I began to fall, and probably fall off the trail down the hill side, he grabbed me on the run by the collar and held me up until I got my feet under me again. That would have been another chit, I'm sure.

In OCS, there wasn't a lot of classroom learning; mostly we learned about our weapons, First Aid and Marine Corp history, which was so important in Marine Corps training. It is this instruction into the Marines' history that makes Marines understand that they are part of the greatest fighting force in the world and understanding that "Once A Marine Always A Marine." Courage, Honor, Fortitude and Determination never to be defeated are the very essence of the Marine Corps.

A few good men is not just a catchy phrase; it is the Marine Corps.

It was a while before I realized what the basis of our training was. It was mostly physical to get us in shape, but more than that it was to push us to the brink and force us to keep going further than we ever thought we could go. It was also to break and weed out the weak-willed and weak-spirited, for it was better to find out there in training who couldn't hack it rather than in combat when they would be leading forty-five Marines as a Platoon Commander. It was the reason that very time the DIs would find a weakling they would jump on them with both feet and never let up until the candidate broke or showed they could take it.

My game plan was to blend into the crowd and never stand out too much unless it was to be very good at something.

In our platoon we had this smallish mousy guy and I don't remember his name, only that the DI called him "House Mouse #1" and another weak-looking guy he called "House Mouse #2." The DI stayed on these two guys relentlessly. For the reason I just mentioned. But other guys seemed not to be bothered by the verbal abuse that we all received.

My buddy Dave "Shitty" Anderson was one of those. Dave was a big guy with a happy disposition. He would laugh at the DI's antics and one time when we were standing in formation out in the snow the DI asked Dave if he thought that some episode of verbal abuse was "funny." Most normal candidates would have replied "No, Staff Sergeant!" but not Shitty. He said "Yes, Staff Sergeant!" And with that the DI hit him with a snow ball right in the head. That set us all off laughing like crazy. I believe that earned us a two mile jog.

This particular DI was a black Staff Sergeant with a large repertoire of great verbal abuses and they were funny even if they were directed at you. Well, maybe not at first, but after you got used to them and learned not to take them too personally. Of course, one of the Marines' favorite sayings was, "You better get squared the hell away."

You could get into trouble for just about anything; one time I got caught singing in the shower and the DI made me go to each platoon in the company still in my bath towel and sing to them. You could imagine the response that I got with my serenade. But by this time I thought it was funny and didn't let stuff like that bother me.

Our Platoon Sergeant was Staff Sergeant Neisley, who was a great guy, and like most Marines at the end of your Boot Camp or OCS training, you would love these guys who helped make you into a Marine. Our other DI and assistant Platoon Sergeant was Sergeant McCauldy who was somewhat of a character also. He had a mustache and reminded me of a British Army sergeant by the way he looked. He was a buck sergeant with four hash marks on his sleeve. Each hash mark represented four years in the Corps and he was only a three striper. There were several stories of how he had been busted, but I don't know what the real story was.

Each one of us candidates had to stand fire watch duty at least a couple of times during OCS. You had a one-hour watch during the night in which you patrolled the barracks in order to make sure that the barracks were safe and that if there were a fire to break out you could sound the alarm. Well, one end of the company's barracks was right next to the railroad tracks, like about twenty feet away, and there was a passenger train that came through at about 2:00 AM every night. I think the Marine Corps must have paid the engineer to blow his whistle just as he passed the barracks in order to

Ron Boehm

scare the hell out of all the OCS candidates. Guys would be startled out of their sleep, sit up in bed and let out a scream as the train passed by. It was quite a sight when I had the watch at that time. I would look at my watch and anticipate the train whistle event. There was a railroad crossing in front of the barracks, so I guess there was a reason to blow the train whistle, but it was still another source of torture for the candidates.

The barracks we lived in was right on the Potomac River which provided a great view if you could enjoy a view while they were putting you though a meat grinder. The barracks was a two-story building covered with white weather boards. They called them the "White Elephants." Later on when I was in Vietnam there was club in downtown Da Nang called the "White Elephant." It had quite a reputation for drunkenness and rowdiness.

In OCS you learned all kinds of new words and phrases. Some were just military, but some were Marine Corps like: "You better get your asses squared away," or "Belay that order," meaning cancel that, and all Marines will remember, "What is that Irish Pennant hanging from your uniform for candidate?" An Irish Pennant was a green thread hanging for your uniform. Your heard the phrase, "Bounce a quarter off your bed." Well, that was more than just a phrase—that is how we had to make up our beds; tight enough to bounce a quarter.

Another screw-with-you ritual was "Get in your rack, Get out of your rack." The DI would come into the barracks and inspect us prior to lights out and getting into bed. We would stand at attention in front of our bunk beds, "our racks," and he would shout "get in your racks," and we would jump into our beds and lay at attention. Then he would say "get out of our racks," and we would have to get out and stand at attention in front of our beds just to be told again to "get in your racks." This went on for several times and the Sergeant would find that we were too slow at getting in or out of our racks and we would have to do it again. My problem was that I was in the top bed of the bunk bed and at five six, it took one foot on the lower bed and a high jumping technique to get into the top rack. After about my fourth or fifth attempt my jump was not quite as high as the one before and I was banging my crotch off the bed frame; that didn't feel very good.

And one of my favorites was "The Uniform of the Day." The uniform of the day would be posted or passed on and as soon as you got dressed, it would be changed.

Another drill was pushing our foot lockers around the floor of the barracks like a train saying "choo choo, choo choo." The Sergeants seemed never to run out of harassment techniques.

On the weekends, we would get off training around noon on Saturday and go out of the gate into the town, Triangle, Virginia. There we would wash our clothes, maybe get a burger or something like that. But you spent a bunch of time cleaning your gear and polishing your shoes and stuff like that. After so many weeks we were allowed to leave the base and the town of Triangle and go off to Washington, D.C. But by the time you got to D.C., had a couple of beers and something to eat, you just wanted to go back to the hotel and rest. Because of our training schedule, we were not used to staying up very long after dark. My buddy Phil Vannoy recalled that as we were sharing a hotel room in D.C., I would call my sweetheart Eileen and fall asleep in the middle to the conversation, and he would end up talking to her.

Phil was a great guy with a very pleasant disposition and a constant smile on his face, like Dave "Shitty" Anderson in that respect. The three of us were good friends, along with Marty Steele who was already a corporal involved in the OCS training when he got accepted as a candidate to OCS.

Marty was an outstanding corporal who had been to Vietnam already with the 1st Tank battalion and was serving as an instructor at OCS when he was recommended for OCS by his commander. His bunk was next to mine and all of us in the platoon benefitted from his advice on handling the rigors of training and this new life in the Marine Corps. Marty had a very distinguished career in the Marine Corps, retired as a Lieutenant General and a one point was in consideration for Commandant of the Marine Corps. He would become the highest ranking tank officer in the history of the Marine Corps. (Source: *Boys of '67*, by Charles Jones)

Dave Anderson would later be a platoon commander in Vietnam like most of the guys from our OCS and The Basic School classes. He was only in country a short time when he was shot in the chest in an action when his company got into a firefight with an North Vietnam Army regiment. He and his men had to be rescued by another friend, Ray Smith's, company. Ray would come to be one of the most decorated Marines of our era and retired as a Major General. He, Marty Steele, Jim Jones and Les Palm, in all of our OCS and TBS classes, would go on to become Marine Corps Generals and those whose careers and exploits are written about in a book titled Boys of '67 by Charles Jones. The book is mostly about these great Marines but as the title says it is about the Marine Officers of The Basic School of April 5, 1967. We would become one of, if not the most, heralded Basic School Class in Marine Corps history.

But I don't want to get too far ahead of myself. I mentioned that the Corps was trying to find people to be officers who could take the pressure of leading forty-five Marines in combat and try to get rid of those that couldn't hack it there in OCS rather than have them break in combat. One of those guys in our platoon did crack and got into a fight with an officer in Washington on one weekend. So he was taken out of our platoon and they later found him walking down the runway at the Quantico airfield in the middle of the night and acting strangely. He had snapped and was gone.

This comes under the "It's a small world category." As my platoon was marching to or from class we passed another platoon going the opposite way and this guy waves to me and shouts "Ronnie!" It was my friend from college, Dan DeBlanc. I didn't even know that he had joined the Corps. I would later cross paths with him again in Vietnam.

The physical aspect of OCS was tough, (the former enlisted guys who went through Boot Camp would laugh at that statement), but it got a little easier as we got into shape, all except for the forced marches on the Hill Trail—that never got easier. It was always a ball buster. We had the PFT (Physical Fitness Test), the PRT (Physical Readiness Test) and the O Course (Obstacle Course.) The PFT was a series of physical drills that you had to complete by doing a set number or do it in a certain time frame. It was designed to push the hell out of you and it did. The PRT was a three mile run with full pack, rifle, boots, helmet and gear that you had to complete in a certain time frame. It was a tough test for me, but I would make it, though it was nothing to brag about. The O Course was my favorite event and on one occasion I beat the company stud, a former jock, head to head. I had a good technique of rolling over the series of logs about four feet off the ground and we hit the last obstacle, the twenty foot rope climb even. But he tried to climb the rope with his arms, and I knew the trick of using the rope like a ladder, using my legs and feet to climb up. I slapped the top just before he did.

The Rifle Range

My favorite part of training was the rifle range. I can remember the feeling I had the first time that we went to the armory and signed out our M-14. Man, that was sweet. I learned very fast not to say "my gun"; it was a "rifle" not a "gun." The DI's would make you say to all in earshot, "This is my rifle" (while holding up your rifle) "and this is my gun" (while grabbing your crotch); "one is for killing, the other is for fun." But for me shooting was fun; I fired expert the first time I fired the M-14. That is a great rifle and still in use in the Corps.

At the range we fired standing up, in the "off hand" position, sitting, and in the prone or lying position. When you fired at the target, the guys manning the targets would mark the hit with a circular marker at the end of a stick. This way you could adjust your sight for "windage" and elevation or as they called it "putting in your rifle dope." If you missed the target completely, they would wave a red flag, which was called "Maggie's drawers."

Years later, I read a book about the Battle for Khe Sanh and the author began by describing the morning reveille scene with everyone standing up in their fox holes with helmet and flack vest on saluting the flag when the thump of mortars coming out of the NVA mortar tubes was heard. Everyone got back down in their holes. When the mortars ceased their explosions, someone waved a red flag, Maggie's Drawers. That said an awful lot about the Marines at their embattled hill top at Khe Sanh.

Marksmanship is paramount in the Marine Corps, where it is said that the most deadly weapon in the Corps is the rifleman and that every Marine is a rifleman first. If you don't have an Expert Rifle and Expert Pistol Badge, it is noticed. I wasn't so good with the .45 pistol; my first time to qualify, I qualified as Sharp Shooter, but my next time to qualify I fired Expert.

OCS lasted ten weeks and I was pretty excited as we approached the end of the course. We had been fitted for our officer's uniforms and sword and I made a loan to pay for everything. Officers buy their own uniforms.

Graduation day had come and my family or part of them took a train all the way from New Orleans to Quantico. My dad worked on the railroad and got a free family pass. It was my dad, my mom, three of my youngest sisters and my youngest brother on the longest trip my family had ever taken. On graduation day, the Marine officers to be commissioned and their families and friends were all gathered in the auditoriums. I looked up and spotted my family in the balcony and was happy to see them. When we were pronounced Officers in the United States Marine Corps and the band played the Marine Corps Hymn, I thought my chest would explode it was so expanded with pride. I looked up in the balcony and saw my dad with tears in his eyes. I had never seen that in my whole life, neither before or after. He was a tough guy who didn't show much emotion and gave very few compliments, but that put tears in my eyes, too. I'll never forget that moment.

So OCS was over, I had made it and I was now a 2nd Lieutenant in the United States Marine Corps. After a short leave I was to report to TBS or the Marine Corps' The Basic Officer's School.

On my flight home from OCS as a very proud 2nd Lieutenant in my green uniform with spit-shined shoes and spit-shined brim of my cover (hat, but don't ever say that in the Corps) I took my seat on the airplane and the stewardess said, "Here, let me take your hat" and put a thumb print right in the middle of that spit-shined cover's brim. I worked on that brim for hours to get it to shine like that. But what the hell, I was now a Marine Officer and heading home

OCS 3rd Platoon E Company —
Marty Steele and yours truly are holding the sign

TBS

The Basic Officer's School for Marine officers wasn't like OCS, a ball-buster; it was about learning to be a Marine Officer and learning the skills and the use of the tools that we

Ron Boehm

would use in combat. Vietnam was going strong and nearly all of us would see combat, most before the end of the year and those of us who went to flight school a year and a half later.

In Basic School I was assigned to the 1st Platoon of Mike Company. Assignment was based upon the alphabet so the last names of all the guys in my platoon started with A, B or C. In my squad of fifteen men and my fire team of five men was Fred Bonati, Tom Broderick, Pete Barber and Bob Bracken. All of us but Bracken would become pilots. Bob Bracken was legally blind I was told and shouldn't even be in the Marine Corps. Dave Cummings was in our squad and would go straight to Vietnam after Basic School like most of the 516 2nd Lieutenants from the TBS class of 5/67. He got wounded in Vietnam then went on to flight school after his rehab.

We all became good buddies and did most of the training and exercises together. Tom and Dave would go to Naval Flight School in Pensacola. Fred, Pete and I would go to the Air Force Flight School in a new program set up with the Air Force to train about one hundred Marine jet pilots a year. We would be in the very first classes of Marines to train in the Air Force's UPT (Undergraduate Pilot Training) program.

One of the first things that stood out to me at TBS was the training. Basic School trained all the officers to be platoon commanders no matter what MOS (Military Occupation Specialty) you would later become. Just like all Marines are trained to be riflemen, all officers are trained to be platoon leaders. It wasn't all about being trained by the book as written years ago in a different war, but rather, they were trying to train us from the experience of combat vets both enlisted and officers who had just returned from Vietnam. They were teaching us the most effective ways to do our jobs, the way that they learned in combat.

Also, the most important thing was to learn the subject matter and not just to pass a test. So immediately after a test we went over the test and learned the correct answers while it was still fresh in our minds.

Our M Company Commander was a short but tough stud of a guy and former Recon officer by the name of Captain Paul. He could run circles around all of us and was a very good leader who had just returned from Vietnam.

One of my favorite courses was Land Navigation where we were taught to read a map and navigate from point A to point B over the terrain or through the woods and of course to find your position by reading the terrain and correctly pin-pointing it on a map. This was also the basis for calling in fire support or air support.

We were taught the skills and techniques in class and then we would go out in the field to practice what we had just learned in class. In the course we had to find a number of ammo cans painted white and stuck on a stake in the middle of the woods. It was pretty challenging and you would see a Lieutenant in the middle of a road or field looking confused with a map in one hand and a compass in the other trying to figure out where he was or where the damn ammo can was.

Then we had a night time compass march, where we had to read the map and navigate through the woods at night to our objective and arrive by a certain time. I was teamed up with Bonati and we were discussing how to best accomplish the task. Fred looked at the map, looked at the sky and said follow me and that star. We took off running through the woods in the direction of our objective looking at the stars for guidance. I thought we made it to the objective first; however, when Fred and I got there Pete Barber was already there and leaving. He had a date or something that night and he didn't want to be late. He must have run the whole way because Fred and I were moving pretty fast through the woods that night. We were all cut up from getting lashed by the branches while running through the woods.

Fred was a piece of work and really smart. I really enjoyed his friendship and we would keep on crossing paths after TBS throughout our time in the Corps mainly because of our alphabetical alignment on orders.

When I went home on leave after OCS and before I reported to TBS I got to spend time with Eileen, my sweetheart, and we discussed getting married, but no commitment was made. However, the wheels were put in motion and after many phone calls back and

Ron Boehm

forth when I went back to Quantico, all of a sudden I was engaged to be married.

When I returned home on leave for Memorial Day in 1967, we got married in New Orleans. We were married on a Saturday and I had to be back at TBS on Monday morning for classes. I had rented an apartment in Woodbridge, Virginia, across from by buddy Tom Broderick and Ray Smith.

Eileen was nineteen and I was twenty-four years old at the time. This started a new adventure for both of us in the Marine Corps.

Eileen, having no experience with the military and its terminology, had some amusing incidents. One was when an MP was trying to giving her a parking ticket for parking in a no parking zone between the hours of 0800 to 1700 hours. She jumped all over the MP and told him in no uncertain terms that she didn't know what that meant and that she had only been here for two weeks. The MP apologized and tore up the ticket.

Another time Eileen and I went to Washington, D.C.- on the weekend with a Brazilian Marine Officer who was going through TBS with us. His name was Mark Agnise, a very nice and good-looking guy who was from a wealthy doctor's family in Brazil and who was dating a Brazilian movie star. Mark spoke several languages, including French.

Eileen was a pretty petite blond except for her chest which was a pretty good size. As the three of us were walking down M street in D.C. we passed two French sailors who stared at Eileen and said something in French. Eileen pretty much knew what they were saying, but asked Mark anyway. Mark tried to be polite and said something nice, but Eileen insisted on knowing exactly what they said; so Mark confessed and said that they had remarked, "Too much sail for so small a craft."

TBS lasted for twenty-one weeks from April 5 1967 through August, 1967, and most of the TBS graduates were to be 0301 Basic Infantry Officers and would be in Vietnam soon after graduating from TBS. There were a number of us who were going to flight school, which would be the Naval Flight School in Pensacola, Florida or so we thought. About a month before graduation, they called a number of us into a meeting and asked who wanted to go to Air Force Flight School. We said, "Why would we want to do that?" And they said, "You will be guaranteed jets." Everybody's hand went up.

A large number of the guys in that room were former enlisted who had a year or more of college, had a high GCT (IQ) test score, had stood out in Boot Camp and were signed up in the MAR-CAD program to become officers and pilots. I was one of the few with a college degree, because most guys out of college went from OCS straight to Naval Flight School; however, as I said earlier, the recruiters talked me into going to The Basic School.

In that room with me was Fred Bonati, Pete Barber, Rick Spitz, Kurt Wilbrecht and about twenty or so others. Kurt was Rick Spitz's good friend since boot camp and would become an F-4 pilot and would later be killed in Vietnam attacking a target when his plane failed to pull out of a dive. He probably took a hit from small arms fire on the way into the target. We would be the first group of Marines to go to Air Force Flight School.

The Boys of 5/'67

Our Basic School Class (TBS 5/67) was one of, if not the most renowned Basic School Class in Marine Corps history. Of the 542 2nd Lieutenants that started in that class on 5 April, 1967, 516 graduated on August 30, 1967. The 516 Marine Officers of this class were awarded twenty-two Silver Stars and ten Navy Crosses for bravery in combat and two Distinguished Flying Crosses.

Most of us served in Vietnam; for the guys that were infantry officers, they would be in combat in Vietnam within a few months after our graduation from TBS and right in the middle of the Tet

Offensive of January 1968. Tet was the Vietnamese New Year and in 1968 the North Vietnamese and their Viet Cong compatriots in South Vietnam started a country wide offensive that went on for months.

Eleven of those Marine officers fresh out of Basic School died within the first three months in country and our class lost a total of thirty-nine of its officers killed in action in Vietnam. (Source: *Boys of '67*, by Charles Jones)

For those of us that went on to be pilots, we would get there about a year and a half later.

Tet produced many fierce battles and many, many acts of bravery and heroism that helped shape the careers of a number of Marine officers that went on to be future top level leaders of the Corps.

Charles Jones' book Boys of '67 is a story about this Basic School Class but mainly covers the careers and exploits of these four Marine General Officers: General Jim Jones, Lieutenant General Marty Steel, Major General Ray Smith and Major General Les Palm.

Marty Steele

Martin R. Steele, my buddy from OCS, had an outstanding career in the Corps. He was a tank officer and rose in the ranks to retire as a Lieutenant General and became the highest ranking tank officer in Marine Corps history.

Marty had a brilliant thirty-five year career in the Corps and served in a whole host of important and prestigious billets including Commanding General of the Marine Corps Base in Quantico, Virginia, as well as being instrumental in getting the wonderful Marine Corps Museum built. Before his retirement in 1999, he was considered for the position of Commandant of the Marine Corps which was given to General Jim Jones.

Ray Smith

Ray L. Smith was a good friend of my buddy Fred Bonati and with whom I car pooled in TBS sometimes from our apartments in Woodbridge, Virginia. He became one of the most decorated Marines in modern history. He won the Navy Cross, two Silver Stars, the Bronze Star and three Purple Hearts along with numerous other awards in two tours in Vietnam and the other battles and operations he was involved in.

He was a 2nd Lieutenant when he took over as company commander for Alpha 1/1 in the battle for the ancient City of Hue where the Marines faced a NVA Brigade of about seventy-five hundred enemy troops.

He earned his second Silver Star at Khe Sanh towards the end of that epic Marine Corps battle.

I followed Ray's career to some extent; he was in Vietnam a year before I was while I was in flight training, returned to the states while I was in Nam and then returned as a Captain and adviser to the Vietnamese Marines the following year when I came home and was stationed at MCAS El Toro, California.

One evening, while watching the evening news I saw a reporter interviewing Captain Ray Smith just after a battle where they stopped the North Vietnamese advance southward at a river. The reporter asked him what he felt about the South Vietnamese Marines that he was with and he said something to the effect of, "Well, we stopped them (The NVA — North Vietnamese Army) here." That was all he needed to say I guess.

He got his Navy Cross on his second tour in Vietnam while an advisor to a group of about two hundred fifty Vietnamese Marines. They occupied a hill top outpost and were fighting off a number of savage assaults by a large NVA force estimated to be about two

Battalions during a period from March 30 to April 1, 1972. Ray's Vietnamese Marines defending the outpost were down to about twenty-eight and air support was no longer available. He attempted to lead his men off the hill to the safety of friendly lines. As they were making their exit, they encountered the booby-trapped barbed wire perimeter fence and an enemy soldier. Ray shot the enemy soldier and threw himself backwards onto the fence, letting his people run over him as he lay on the downed barbed wire, then led his troops to the safety of friendly lines. (Source : *Boys of '67*, by Charles Jones)

Later when I had got out of the Corps, I saw that he was the Battalion Commander who led the Marines who landed in Grenada to rescue the students and after that his unit took over in Beirut, Lebanon for the Marines that got blown up in their barracks in 1983. Two hundred forty-one Marines, sailors and soldiers lost their lives in that attack.

I knew Ray through my buddy Fred Bonati who was Ray's best man in his wedding. They had been enlisted Marines together, and Fred predicted back then in TBS that Ray would some day be Commandant of the Marine Corps. He came close in his prediction, for Ray was considered for that position.

Ray was a warrior in every sense of the word from modern day to those of past history. After his tours in Vietnam, Ray returned to Basic School as a Captain and instructor. He was nick-named "E-Tool" Smith for his heroics in Vietnam when it was thought by his students that in a fierce combat situation he ran out of ammunition and fought off the enemy with his e-tool (a small foldable shovel.) (Source: *Boys of '67*, by Charles Jones)

Ray retired as a Major General and when Ray retired from the Marine Corps in 1999 he was the most decorated Marine living at that time. The term "Warrior" fits him very well.

Fred Bonati told me a story about when he and Ray Smith were going through the MARCAD processing (a program to promote enlisted Marines to flight school) at Camp Pendleton and they were being interviewed by officers on a selection committee.

He said, "We were going through the process for the MAR-

CAD program, and we had to jump through a bunch of hoops. One was we had to individually go before boards made up of three, four or five officers, Captains, Majors and Lieutenant Colonels. They wanted to see how you handled yourself. Poise. Confidence. They asked all sorts of questions in order to ascertain whether you were officer material and your intentions were sincere. For instance, they'd put words that you may or may not know in their sentences just to see if you knew the meanings. Like siblings, peers, etc. They asked Ray if he had any peers, and he answered yes, that the members of the board for instance, were his peers. One of the officers, being stunned by his reply, asked him if he really knew the meaning of the word peer. Ray says, 'The Constitution of the U.S. says that you are my equal.' Doesn't sound like a big deal, but I was scared shitless when I went in there. In fact the board thought I was aloof and cold, when actually I was catatonic. So, Smitty goes in there and pulls that off. Pretty cool."

Oddly enough, Marty Steele and Ray Smith were both former enlisted Marines and roommates in The Basic School.

Jim Jones

I didn't know Jim Jones, but if you were a Marine in that era you heard of James L. Jones. He got his baptism by fire in a battle in Vietnam where his company was battling a NVA battalion in an area called Foxtrot Ridge. His credentials were built over the years as he rose through the ranks to become the 32nd Commandant of the Marine Corps, Supreme Allied Commander of American and NATO Forces in Europe and Africa, then National Security Adviser for President Obama.

　　　　　　　　　　Ron Boehm

Les Palm

eslie M. Palm was a 2nd and 1st Lieutenant artillery officer who earned his combat pay with the 1st Battalion 13 Marine Regiment at Khe Sanh and Hill 881 South in Vietnam from December 1967 to December 1968. He later commanded the 10th Marine Regiment in August 1990 and participated in Operation Desert Shield and Desert Storm. Les Palm had a great thirty-one year career in the Marine Corps and retired as a Major General. After his retirement, he served for twelve years as Publisher and CEO of The Marine Corps Association which publishes the Marine Corps Gazette and the Leatherneck Magazines. (Source: Wikipedia)

TBS M CO

CHAPTER 3

Flight School, A6A Training

Orders to Air Force Flight School

After graduation from TBS, I was given orders to report to the U.S. Air Force Flight Training at Craig Air Force Base in Selma, Alabama, to start my training on October 25, 1968 with the UPT Class of 69-03. I had a two week leave back home in New Orleans and then recruiting duty in the New Orleans area until I reported to Craig AF Base. I was very excited and could hardly wait to go. Eileen, my new wife, and I enjoyed being home for awhile, but we were both anxious to start our new life.

My Flying Buddies

A number of my buddies also received orders to flight school around that time; they were: Fred Bonati — Williams Air Force Base, Arizona; Tom Broderick — U.S. Naval Flight School, Pensacola, Florida; Dave Cummings (after his first tour in Vietnam as an infantry officer)- Naval Flight School, Pensacola, Florida; Pete Barber — Craig Air Force Base, Selma, Alabama; Rick Spitz- Laughlin Air Force Base, Del Rio, Texas.

My friends from college and the New Orleans area who received orders to flight school were my roommate at Southeastern Louisiana College, Jerry LeBlanc USAF — Shepherd AFB, Wichita Falls, Texas; my friend from college, Dan DeBlanc, USMC — US

Naval Flight School, Pensacola, Florida; from my neighborhood in New Orleans, Charlie de Gruy, USN, U.S. Naval Academy graduate — Naval Flight School Pensacola, Florida.

From my high school class was Arlan Hanley, USMC Naval Flight School, Pensacola, Florida, and Danny Phillips, Naval Flight Officers' School, Pensacola, Florida.

Charlie de Gruy had a great career in the Navy; he joined as an enlisted seaman in the Navy Reserve at seventeen years old, went on to Southeastern Louisiana College with a bunch of us from the Lakeview neighborhood in New Orleans, and then received an appointment to the United States Naval Academy.

He flew F-4Js with VF 96 in Vietnam, commanded an F-14 squadron VF-211 and a F-4 training squadron VF-101. He was XO of the USS America CV 66, was a Navy test pilot, and commanded two ships, the USS Austin (LPD4) and USS Saipan (LHA2). He served as a Chief of Staff of Naval Doctrine Command. Charlie retired as a Captain in the United States Navy, just missing by a bit the rank of Admiral.

All of us earned our wings of Silver or Gold and for us Marines who went through Air Force Flight School, we earned our Silver Wings, and then we had to earn our Navy Wings of Gold, so we had both.

The Marine Corps set up a program with the Air Force in 1968 to train about one hundred Marine pilots a year. This lasted for only a few of years as Vietnam was coming to an end. The story I heard was that there wasn't enough room to train the number of Marine pilots in Pensacola that the Corps needed so they sent the potential jet pilots to Air Force UPT training and most of the other Marines that went to Pensacola ended up in helicopters.

It was a pretty unique experience to be one of only about six Marines on an Air Force Base. Green really stood out.

Of those buddies listed above, all had good careers in the military and most served in combat in Vietnam.

Fred Bonati and I would cross paths again and again, flew to Vietnam on the same flight and were "hootch-mates" for awhile in Da Nang until he was transferred to the air base at Chu Li. We would get together again in El Toro Marine Air Station in California when we returned from Vietnam.

Tom Broderick would end up flying Huey gunships in Nam and crashed one in Da Nang Bay which almost cost him his life. An Army "Skycrane Helicopter" tried to rescue the downed crew when his Huey helicopter went down in the water, but the 125 miles per hour downdraft from the rotor blades of the big helicopter pushed him under the water. Tom was a very good swimmer and was on the college swim team in Wisconsin, but he couldn't handle the force of the downdraft from the rotor blades. He had one of the other crew members in his arm trying to keep them both afloat but couldn't hold on any longer and let him slip away. He told me that he had thought it was all over, put his head down, asked God to protect his family and was entering a peaceful end when he felt something hit his helmet. He put his hand up and felt the runner of another helicopter. Someone pulled him into a Huey chopper that had set down into the water, flew him to a medical center on the beach and saved his life, then flew away.

Tom tried to find out who had saved his life, but there were no record of any helicopter flight like that around that area at that time. Tom said he now believes that it was maybe an unauthorized flight by a crew chief or someone who just took the Huey for a joy ride. But he was pretty thankful that they did. He was the only survivor from his flight crew.

Tom had several other brushes with death in his Marine Corps flying career having crashed some other aircraft. Tom's brother also nearly bought the farm when the aircraft he was flying went into the drink after taking off from an aircraft carrier. He just barely got out of the ditched plane when the huge ship ran over him. He was pretty much given up for lost, but a destroyer doing search and rescue picked him up. I guess it runs in the family.

Rick Spitz is another friend with whom I share a lot of stories. I didn't know him in TBS; we met in the A6A training squadron VMA (AW) 224 at Cherry Point, North Carolina, and became fast friends and remain close even today. We were roommates in Da

Nang, were in the same squadron VMA (AW) 242, went to Jungle Survival School and FAC School together.

Dave Cummings, Fred Bonati, Tom Broderick, Pete Barber and I were squad mates in the 1st Platoon of Mike Company in TBS and we all became pilots.

Dave flew Cobra gunships in Vietnam and received the Distinguished Flying Cross for some very heroic flying. I was told the story that Dave was flying a two seat Cobra gunship and heard the call for an energy extract of a wounded Marine on the side of a mountain. The CH-46's rescue helicopters couldn't get in because of the low clouds surrounding the mountain, so Dave went in for the rescue slowly letting his Cobra down the side of the mountain in the fog or clouds. He set the chopper down, got out of his bird, put the wounded Marine in his seat, hung onto the small wing that holds the rocket pod outside the aircraft, as the other pilot flew all three of the Marines off the mountain. I also heard that his CO almost court-martialed him, but then put him up for the DFC (Distinguished Flying Cross).

Rick Spitz and Dave were two of the guys from our Basic School class to receive the DFC.

Pete Barber was in the flight school class ahead of me at Craig AFB and was selected to fly F-4s after graduation from Air Force flight school as was Fred Bonati. All three of us ended up at Cherry Point Marine Air Station in North Carolina.

Forty years later at our reunion, I was so overwhelmed by the experience of meeting these wonderful old friends and Marines again, listening to their stories in informal gatherings after the scheduled events, that all I could think to say when I addressed the group after dinner at the Marine Corps Museum was, "I'm not a hero, but this room is filled with them." And that was not mere flattering comment; it was the truth and an understatement at that.

It was August of 1967, Basic School was coming to an end and I had my orders to Air Force Flight School at Craig AFB in Selma, Alabama. I was to report for flight training with the UPT (Undergraduate Pilot Training) Class of 69-03. I had a couple of weeks leave at home in New Orleans and then I was assigned recruiting duty for a short time until Flight School Started. I was excited and a little bit nervous about flight school; I didn't know how I would do. This was a whole new adventure and I had only been in a small airplane once and in an airline plane twice. But I was looking forward to it very much. It was of some comfort to know that I had Eileen with me for moral support. It seemed that every new thing in my life I had to face all alone; little league, high school, college and OCS I had done all on my own. So this was going to be a great experience for both Eileen and me.

Flight School

I reported to Air Force Flight School at Craig AFB in Selma, Alabama in October of 1967. UPT Class 69-03 started on October 25, 1967 and lasted for fifty-three weeks. Of the sixty-six green flight school enrollees that started training, fifty-one of us would eventually earn our Air Force silver wings on December 3, 1968.

We started our flying lessons in T-41s which was the Air Force's version of a Cessna 172, and I loved every minute of it. Every take off and every landing I thought was thrilling, some a little more than others. I would come home and tell Eileen everything that we did or learned that day. We were learning new flying terminology and procedures all the time, and we were issued our official aviator's sun glasses. We were cool or thought we were.

We started out in the classroom and then in the Link Trainers. From there we moved on to our first flying lessons in the T-41 at the municipal satellite field called Selfield with civilian instructors. The sections alternated with one section going to class in the morning and flying in the afternoon and then switching to morning flying and afternoon classes. There were plenty of crazy stories and funny incidents with that many trainees learning the new skills of flying.

Our class was divided up into two sections, "A" and "B" Sections. We had three captains in our class: Captain Mike Nelson, USAF, was student commander of "A" Section, Captain Kevin Sliwinski, USAF, was "B" section's student commander and Captain Jack Rippy, USMC, who was my Marine counter-part in the section "A." Mike Nelson and Kevin Sliwinski were already navigators in the Air Force and had all of that experience in aviation going for them.

Each class had two Marines assigned to it, one in each section. Jack Rippy was the Marine in "A" Section and I was in "B" Section. We became great friends, graduated flight school together, went through A6A training together, were in the same A6A squadrons VMA (AW) 224 at Marine Corp Air Station Cherry Point, North Carolina and VMA (AW) 242 in Vietnam and again at MCAS El Toro, California, when we returned from Vietnam. Jack was a funny guy and a bit eccentric. He was already a lawyer when he joined the Marine Corps and he was very good at arguing a point no matter how insignificant it was. We had many a crazy story between us.

I completed my first solo flight on November 17, 1967. When you came back after your first solo flight you would cut a piece of your tee shirt off, put your name and the date of your "solo" on it and pin it to the bulletin board in the flight shack. That was quite a day. I was very nervous, as were we all, walking out to the airplane to be all alone flying an airplane for the first time. In the back of your mind was the thought, "What if I freeze up or forget how to fly, or worse, forget how to land?"

Solo Tee Shirts

The physical part of flying, the coordination, came easy to me, probably because I was an athlete my whole life. I later had difficulty in the instrument phase in T-37s.

One of the first things we had to learn was the proper radio procedures and terminology to use while flying, like making position reports while in the traffic pattern. We would fly around in the pattern doing touch and goes and calling our position like "down wind," "base" and "final." The guys who were not flying would gather around the radio in the flight shack while waiting for their turn to fly and listen to the other guys making their position calls. I had this very thick New Orleans accent back then saying things like "warta" for water and "French Quarta," things like that. A lot of guys, if they hadn't been to New Orleans and heard that "Nu Arlins" accent before, thought that I was from New York or New Jersey. It turned out that listening to me make my position calls was one of their favorite things to do. They just loved to hear me on the radio.

About two years later, while flying a combat mission over Laos and sometime in the middle of the night, I had checked into the 7th Air Force controlling agency radio call sign "Moonbeam."

I reported into "Moonbeam" with my call sign, "Marine Ringneck 54," my aircraft type—Alpha 6 and my ordinance on board—22 Delta 2's (five hundred pound bombs.)

At the same time there was an Air Force F-4 on the same frequency and he came up on the radio and asked if this was Romeo Bravo (phonetic alphabet for R B and in this case Ron Boehm) from Selma, Alabama?

I responded, "Affirmative."

It was my flight school classmate George Driscoll who recognized my voice two years later, half-way around the world while flying an Air Force F-4 on combat mission over Laos. What a small world.

Another guy in our class with a memorable accent was the tall slender Joe Jackson from Alabama. He claimed he was from East Taboga, or East of Boga, Alabama, or someplace like that. Like I said, he had a pretty thick Alabama accent. I'm not sure there really was a place by that name or it was just Joe's joke. To say that Joe had a southern drawl would be an understatement for sure.

He would say things like, "You godda get tight", or "Eassse off" and "Whar ya at." He kept us laughing all the time. You just couldn't help loving the guy.

We had three foreign students in our class, a Norwegian, Finn Berg, and two Iranians. One of the Iranians was from an upper class family and the other was just from the military ranks. Finn was a smart guy and very likable who fit in with all of the rest of us and was an excellent student. The Iranians were very different and never fit in with the class. One of the Iranians was terrible at flying and had trouble with the English language. I thought he would either kill himself or someone else before long.

One day while flying in the T-41, he was turning final approach as the tower had cleared another plane onto the runway for takeoff. The tower tried to tell him to wave off and go around, but he kept on coming just as the other aircraft taxied into the runway. We looked out from the flight shack in horror, expecting a collision. The Iranian touched down right behind the other aircraft which was getting ready to take off, and amazingly gave it the power and hopped over the other aircraft and did a touch and go (touch down and take off without stopping). I don't know how the two aircraft missed each other or how the Iranian pulled off that recovery. It was amazing.

That one Iranian didn't last much longer after that. Actually, that might have been his last flight. On the other hand, Finn the Norwegian was one of our top pilots. He was at the time a Sergeant in the Norwegian Air Force and was a cool and overall pleasant guy to hang with.

One of our big unexpected events was when a Marine F-8 pilot lost his radio while flying in the weather over our area, found a hole in the clouds and spotted an airfield. He descended through the opening in the clouds and, because it was the weekend, landed at an unmanned satellite field called Vaiden Field that the T-37s and T-38s used to do touch and goes. He used his survival knife to break into the radio shack, turned on the radio and called to find out where he was. I remember being very impressed when I met the pilot and thought to myself, "Wow, he's a Marine jet pilot and he just landed at our airfield." It was a little bit of hero worship on my part.

T-37

T-37 Phase

We finished up T-41s at Selfield and moved on to T-37s, a very small two-seat primary jet trainer that made a loud whistling sound. They called it "a three thousand pound dog whistle." It was so small that to pre-flight the cockpit you just leaned over the canopy rail and reached in. I was really excited to get to fly a jet. This was getting close to being a real pilot and I remember being thrilled when we checked out our new equipment: a G-suit worn like cowboy chaps that inflated under G forces to help keep your blood from pooling in the lower part of your body, helmet and parachute. Wow, that was so cool.

However, my first ride in the T-37 was a blur because everything went so much faster and I had a very tough time with a feeling of claustrophobia. In the T-41, you were in a fairly large and open cockpit and you wore your flight boots, flight suit, hat (called a cover in the Marine Corps) and sunglasses. Now in the T-37 you were in a little, tight cockpit and wore a G-suit, harness, parachute, helmet with visor and oxygen mask. It was so confining that I had to fight that terrible claustrophobic feeling.

I told my wife Eileen that I didn't know if I could handle it. She told me that I was a Marine and I had handled everything they had given me so far and that I'd come too far to turn back now. I fought it for another flight or two, but as soon as I started to fly the airplane I got so involved with the flying, I didn't have time to think about anything else and it was never a problem again.

Another early memory regarding the T-37 phase was that of my first time actually flying the aircraft in the traffic pattern; it went so fast that I thought, "There is no way I will be able to enter into the break, throttle back, lower flaps, drop landing gear, and make a radio call all in that short time frame." But I gradually caught up with the airplane and did it with ease.

The T-37 was fun to fly, and after getting proficient at taking off and landing the bird, we soloed and then came one of my favorite phases of flying, formation flying. The first time we edged up next to another airplane in the middle of the sky I was awed by the sight of flying just a few feet away from another airborne aircraft. In close or Parade Formation your aircraft's wing-tip is positioned three feet from the lead aircraft's wing-tip on three planes; horizontally by three feet, vertically by three feet and set in back of the lead's wing by three feet. To look out and see another aircraft so close and suspended in mid-air seemed magic to me. I loved it and was one of the first in my group to solo in formation flying.

Your whole reference with regards to flying in tight formation with another aircraft is just a reference point on your aircraft lined up with a reference point on the other aircraft. The pilot in the lead aircraft flies and directs the wingman, the wingman just flies that relative position off the lead. It's great. In a loose formation, you fly your aircraft and maintain a relative distance and position to the lead.

Ron Boehm

One of our favorite instructor pilots in T-37s was "The Bear," a Major whose real name I don't remember, but he was a burly guy with big bushy eyebrows, a good sense of humor and patience. He had a way of making you comfortable while being able to get instruction over to you.

Our flying now was out of Craig AFB with air work in the designated Craig training area and shooting touch and goes at Vaiden Field.

We had a control booth of sorts on the side of the runway where an instructor and students would monitor the traffic pattern; T-37s where on one runway and T-38s were on the other runway in opposite hand patterns. In the duty in the control booth, you would receive the position radio calls from the planes in the pattern and check for the landing gear being down and things like that. The T-37 control booth's call sign was "Henhouse." One day I was on duty in the "Henhouse" when a position call came in from an aircraft whose pilot must have been a former Craig student or instructor when he said his call sign and reported, "On initial approach at flight level 800;" that would be 80,000 feet. We figured that he must have been flying a U-2 to be that high.

Eileen and I lived in a little one bedroom house we rented from a wonderfully nice lady named Mrs. Hardin. Our house was in back of Mrs. Hardin's farm house out in the country and since Mrs. Hardin was an antique dealer she had furnished our little house with antiques. It was great and perfect for Eileen and myself. We would throw parties outside for the squadron and I would go dove and quail hunting in the fields behind the house.

Mrs. Hardin's son, Buddy Hardin, was a few years older than me and had played football for Bear Bryant at The University of Alabama. The whole family were just very nice people.

I did fairly well in the T-37 phase; flying the aircraft as physical exercise came easy to me. It was the instrument portion that I had difficulty catching on to. I was getting all up tight when I had an instrument hop and I was worried about my status for the first time in my training.

One of the neat things about flying the T-37 was that you got to stall and spin it, then recover from the spin and stall. In most jet aircraft a spin would be game, set and match, game over, but the "Tweet" had straight wings and you could spin it all day long. Once you stalled it and held one rudder pedal down and the stick back to induce a spin, then you began the recovery from a fairly flat spin as the plane rotated and bobbed up and down slightly. That was fun to me as was aerobatics in general, but some guys didn't like it at all.

T-38

Moving on to the T-38 phase of our training was looked upon with great excitement by myself and the class. The T-38 was a sleek white dart, fast and very maneuverable. The engine tolerances were tight and a piece of paper or some small amount of debris on the runway could FOD (foreign object damage) the engine. However, it was supersonic and everyone got at least one chance to break the sound barrier, which was cool but anti-climactic. When you went through the barrier you felt a little stick movement and some of the instrument needles jumped slightly but not some great experience. But then again how many people get to go supersonic?

Ron Boehm

Again, I did fairly well in the flying aspect of the T-38 phase; I was one of the first to solo again and fast in getting the formation flying down, but I struggled in the instrument phase and even busted a check ride. I was uptight and just couldn't see the big picture. Things changed for the better for me when I was taken under the wing of Major Smithwick. He said that I would only fly with him, and he went about the task of relaxing me and getting the concept and technique of instrument flying over to me.

The breakthrough came to me on a flight with the Major when he told me that the whole idea was to "Take-off, climb to an altitude, turn on course, descend and make turns to line up on final for the airport you are going to and land."

"Everything else is just a difference in altitude and heading."

On one flight, he said to me he was just along for the ride, that he had a book to read and that I should take the airplane, do whatever I wanted to do and have fun.

He said to call him when we were on final approach.

That was the turning point for me; I relaxed and realized flying was fun and that I could understand the instrument part of flying OK.

It was kind of ironic because I ended up flying the A-6 Intruder which, along with the Air Force's F-111, was one of the two most sophisticated all-weather attack instrument aircrafts flying at the time.

I give the Major all the credit of getting me over that big bump in my training. He saw in me what I was having doubts about and was hurting my confidence. He knew what I needed and made sure I got it right. I can't thank him enough.

My buddy Jack Rippy had a similar situation in that he had a difficult point in his training also and gave credit to his T-38 IP, Bill Sterling, for getting him through.

One of our instructors who got my attention was a Major who had been a "Wild Weasel" pilot in Vietnam before becoming an instructor. These were the guys with big balls whose job was to attack the North Vietnamese missile sites and protect the F-4s and F-105 strike aircraft. That was a deadly and dangerous mission. They had missiles being shot at them and then attacking those same sites that were shooting at them. But they did a great job of protecting the various flights going to attack targets in Laos and North Vietnam.

In Jack's section, he had a former RF-101 Voodoo reconnaissance aircraft pilot as an instructor. Jack said that there was a contemporary puff flick about the reconnaissance missions called "Alone, Unarmed and Unafraid," and this guy's comment was, "Well, two out of three ain't bad."

Instrument training, as every instrument pilot will attest to, involved "time under the hood," which meant that you would be flying with a hood over your eyes so as to keep you from seeing outside the cockpit and therefore flying only by seeing the instruments. You had to constantly cross-check the instruments to keep your course, altitude and airspeed correct. The technique involved moving your eyes from instrument to instrument in a constant scanning motion and not staying on one of them. Vertigo could make the task about twenty times more difficult, because your mind was telling you one thing and the instruments were saying something else. You had to force yourself with all your will power to believe the instruments and not your mind.

You might be flying while leaning over about thirty degrees trying to keep the airplane level. There was a saying in instrument training that, "One peek from under the hood was worth a thousand crosschecks," and it was true.

Ron Boehm

Scanning outside the cockpit was very important while flying VFR (visual flight rules); you had to look out for other aircraft. I drove my wife nuts while driving by scanning the area while driving telling her that I was practicing my scan technique. She said, "It would be best to look straight ahead before we got into a crash." Eileen was very wise for her young self. She was only nineteen when we got married and I was twenty-four. Wow! We were kids, but it wasn't unusual at that time for people to get married at that age.

One of my funny memories in the T-38 phase was when we were taking off in the late afternoon and landing after dark getting some nighttime flying time and landings. One of the guys in our class thought he was going blind as the sun was setting and it got darker and darker. He was in a bit of a panic thinking he was losing his eye sight and wondering how he was going to be able to land his aircraft when he reached up and lifted his dark visor up and then touched his sun glasses on his face. He hadn't realized that he was wearing his sun glasses when he put his dark visor down thus rendering himself almost blind when the sun went down. Needless to say, he was very happy to find that he was not going blind, just absent-minded and feeling kind of dumb. But all of us had at least one dumb moment, if not several, in our training experience.

One of my dumb moments was when I was out solo in the flying area practicing aerobatics. On the side of the canopy rail was a yellow caution warning which stated "Caution — Do Not Engage Full Lateral Stick Travel." So I thought, "Why, it can't be that bad." So I decided to try it. I pushed the stick fully to the left and the aircraft did a violent snap roll to the left, my head and helmet bounced off the canopy and the aircraft did at least two, maybe three very rapid aileron rolls before my eyes uncaged and I could see straight. Then I said to myself, "Wow! So that's why they have that caution sign on the canopy rail, dumb ass!"

I loved formation flying and as in T-37s I did well in that phase of T-38 training. Taking off and landing in formation was great as was flying a few feet away from a beautiful bird like the T-38.

If just gave me a wonderful feeling seeing the other bird suspended in mid-air just a few feet away.

One of my instructors was paranoid of close-formation flying and would not let you get into the proper aircraft separation of three feet. He had an iron grip on the stick, but I guess flying with numb-nut students all day and being just three feet away from a mid-air collision, I might have done the same.

Our final instrument check ride was pretty much the end of our flight school training; once you passed that check ride you were home free with a great feeling of elation. After that, we had some more flying but it was just more or less getting flying hours after that. We finished up and Jack Rippy, my Marine class counterpart, and I both got orders to MCAS Cherry Point, North Carolina, for A6A Intruder training.

Our graduation day at Craig AFB was December 3, 1968; we had a short leave and then reported to MCAS Cherry Point in mid-December of 1968.

Lt. Ron Boehm

Capt. Jack Rippy

Ron Boehm

Cherry Point

As I was checking in at Cherry Point, there was a big commotion with sirens wailing and emergency vehicles running around. An F-4 jet had crashed on takeoff and the pilot and RIO (back seat - Radar Intercept Officer) had ejected. I found out later that day that the pilot was my friend from TBS and flight school Pete Barber who ejected from the aircraft after his RIO and at a low altitude as the aircraft was rolling on its side. The low altitude and the plane's position didn't give Pete's chute time to open and he landed while still in his ejection seat in the fuel pits. He was badly injured but still conscious. It was almost a miracle, but the seat hit back first and saved him. Pete was in the flight school class just before Jack and my flight school class at Craig AFB and was in my squad in The Basic School at Quantico.

Pete's arm and shoulder were badly broken in the ejection from the F-4. The usual procedure to initiate an ejection from a Navy and Marine jet was to pull the face curtain from the top of the seat down over your face with the secondary ejection handle in the seat between your legs. But we had gone through the Air Force training and their jets had the primary ejection handle on the side of the seats where an arm rest would be with the secondary handle also being between your legs. I don't know if that had any bearing on his pulling the handle between his legs; maybe this was just the closest handle to grab, but when Pete pulled the eject handle upwards his arm got up into the wind stream after the canopy was blown off and this was the cause for the damage to his arm and shoulder. Had Pete used the face curtain rather than the seat handle his arm may not have been damaged as much. But a fraction of a second probably saved his life and to have survived leaving a jet fighter low to the ground and ejecting on a ninety degree angle without the chute opening is very close to miraculous. I understand that Pete recovered enough to fly again.

Jack and I checked into MAG 24 and were assigned to the A-6 squadron VMA (AW) 224 then TADed (temorary additional duty) to the to the TA-4 training squadron VMAT-103 to get some training and familiarization with Naval Aviation procedures. This program was brand new and we were in the first few groups to make the transition from Air Force to the Marine Corps aviation.

And since we were the first groups of Marines to go through Air Force flight training instead of Naval Flight School in Pensacola, Florida, they had to figure out how to get us up to snuff and transitioned to Marine Corps aviation. We were a bit of an experiment. As Air Force trained pilots, we had just one year of training and were instrument-qualified to fly jets when we received our wings, but our Navy-trained counterparts had a year and a half of training which included carrier landings, gunnery, air to air tactics and bombing training. They were much further along in the training then we were. I felt like I learned to fly combat in Vietnam.

In the TA-4s we got some flying time, got to drop some little blue practice bombs, got some SATS runway experience (arrested landings and catapult take-offs on a landing field,) to simulate carrier flight operations. We were then sent to the A6 training squadron VMAT (AW) 202 to become A6A Intruder pilots or for some guys EA-6 Prowler pilots and BNs. V is for fixed wing, M is for Marine, A for attack, (AW) for all weather.

All weather is what the A-6 was all about. It had the capability of attacking a target in all weather conditions and was one of the most sophisticated aircraft weapon systems flying at the time. I'll never forget the first time that I sat in the A-6; it was a lot bigger than anything I had flown in before. The cockpit was also much higher off the ground.

Our sister squadrons at Cherry Point were VMA (AW) 332 Moonlighters and VMA(AW) 121 Green Knights.

It was also in my first weeks in VMA (AW) 202 that I met Rick Spitz who was in my Basic School Class but in a different company. Rick or Dick as we called him then would become one of my best friends and that friendship would last for a lifetime. We would later become roommates in Vietnam.

Another friend from Basic School was Fred Bonati, my buddy and squad-mate, who along with Pete Barber from Basic School, ended up at Cherry Point also. They were in the F-4 training squadron VMFAT 101. Fred went through Air Force Pilot Training at Williams AFB in Arizona, Rick went through Laughlin AFB in Del Rio, Texas, and Pete went through Craig AFB with Jack and me in Selma, Alabama.

So out of the 1st Platoon of "M" Company at TBS we had five guys all in the same squad become pilots; Fred Bonati flew F-4s, Pete Barber F-4s, Tom Broderick Huey gunships, Dave Cummings Cobra gunships, and I flew the A6A.

Training in the A-6 was a bit different in that this was the aircraft that we would fly in combat, so I guess I was more conscious of the training. We went through simulator training, had a few flights in the right seat with an instructor and then flew our first flight as a pilot. The A-6 was a great aircraft. It was made by Grumman Aircraft and typical of Grumman aircraft, it was a very sturdy and well-built aircraft. Some called them the "Lead Sled." It was a great bombing platform and could carry twenty-eight five hundred pound bombs but usually we carried twenty-two, leaving the two bombs off next to the landing gear doors for clearance.

But the most important feature of the A6A was that it was one of the most sophisticated electronic system aircraft at the time. Its main mission was that of an All Weather Attack Aircraft, that could attack a target in just about any weather without visually seeing it. The A-4s, A-7s, F-4s, F-105s had to have a visual on the target to attack them. Only the Air Force's F-111 had a similar capability as the A-6.

The cockpit was set up with the pilot on the left side and a BN (Bombardier Navigator) on the right side sitting side by side, as opposed to the F-4 where the pilot and RIO sat front and back. Some of our training was to run "road wreckies" on the highways in and around North Carolina where we would lock on to cars or trucks traveling down the highway and run a simulated attack on them.

The A-6 had the capability of seeing with its look down doppler radar and our computer weapon system could locate a vehicle moving at four miles per hour plus, relative to the surroundings. The BN could then lock onto that vehicle and we could drop our bombs with deadly accuracy. This was our primary mission in Vietnam and Laos. But in Nam we were looking for trucks at night in a triple canopy jungle and not on a wide open highway. Oh yeah, and people on the ground were shooting at us.

We had this bombing practice run up to an airfield in New Hampshire where we carried a small blue practice bomb and tried to pick up and bomb a remote controlled tank that they ran up and down the runway. That in itself was OK, but the neat thing was that the mission was always scheduled on Fridays and the squadron would place our lobster order with a local fisherman on the day before and the flight crew would then land at a near-by airport and pick up our lobster order. We would load them in a wing tank that was modified with a little hatch door in which we loaded the lobsters for the flight back to Cherry Point for that evening's Squadron lobster boil party. That was pretty cool.

The new pilots got to fly in the A-6 weeks before the BNs did. Their training was in a larger aircraft that had several BN consoles set up inside where they ran their systems and practiced their skills. The A-6 trainee pilots would train in the A-6 itself with experienced BNs instructing us in our missions. After a while we finally got to fly with the trainee BNs, "nugget pilot, nugget BN."

After we completed our A-6 initial training phase and got our rating as A-6 pilots, we were transferred back to VMA (AW) 224 to complete our training and get us ready for Vietnam. It was also at that point that we were given our Navy Wings of Gold. We were supposed to get carrier qualified on the USS Lexington down in Pensacola but the ship was down for repairs and they needed to get us to Vietnam, so we got our gold wings when we were transferred back to 224.

VMA (AW) 224 was the Snoopy Squadron with "Snoopy" as our tail insignia and "Lucy" as our call sign.

Ron Boehm

My buddy Rick Spitz got to fly with Carl Wadell, a BN, on Carl's very first mission in the aircraft. It would turn out to be quite an adventure for them, especially for Carl. They were flying a training mission up at about thirty-one thousand feet or so when Rick decided to take off his oxygen mask and eat a peanut butter sandwich and have a sip of his coke. He quickly got hypoxic and then went unconscious. Rick had the aircraft trimmed up pretty good so it was flying straight and level. Carl noticed Rick's head rolling around and realized what was happening and tried to reach over and put Rick's oxygen mask on, but without success.

Carl then radioed the Flight Center, "This is Marine Lucy 02, an Alpha 6 at thirty-one thousand feet requesting an immediate descent."

The controller replied, "Negative, Lucy 02, climb to flight level 330."

Carl said in a more urgent voice that he was the BN and that the pilot was unconscious.

At which time the controller asked, "Who is flying the aircraft?"

Carl replied in an elevated voice that he was, but that it was his first time in the aircraft and that he was the BN.

The controller said, "Roger, you are cleared to descend."

There was no control stick on the BN's side of the aircraft, so Carl was leaning over with his left hand trying to push the stick forward to get the nose of the aircraft down in order to descend below ten thousand feet, whereby Rick would get enough oxygen to recover consciousness. However, when he pushed the nose down and begin to descend, the aircraft would gain speed and level off again. Carl fought with the aircraft for awhile and finally got it down to about eighteen thousand feet when Rick finally came to and asked what was going on.

"You were unconscious," Carl said and related the whole story.

They landed at the Air Force Base in Kansas City and then continued on with their weekend and flight plan. Rick told Carl that they should keep this to themselves, but when they got back to the squadron in Cherry Point, Carl was worried about Rick's health and told the CO. The CO called Rick into his office and asked if there was anything that Rick wanted to tell him. Rick said that there was nothing that he wanted to tell the CO. But the CO said that Rick shouldn't hold it against Carl, but Carl was worried about Rick and had told the skipper what had happened.

The skipper gave Rick a talking to and at our next squadron briefing Rick had to give a talk on hypoxia and the dangers of removing your oxygen mask at altitude. Our squadron's tail insignia was that of Snoopy on his Dog House, so Rick drew up a poster showing Snoopy on the Dog House with the caption saying, "He who don't have oxygen mask on will have a breath-taking experience."

The aircraft that Rick and Carl were in had a prior write-up about difficulty in holding cabin pressure. Rick had flown it down to NAS Roosevelt Roads in Puerto Rico a week before and had to keep the thermostat up to keep pressure and they were burning up inside because of the heat.

Speaking of NAS Roosevelt Roads, there were a couple of amusing stories that came out of our squadron deployment there. Both involved my buddies, Rick Spitz and Jack Rippy. The Squadron had deployed there in order to get some live bombing practice instead of dropping those little blue bombs in North Carolina. We would fly our missions from Roosevelt Roads airfield to the little Island of Viegues. There was a restricted bombing area on about half of the island, but the island was also inhabited with farms and livestock. Jack was sent out on a night bombing hop to drop napalm on the target. The BN wasn't very happy with the idea of dropping napalm at night and knew it was a dangerous evolution for guys with so little time in the aircraft, especially since we hadn't had much visual bombing practice and very little night practice at this point. And dropping napalm at night was something we never did in Vietnam, but we had to get the night bombing in to complete the A6 training syllabus.

The target controller wasn't being very helpful with the info he was giving so as they were making their target run the BN said, "It looks good to me, drop it and let's get out of here." Jack said it was a ten degree dive, in hilly terrain at night—miss the target by a few feet

Ron Boehm

and the canister would clear the ridge line and go way down range—which it did. The controller then knew he had induced the problem and acted all PO'd to cover his own short comings. For the rookies that we were, it was important to get good info for the experienced BN in an unfamiliar situation like that, which it didn't sound like Jack got.

So the result was that the bomb missed the target, went downrange and napalmed some poor farmer's goat which the squadron had to replace in order to appease the farmer. Well, we loved to kid Jack about it but considering the circumstances it could have happened to any one of us nuggets.

Jack also got a goat kill in the Naval Gunfire impact zone on San Clemente a few years later after we had come back from Vietnam.

Historical Note: Commander Laird USN was the only pilot who I know of that had a kill in both the Atlantic and Pacific theater in WWII having shot down a Japanese and German plane in the two theaters. Colonel Jack Rippy is the only guy I know of who had a goat kill in both the Atlantic and Pacific theater; Vieques, Puerto Rico 1969 and San Clemente Island, California 1974. "Jack the Goat Killer"—it has a nice ring to it.

In the evening, we would get dressed up to get some night life and go to the gambling casino. There was a dress code, coat and tie, but Rick didn't get the memo I guess. When we got to the casino they wouldn't allow Rick in without a coat and tie. But the guy at the door said that they had some coats and ties that Rick could borrow. Well, the jacket was some god-awful color that didn't match his pants and the tie was even worse. He looked like he had been shopping at the Salvation Army store on an after sale day when everything had been picked over. But he got in, even though we were embarrassed to be with him.

Let me inject here a little background on Rick which will show up time and time again in this book since he is my good buddy and the subject of a number of stories. Rick is a very smart guy who you would never characterize as "lacking in self-confidence." One of his buddies who he grew up with in Minnesota told us a story about him while on a salmon fishing trip in Alaska: that Rick's teacher in high school sent a note home with his report card stating that Rick didn't sufficiently apply himself to his studies or live up to his potential and gave him a grade of "A." Rick , I guess could make "As" with little effort.

Rick figured that he was smarter than most of the people making the rules (which was true most of the time) and, therefore, it was OK for him to bend the rules, because the rules usually didn't make sense to him and/or didn't fit his agenda. And I figured that I wasn't as smart as him, so I usually went ahead with what he said, even though I would occasionally question the validity of the proposed idea or how much trouble it would get us or him into.

As we were just getting close to finishing our A-6 training and getting ready to be sent over to Vietnam, our buddies and classmates from Basic School who were grunts were returning from their Vietnam tour. On one occasion Rick ask if I wanted to go with him to the "O" Club to see a friend of his, Robert Belsar who had just returned from Nam and was stationed at Camp Lejeune.

Belsar had won a Silver Star and a Purple Heart and had gotten the lower part of one leg shot off. He also had little or no feeling in one of his arms.

We were at the bar drinking when he said to Rick, "Take a look at this," and put a cigarette out on his forearm. He had very little feeling in his forearm.

We were listening to his stories and drinking a few rounds when he took his prosthesis off with a sock and spit shined shoe on it, placed it on the bar and said, "Bartender, fill this up with beer, it takes 2.3 liters."

So there we were three Marine 1st Lieutenants drinking out of his wooden (well, fiberglass) leg when a Bird Colonel walks by with his wife, and I said, under the influence of alcohol, "Colonel, you don't have a hair on your ass if you don't take a drink out of this combat vet's wooden leg."

The Colonel grabbed the leg turned it up, took a swig, put a ten spot on the bar and said, "The next one is on me, carry on gents."

The Colonel was cool, but his wife just rolled her eyes and kept walking.

Cross Countries

Cross countries were great; they gave us rookie pilots flight time and a lot of experience in flying the aircraft, having to deal with planning our flights, navigating, getting in required syllabus training and dealing with all the unexpected things that came up on a long flight, like a broken aircraft. But the best part of all was you could go pretty much anywhere you wanted, and of course knowing where the best "O" Club parties were and on what night was also important. I think it was Tinker AFB in Oklahoma City on Friday nights that was good and so was NAS Alameda across the bay from San Francisco on Saturday nights.

One of the most memorable cross countries was with Ken Poulsen, my BN of that weekend. We were both nuggets and Ken was from the San Francisco area so we planned a trip to San Francisco and back. It just so happened that that was the same time when the astronauts landed on the moon for the first time.

We took off from MCAS Cherry Point on Friday July 18, 1969 and flew the first leg to NAS Pensacola. That was a fun hop because we flew the whole flight navigating at low level whereby we would hit visual check points according to time and heading and getting that part of our training syllabus out of the way. We dropped off some aircraft parts at NAS Pensacola, refueled and flew to NAS New Orleans on a flight path along the Gulf Coast of Florida, Alabama and Mississippi. We flew along the beach at about one hundred feet above the waves and flew past Biloxi, Gulf Port and Bay St. Louis and on to New Orleans.

The Mississippi Gulf Coast is the same area that one month later would be wiped out by Hurricane Camille which hit that area on August 17, 1969. Camille was the second strongest storm on record to hit the U.S. at that time. I remember thinking at the time that its pressure recorded at Bay St. Louis of 26.84 was the lowest pressure I had ever remembered hearing of. Camille had a storm surge tide of 24.6 feet when it came ashore at Pass Christian, Mississippi. My grandparents had a summer home there when I was a kid and we spent our summer vacations there. Camille just wiped out that area. Then Hurricane Katrina did the same thing thirty-six years later and also devastated New Orleans.

Part of my family was there at NAS New Orleans to meet us when we landed. We taxied onto the ramp and shut down with my family waving. After shutting down we climbed out and I introduced Ken to my family. We stayed the night in New Orleans and went back to the airport the next morning which was Saturday, July 19. After filing our flight plan, we went out to our aircraft, did our pre-flight checks, fired the A-6 up, and taxied out past my waving family.

From New Orleans, we headed to Holloman AFB in Alamogordo, New Mexico. Along the way we did whatever syllabus training that we had to get in, like running "road wreckies" along the highways, low level navigation or instrument approaches.

We would track vehicles on the highway, run a simulated attack on them in which the BN would acquire the target on his radar, lock onto them which sent the attack info to my VDI (Visual Display Indicator) and I would fly the "video-like game" until we got a simulated bomb release. We showed no mercy, we attacked trucks, family cars, or anything moving over four miles per hour.

Coming into Holloman, we flew over the White Sands, home of the White Sands Proving Grounds. They are truly white and are a really great sight to see. We were told that most of the animals that live on the White Sands are white also, which makes good sense.

After landing, we refueled, filed a flight plan, and, upon starting up, found out that we had a problem with some piece of equipment that we couldn't get working. We called back to our squadron in Cherry Point for help with getting the problem fixed. It took several calls and tries to fix the problem, but we finally got things working and took off for the next leg of our flight.

From Holloman AFB, we headed west again, this time heading for the San Francisco Bay area and Hamilton AFB in San Rafael just across the bay and north of San Francisco. On the way, we headed northwest and flew over the Grand Canyon at a fairly low altitude. It was my first view of the Canyon and it was awesome. We thought about flying down into the Canyon, but we were nuggets, and I guess not salty enough to avoid a flight violation for going into the Canyon so we just saw the sites.

After the Grand Canyon, we continued on our northwest heading and flew over Lake Mead and Hoover Damn. That was a great sight, also and from there, we got down low across the desert again for some low level navigation work. I loved getting right down on the desert floor about fifty feet or lower, hauling ass at about three hundred knots, just blowing and going.

On one leg of our planned flight path, we were following a section of highway and came up on a hill. Just as we topped the hill at about fifty feet above the surface of the highway, we met a truck coming the other way; I pulled up slightly and could see the driver in the cab. I would imagine the driver had to stop and change his underwear after getting the hell scared out him by a low level A-6 coming straight at him at three hundred plus knots. Just the sound would scare the hell out of you. We continued onto Hamilton AFB in San Rafael, California.

After landing, shutting down and taking care of all the post-flight stuff you go through, Ken called a couple friends who came and picked us up and we went on a short tour that evening of the area, including going over the Golden Gate Bridge, which was my first time to see it. For that matter, it was my first time in California. We spent the night in San Francisco and Ken showed me around some.

Sunday July 20, 1969

On Sunday July 20, 1969, we got back to the airport and started to prepare for our flight and file our flight plan when everybody was abuzz about what was happening on television. Someone said, "Come over here and watch; the astronauts are about to land on the moon." We went over to the TV and watched the Apollo 11 astronauts land on the moon.

After watching this monumental event, we went back to our preparations for our flight to Tinker AFB in Oklahoma City. We filed our flight plan, went out to our aircraft, did our preflight, climbed in and cranked the Intruder up. Soon we had permission to taxi and then cleared to take the runway and takeoff.

As we lined up on the centerline of the runway, I got that thrill that I got every time that I looked down the centerline of runway stripes and moved the throttles forward. Every time, it never failed; every time was a new adventure. We rolled down the runway and lifted off, climbing out into a clear blue sky heading east.

Somewhere over the vast desert in route to Tinker AFB, we ran into some weather; thunder clouds were building and we were trying to circumnavigate them. We asked the flight center for a higher altitude trying to top the clouds. We were up at about thirty-seven thousand feet or so, which was getting close to the limit of the A-6. I got it to forty thousand feet one time, but it took some time to get there and it was barely flying. We were in the clouds and I was manually flying when the stick felt like it was in a bowl of mashed potatoes. I could move it around with little effect on the aircraft. I then looked at the altimeter and the vertical velocity indicator which was showing a descent and realized that we were in a stall. I pushed the stick forward and recovered after losing several thousand feet and I notified Center that we had to make an immediate descent due to weather.

Ron Boehm

We were getting bounced around pretty good and then we got struck by lightning. That made things even more tense with the weather, stalling out and then getting hit by lightning. We also had our first experience with Saint Elmo's Fire while in the middle of the thunderstorm. The edge of the wind screen and the leading edge of the wings were aglow with a weird green sparkling light. The whole thing was a bit eerie. Don't forget that both of us were nuggets with not a whole lot of experience between us.

We finally cleared the weather and the rest of the flight was more or less uneventful. We landed at Tinker AFB and rushed into flight ops to check on what was happening with the astronauts.

At 0239 UTC "Greenwich or Zulu time" Monday, July 21, 1969, and 09:39 PM CDT, Sunday, Neil Armstrong opened the hatch of the Eagle Lander, stepped out on the ladder, and turned on the TV camera in the equipment compartment on the side of the Lander. At 0256 Zulu at Tinker AFB in Oklahoma City, Ken and I watched Neil Armstrong descend the ladder, step onto the surface of the moon and say those famous words, "One small step for man, one giant leap for mankind." That was an incredible moment and all of us in the flight ops room were cheering. It was one of those moments that you will always remember where you were and what you were doing, like when we heard about the assassination of President Kennedy or the attacks of 9/11.

We spent the night at Tinker and flew back to Cherry Point the next day. That leg of our cross country excursion was uneventful.

It was great to be back home. I told Eileen all about our flight and asked if she had seen the astronauts land on the moon and what she had done while I was gone. She said with her typical Eileen wit, while rubbing her pregnant belly, that she had been busy making fingers and toes.

While in the process of writing this book I was reminiscing with my long time buddy Fred Bonati about our experiences flying cross country, and he said, " Hey, Ron did you ever go on cross countries to specific airdromes just to get an airplane fixed, because your group didn't have the expertise or the parts? We did that a lot, landing at Naval or Air Force fields and downing the airplane so that they had to fix it. Scotty Michelson and I traded a leather flight jacket for center line baggage tanks full of drag chutes at a F-4 airbase in Texas, I think. (VMFA) 251 didn't have enough chutes to fly until another flight landed. We were celebrated with a party. The airbase had a pile of chutes at the end of the runway about fifteen feet high. We commandeered the van driver that picked them up for repacking, and he went for it. Repacking. That was another joke. We would stuff them back in with a broom handle, while standing on a bucket, during preflight to the amazement of the AF (Air Force) guys hanging around. Sweet!

A lot of laughs, the AF. Like some AF guy dressed in pure white utes (utilities uniform) checking under the plane at Udorn (Thailand) and having a quart of hydraulic fluid leak out and drench him. Or having them say, 'You're not really going to take off on those tires, are you sir?' Or 'Aren't all those zuse fasteners supposed to work, sir?'

The AF was just too, too. We used to fly to Ubon for three day R and R's and switch air crews, and before I got to VN (Vietnam), a Marine F-4 crew was forced by the base commander at Ubon to wash their plane before they could take off. And, from all reports the pilots and RIOs did just that.

Man, Ron, this is bringing all sorts of stuff out of the brain woodwork. How about flight specific planes. In Chu Lai, because of maintenance problems, we had airplanes that could only fly near the base, planes that could only fly VFR, in the daytime, had to be parked outside the revets (revetments) 'cause the wings wouldn't fold, and could only carry certain ordinance.

When we got back to El Toro, they drop checked all our planes for missile capability. Turns out we were flying MIG-caps and couldn't crank off a sidewinder or a sparrow even if we had to. Looked good, though.

War is Hell, Ron."

—•••—

Ron Boehm

CHAPTER 4

Vietnam

Vietnam

I was scheduled to go to Vietnam in August, but since Eileen was due in September, I was able to switch my leave date with Rick Spitz. He was a bachelor and it didn't make any difference to him. My daughter Laura was born on September 18, 1969. Eileen left Cherry Point before me to go to New Orleans and be with family and to find a place to live while I was in Vietnam. I then went on leave and joined her in New Orleans and eight days after Laura was born I caught a flight to Norton AFB in California from where I was to depart for Vietnam.

It was around 2:00 AM and I was sitting in this very empty terminal building in Norton AFB thinking, here I am going to war sitting all alone with an uneasy feeling in my stomach when a big black Navy Chief walked by.

I guess he saw the solemn look on my face and said, "How you doin' Lieutenant?"

I said, "Fine, Chief, how about you?"

And he said to me, "You know, you can always tell a Marine, but not very much."

That made me laugh and put a smile on my face and I said, "Thanks, Chief." I needed that.

A few moments later up walks my good buddy from Basic School, Fred Bonati. He was on his way to Nam also. We were constantly on the same set of orders since our names were next to each other alphabetically. It was a long flight ahead for us. I think we flew to Guam first and then to Okinawa. We were on a commercial charter flight and everybody there was in the service and going to Nam so it was pretty somber. At some point one of the stewardesses walked down the aisle with a small box in her hands that made laughing sounds and it lightened up the whole airplane.

Somewhere along the flight, Fred, who was sitting next to me, looked out over the vast expanse of water and asked me, "What are your thoughts?"

I said, "There is a lot of water out there."

And Fred answered, "Yeah, war is hell."

Then we both kept up with a whole bunch of clichés, and for some funny reason, we both remembered that and would say that to each other every so often.

From Guam, we went to Okinawa. At Camp Henson we spent a few days checking in getting our jungle utility uniforms, and a bunch more shots. We had received about fifteen immunizations before we left North Carolina and now we were getting about a dozen more. You will never forget the Gamaglobulin shot. The needle looked like it was six inches long and as big around as a silver dollar. They shot so much vaccine into your butt that you had a big knot there for a day or so. We were issued our camouflaged utilities and then we were ready to proceed to Vietnam.

I don't remember very much about that stay in Okinawa, but Rick Spitz and I went back there a month or so later for Sea Survival School, which provided more interesting stories. It seemed like whenever Rick and I teamed up we would get into some kind crap that made for great stories later.

I do remember our arrival at Da Nang, Vietnam. As we approached Da Nang in this commercial 727, the pilot came on the speaker to announce that there had been fire near the south end of the runway earlier so that they would be making a tactical approach to the runway. What we didn't expect was for the pilot to put this airliner into a fighter plane type break. You know airliners come with gentle turns and slow descents to a straight in approach. But no, this guy comes in level at about three hundred knots over the end of the runway, racks the plane into a ninety degree bank, pulling Gs and goes into a descending turn to a solid touchdown. In the middle of the break, Fred, who was a F-4 fighter pilot looks at me, an A-6 attack pilot and says, "Son-of-a-bitch!" I don't know if it was a dangerous situation that called for an extreme maneuver or just an airline pilot who always wanted to be a fighter pilot, or a fighter pilot who became an airline pilot. But it got our attention. "Damn, we are in a war zone, welcome to Da Nang, Vietnam September 1969."

Fred and I and some other Marines were taken to a check-in facility and there I got in touch with my new squadron VMA (AW) 242. Rick Spitz came to pick me up and take me to squadron headquarters. After checking in there, I was assigned a locker in the ready room and then assigned to an Asian hut or a "hootch," as they were called, to live in. They were not exactly the Holiday Inn, in fact they had a plywood floor, plywood walls about four feet high, and screens above the walls to the roof. It had two partitioned bedrooms, and no toilet. Still, it was better than the grunts in the field had.

We had a bomb shelter just outside of several hootches made of sand bags, but if you shined a light in there at night you would probably see some rat eyes looking back at you. It would have to be a serious rocket attack to go into it at night or for that matter during the day time.

Later on, Jim Jurjevich, a BN, and I would sit on top of the bomb shelter after the end of a late night or early morning mission, drinking wine and eating summer sausage his mom had sent him to unwind after the night's mission. Watching the sun come up sitting on a bomb shelter with a bottle of wine should be a scene in a movie. What an image.

Squadron HQ VMA (AW)242

In our check-in briefing we were told about the rocket alert sirens, that they would sound off if we were under attack and that we should seek shelter immediately when they went off. So of course, on my first night there in that plywood hut and rat-infested bomb shelter, the sirens went off. I was sitting on the steps at about 9:00 PM in my green skivvies, tee shirt and unlaced boots when the siren sounded an attack alert. Remember this was my first day in war, so I ran inside, grabbed my flak vest, helmet and pistol and ran down to "Boys Town" which is where Rick and Fred stayed.

"Boys Town" was what we called the area which had a few Quonset type metal huts that each housed a number of air crews. The huts were surrounded with fifty-five gallon drums filled with sand and stacked two high for rocket protection. That sounded to me like a lot better protection than my plywood hootch. In the Boys Town hut were three or so rows of military beds each consisting of a metal frame and thin mattress set on a concrete floor for the pilots to sleep in and that was about it. You couldn't really call it living space, just where you slept and kept your stuff. It was kept in the dark because some guys flew during the day and others flew at night.

I knew that Rick was in the center row and the eighth bunk from the door. I don't remember if I had actually heard a rocket explode or not, but this was war and I was seeking safety. I got to the door of the Quonset hut after a block long sprint, opened it and went down the line counting beds, "one, two, three," and so on until I counted eight. There was no place to sit so I jumped into this single bed with Rick.

He awoke in a startled state and said, "Who is that?"

I said, "Rick, it's me, Ronnie."

"What the hell are you doing in bed with me," he said.

"We are under a rocket attack," I replied.

"Well, that's not a reason to get in bed with me. What is that in your hand?"

"My pistol," I replied. "I've got my helmet, flax vest and boots on also."

"For God's sake, Ronnie, put your pistol away, go back to your hootch and go to sleep. The sirens go off all the time."

Ron Boehm

Asian Hut—
My Hootch

So Much for My First Day in the War

I stayed in the Asian hut for a week or two and then moved into better quarters with my buddy Fred Bonati as my roommate. These quarters were two-men Quonset huts with an air conditioner, one of those little table refrigerators, two beds and a table. There was a large shower and toilet facility (head) close by that served all the officers from the huts in that area. This was very special toilet facility made of wood studs and plywood and was called the "Erudite Shitter." No profanity was allowed on the walls; graffiti yes, profanity no. Only noble writings, deep or eloquent thoughts, poetry, quotes from Shakespeare, or some Greek philosopher and things like that were to be found on the walls of the "Erudite Shitter." It was incredible; sometimes I thought I should bring a dictionary in there to understand what I was reading. When the squadron left Vietnam to return to the states, they took the plywood walls and stalls with all the writing on it and brought it back with them to MCAS El Toro.

Quonset Hut — Fred's and my Hootch

My favorite writing on a stall door was simply, "I had nothing vulgar to say, so I drew a rose." And it was a nice rendering of a rose.

Jack Rippy remembers one writing that stated under the classic "God is dead, Nietzsche" and "Nietzsche is dead, God" was a variant - "God is dead, Nietzsche" with the reply; "No, He's not, He's alive and well and living on the Air Force side!"

In Da Nang the Air Force was on one side of the airbase and the Marines and Navy were on the other side. With the Air Force everything was first class, with the Marines everything was third class or coach and you had to make do with what you had. The Air Force side of the airbase had paved streets, the old Holiday Inn-like living quarters, very nice dining halls, an "O" club, and a swimming pool.

We had sand streets, Asian and Quonset Huts, outdoor shitters, plywood mess halls, an "O" Club, and water shortages that we claimed were because the AF was filling their swimming pool.

There were other head facilities located around the compound; these were the two-hole and four-hole out houses which had a bench like seat with a hole to sit on. Underneath was a fifty-five gallon steel drum cut in half and filled with diesel fuel. On a regular basis, once or twice a week or something like that, they would service the outdoor heads by pulling out the steel drums and setting the diesel on fire. This was called "burning the shitters." No Marine who has ever experienced the ritual will ever forget that unique smell.

Ron Boehm

There was another part to the servicing of the heads and that was done by the infamous "MAG 11 Pee Pee Pumper." The Pee Pee Pumper was a tank truck equipped with a pump, hose, and a yellow rotating warning light on top that was on when in the operation of pumping out the heads. I guess the yellow rotating light was a warning of sorts like, "Danger, stay clear, Pee Pee pumping in progress." Man, I just wish I had a picture of that, because everybody who was there would remember that truck. It was 1st Marine Air Wing folklore.

I got into the routine fairly quick: got issued my flight gear, pistol and shoulder holster. I remember thinking that was a little bit like the old west, with everybody packing heat. Some guys didn't want to go with the standard 38 caliber revolver and would get their own weapons. One BN that I flew with had this real long barrel big ass 44 caliber pistol that would have made Clint Eastwood proud of him. I was amazed that he could carry that big thing and still fit in the cockpit's seat. But he said that if he ever went down, he wanted a fighting chance.

The daily routine depended upon whether or not you flew that day and what time your flight was scheduled. The A-6s flew all day long but a lot of our missions were in the middle of the night, since we were an all-weather electronic attack plane. The F-4s and the A-4s flew most of the day hops because they were visual attack aircraft. The F-4s were fighters, but in 1969 and '70 there wasn't much air to air fighting so they were dropping bombs for a living also. The A-4 was a great visual bombing platform and those guys were very good at what they did—close air support.

It wasn't a rule, but I thought for some odd reason that they put the tallest pilots in the tight little A-4 cockpit and the smaller guys like yours truly in the spacious A-6 cockpit. I think that I was the only guy in the squadron that could stand up in the cockpit; maybe Roger De Jean or Dave Clary could do it also. But I did do it later to take a piss half way over the Pacific on a trans-pacific flight.

First Flight

Your first flight in- country was a "Fam Hop" or familiarization flight, in which you went up with an experienced pilot with the new guy riding in the right seat. The pilot would fly you around the area and point out various landmarks, flying procedures and things you needed to know about flying around Da Nang, Vietnam. In my case, I flew with Dave Clary who I knew from training in my earlier squadron at Cherry Point. Dave had been in- country for several months, was a very good pilot and had a little bit of a crazy streak.

We took off from Da Nang and he showed me Da Nang Bay, the Qua Son Mountains south of the base and then we flew up the coast, where he pointed out some of the now-famous battle areas, the walled city of Hue, Phu Bai, then Quang Tri and Dong Ha. And as we approached the DMZ separating North from South Vietnam, the missile warning light went off with that very urgent warning sound of "Dooo, Dooo Dooo!" All of a sudden Dave made a violent bank to port and then to starboard, then went inverted into a split S as he yelled out to me over the intercom "SAM," which was a surface to air missile. My ass got real tight real fast and I began looking for the missile smoke trail. They briefed us that if you can see the missile you can beat it by breaking into it in an evasive maneuver whereby the missile can't turn with you and goes ballistic allowing you to escape. I was straining to find the SAM when Dave said, "Just kidding." He had set off the missile warning light while I was distracted looking out the cockpit.

But that wasn't the end of his FAM experience for me.

He slowed the A-6 to landing gear speed, lowered the flaps, dropped the landing gear and said to me, "Are you a member of the Clam Shell Society?"

Ron Boehm

I said, "No, what is the Calm Shell Society?"

He said, "I'll show you," and began opening the canopy, which you just don't do in a modern tactical jet; everything began flying out the cockpit and then he took a grease pencil and made an X outside on the windscreen and gave the pencil to me.

"Your turn," he said. "This is to prove that we did open the canopy in flight and are now members of the Clam Shell Society."

Jack Rippy said that Dave had another trick that he would pull on the new guys. He would do the slow down routine and say the cockpit was awfully dirty, open the canopy and turn the aircraft inverted whereby everything would fly out and Dave would say, "Now that's much better." Dave, as I said was a little bit crazy.

I got snapped into the routine and soon I was flying missions. This was what it was all about—flying missions in combat. It was like practicing for a football game, then finally getting into the real game. This was the real game with a lot more on the line.

I remember the first time I went into the locker room where we hung our flight gear, helmets, flight vests, and our "G" suits. There was mine with my name tag sewed on - R. Boehm and next to my locker was the flight gear of another guy—R. Boehm. I was Ron Boehm and he was Robert Boehm. I was five feet, six inches tall and Bob was six feet five inches tall. Thankfully we never got our flight gear mixed up. I pronounced my last name "Bo-em" and he pronounced his name "Beam," so the CO called him High Beam and me Low Beam.

Your first flights were with an experienced BN who led you through the hop, got you to the target, set up the ordinance and ran the systems attack on his computer then showed you the way home. At first you did simple radar guided TPQs in Vietnam, whereby you would be flying about eighteen thousand feet or so and the ground-based radar controllers would guide you to the target and tell you when to "pickle" or drop your bombs. These hops were for the beginners and usually were not anywhere near our troops.

After the TPQ missions, then you got to fly some in-country (in Vietman as opposed to Laos) A-6 system hops. The RABFAC (Radar Beacon Forward Air Control) beacon hops in support of ground troops were only flown by the experienced air crews. In these missions, you were in contact with and controlled by a pilot/forward air controller stationed with the ground units and directing you to the target with a portable transponder.

After you got some experience under your belt two or three months in-country then you got to fly the missions at night over Laos. These were the missions where you could expect some action and often triple A to greet you. The Ho Chi Minh Trail coming out of North Vietnam and through Laos was one of the most heavily defended areas with anti-aircraft weapons in history.

—•••—

First Laos Mission

"They're shooting at us."

My first mission over Laos was with Jim Wingerter, one of the most experienced BNs in the squadron at the time. I was nervous about the flight and the fact that I had never been shot at before. I wasn't worried about getting killed, but rather I was worried about being a coward in a combat situation. Nothing would be worse for a Marine. To act in a cowardly fashion in front of another Marine I thought was worse than death itself. But my first experience with being shot at was nothing like what I was worried about.

We took off from Da Nang around 2:00 AM, headed up the coast and then turned westward just under the DMZ. Soon we were over Laos and leveled off at about eighteen thousand feet. We checked in with the 7th Air Force controlling agency, call sign "Moon Beam," and they directed us to enter a holding pattern. The controller said that our target would be some "movers," trucks moving south along the route package.

The "route package," as we called it, or the Ho Chi Minh Trail was a system of roads coming down from North Vietnam through the mountains, jungle and through Laos, leading down into South Vietnam. This was the route by which the North Vietnamese sent their troops and supplies into the south. The hub of the so called route package was the town of Tchepone where several routes including Route 9 and Route 91 came together. Tchepone was located near the confluence of the Xe Banghiang and the Xe Pon Rivers. Our job was to disrupt that flow and destroy those supplies and troops.

Moonbeam gave us our target, three trucks moving south, our target time and the run-in heading which would bring our bombing run in line with the direction of the road at the point of attack. At night, Laos was pitch black; you were mostly over jungle and you didn't see city lights like back in the States, just blackness and the occasional red "triple A" anti-aircraft fire coming up from the ground, lighting up the sky. That usually indicated where the hot spots were and you hoped they would not direct you to that area where the fire was.

At that time the route package, especially the mountain passes of Ban Karai and Mu Ghia were said to have the most heavy concentration of AAA guns, more so than even the Germans had around their cities in WWII.

I looked out of the cockpit and there was a stream of glowing red balls arching up towards us. But at the vantage point of eighteen thousand feet they seemed to float lazily upward towards us like a fireworks display.

I said to my BN, "Wow! Look at that, that's awesome!"

And he said, "They're shooting at us."

I responded, "Oh shit!" The first of many "oh shits" I would exclaim during my time in Vietnam.

If we had a night flight, which was often the situation, we would go to a daily briefing at the Group Briefing Room in the afternoon and be given specifics regarding the mission: the target area, what kind of defenses we might encounter, our ordinance, the weather and other pertinent information. About an hour before takeoff the pilots and BNs would do their own briefing: discuss the flight plan, the target, the ordinance to be dropped and emergency procedures. If we were flying over Laos, which was the case quite often, since most of our missions were attacking trucks carrying supplies down the Ho Chi Min Trail from North Vietnam into South Vietnam, we would discuss our egress from the target area if we took a hit. The closest safe area was east straight to the South China Sea, but that would mean crossing North Vietnam. If you went down there you would probably be a guest at the Hanoi Hilton or some other prison in North Vietnam. Another choice would be to head west to Thailand, but that meant crossing Laos and if you went down there you had the best chance of surviving but you had a good chance of being killed if captured.

I heard that most of the aircrews that went missing in action in the war and never found went down in Laos. Of course, the best scenario was to keep your bird flying and make it back to Da Nang. But if you did go down, you had a good chance of getting rescued. There were several rescue units with some very good and very brave guys that would risk everything to save you and your crew. The Air Force Jolly Green Giants flying their Sikorsky MH-53 rescue helicopters and the A-1 Skyraiders flying in support of the Jolly Greens flown by the Air Force's "Sandies." They would provide cover fire support for the helicopters.

The Sandies flew the Douglas A-1 Skyraider formerly the AD Skyraider, a large single engine prop plane with a massive 2500 HP radial engine. The A-1 came out in the late 1940s and flew in Korea and Vietnam conflicts. It was a great aircraft for its mission because it could carry bombs, rockets and guns, plus stay on station for a long time.

The South Vietnamese flew the A-1s also and since the pilots were a bit smaller than their American counter parts, I heard that they strapped wood blocks onto the rudder pedals so that they could handle the huge torque that that big engine produced on takeoff.

One Sandy pilot, Major Bernard Fisher USAF in March of 1966 even landed his A-1 while taking heavy fire to rescue another pilot who had been shot down and crash landed on the embattled airstrip of a Special Forces camp. He received the Medal of Honor for his courageous act of valor. (Source: Medal of Honor citation)

Ron Boehm

The Navy and Marines also had their rescue units that saved many lives. Their basic mission was an act of valor. Marine chopper pilots had large balls and their stories of heroic rescues are legendary. It seemed that every helicopter pilot I knew personally was shot down or shot up at least once. But then there is the saying that if your wings are going faster than your fuselage you are already in danger.

Charlie Carr

One of my first hops over Laos was with a BN who was a Marine Corps legend—Charlie Carr. Charlie Carr had more combat missions that any other BN in USMC history and his picture hangs on the wall of the USMC Museum in Quantico, Virginia. Charlie was a one of a kind character, but he was the best and most experienced BN in the Marine Corps and probably the Navy, too. When I was just about finished with my tour in Vietnam with VMA (AW) 242, Charlie was back with my original A-6 squadron VMA (AW) 224 on board the USS Coral Sea aircraft carrier. They were the first Marine A-6 Squadron to go on board the boat in quite some time.

**Maj. Davis, Beman Cummings
Charlie Carr, and Dick Davis
in front of revetments.**

He was the CAG's (Carrier Air Group) lead BN when the A-6s flew off the Coral Sea and seeded Hi Pong harbor with mines in 1970. Charlie started out as an enlisted Marine, then became a warrant officer, and when I met him, he was a Captain, and Major in our squadron VMA AW 242. He was a very colorful person but a very good flying officer. On this particular flight, I had a tape recorder strapped to my leg and plugged into the aircraft's communication system so I could record an actual combat flight. When I played it back later after the flight, I found that every other word was an "F---" or "MF" with some other very descriptive language. But Charlie got you to the target, found the target and put the bombs on the target. He finished his combat tours with six hundred or more missions, two hundred over North Vietnam. (Source: *Fast Movers* by John Sherwood)

Charlie was as infamous out of the cockpit as within. Some of his greatest fame happened in the "O" Club. On one event of flying some special mission or some special number of missions he came into the "O" Club covered, (with his hat on). Marines never say hat, it is your cover. Just like they never say gun; it's your weapon, your rifle or your pistol, never your gun or your hat. The rules of the "O" Club were that if you entered with your cover on the bartender would ring the bell and you bought the house a round of drinks. Of course, drinks were only fifty cents, and there was the special drink of the month that was twenty-five cents. When the bartender rang the bell and pointed at you, you would say, "Shit, I can't believe I forgot to take my cover off," and you pulled out your wallet. The other rule was that you could not hang from the rafters or you would buy the house a round of drinks. But Charlie had a purpose, a celebration of sorts. After walking in with his cover on, he climbed up into the rafters, "dropped trow," his pants, mooned the entire club and said, "Drinks on me."

Talking about drinks, one of the more interesting drinks for us pilots was the "Afterburner." It was a straight shot of alcohol of some type, I don't remember exactly what, that they set on fire and you threw it down trying not to burn yourself up or ruin your throat. If you weren't careful, you could ignite your mustache if you had one and that wasn't much fun.

"O" Club Games

Rolling dice at the bar for drinks was a big past time. One of the dice games was "Ships-Captain-Crew," and I've got to admit I can't remember exactly how the game went. I just remember losing a lot of drinks. Another game was "Acey-Deucey" which was a variation of backgammon. But one of the most famous of the games, if you can call it a game, carried out in the Da Nang Marine "O" Club was "Dead Bug." As everybody was drinking and having a good time, as best you could with no females around, somebody would cry out "dead bug," and everybody dove to the floor putting their arms and legs up in the air like a dead bug. The last person on the floor with their arms and legs up in the air had to buy the house a round of drinks. The floor was concrete, the bar stools were pretty high and people got banged up diving down to the floor. It was an incredible sight to see fifteen or twenty guys all lying on the floor with their arms and legs up in the air. And, of course, these were our best and brightest.

Mag 11 O Club Da Nang

One time I was sitting at the bar with Wally Siller a BN who later became a doctor. We were sitting with this lieutenant colonel who was an alcoholic and got drunk after 5:00 PM at the club just about every evening. The colonel leaned back in the bar stool a bit too far and it tipped over. He hit the concrete floor with an awful sound and just lay there. Hell, I thought he could have been badly injured or worse, dead, and Wally looked down at the colonel and said, "Dead Bug, Colonel?"

China Beach "O" Club

Another game was "Buck-Buck" or as we called it in grade school "Break the Camel's Back." In this game you would get one guy leaning over and grabbing a post or wall or something to hold on to. The next three or five guys bent over the guy in front and wrapped their arms around the guy's waist in front of him.. This was the Camel or whatever. The other guys would line up about ten feet back and one by one yell, "Buck-Buck Number One," and run at the guys bent over, jumping on their backs trying to break the camel's back, break apart the bent over and jointed guys. Then the second guy would yell, "Buck-Buck Number Two" and he would run at the bunch of guys bent over and try to break the camel's back and so forth and so on until the last guy was either riding on the bent over guys' backs or until the structure collapsed. The guys forming the camel's back would say things like, "Is there a flea on our back?" or "When are you going to start?" things like that. Did I mention that a lot of alcohol was involved in this very "adult" game?

It was at The Navy's China Beach "O" Club in Da Nang on the South China Sea coast and the occasion being the Marine Corps' Birthday on November 10, 1969, that this game became a notable event for our squadron. After dinner, songs and many toasts, they struck up a

Ron Boehm

game of buck-buck. Unfortunately, the first guy of the camel was positioned right in front of glass doors. Well, you can see this coming. One guy got a big running start and glanced off the backs of the guys bent over and broke through the glass door. The squadron was on the edge of rowdiness already and this was (pardon the pun) "the straw that broke the camel's back." The Navy threw the whole squadron out.

As all this was going on, Dave Clary and I were down on the beach. China Beach was a beautiful beach with emerald green water and white sand. It was also beautiful at night with the moon light shining on the water and the waves rolling onto the beach. I think our intent was to go skinny-dipping. When we got back to the club everybody was gone along with our transportation.

I asked Dave, "How are we going to get back to the airbase?"

I don't remember exactly how this all transpired, but Dave saw one of those small gray Navy school busses and said, "We'll borrow the bus and take it back to the base."

I looked a bit confused and was kind of drunk so I went along with it. We jumped in, Dave hot-wired the bus if my memory is correct (or the keys were left in it) and we took off back to the Da Nang Airbase which was some distance across town.

After a mile or so we came up to a South Vietnamese police check point with a barricade arm across the street.

I said, "Oh shit, what are we going to do; we're in a stolen bus."

Dave said in a semi-drunken voice, "Get down, we're going to run it!"

Which we did and the Vietnamese guards came running out and opened fire on us with their rifles.

I had been shot at in the air, but this was my first time to be shot at on the ground. Kind of brings a different meaning to the term "friendly fire."

We got back to the base and parked the bus outside the gate and walked into the base. Needless to say, we didn't mention this to anybody with a rank higher than ours. I was tempted to go check out the bus the next day for bullet holes but I figured it was better to stay the hell away from it. War is hell.

Dave was a good pilot, but many of my memories of him involved crazy stuff. Only Charlie Carr who was legendary as being crazy out shined Dave in my view.

Lt. Col Stan Lewis, Dave Clery, and Lt. Earl Smith's last combat flight.

Da Nang AF "O" Club

While we are on the subject of "O" Clubs, I have to tell a little story about the Air Force's "O" Club on the other side of the airbase. As I had mentioned previously, the Navy and Marines were on one side of the field and the Air Force was on the other side. Our side of the field was kind of primitive with sand streets and outhouses; however, the Air Force lived in the former two-story Holiday Inn-type BOQs with a swimming pool and a really nice "O" Club which we visited occasionally. On one such visit I, along with my buddy Roger De Jean, who was only about an inch or two taller than I was, met two Air Force nurses.

Now "round-eyed" women (Caucasians) were a scarce commodity over there since most every woman that you saw was a "slant eyed" oriental. These two AF nurses were a little chunky, but they thought of themselves as queens because of the scarcity status.

　　　　Ron Boehm

When Roger and I met them and introduced ourselves, they looked at us and said, "We thought all Marines were big guys."

I then said, "Depends upon how you define big and were you measure it."

Roger chimed in and said, "Yea, we're big where it counts."

To which they replied, "Yeah, right."

The next day Roger and I went out to one of the A-6s on the flight line to take a picture with a Polaroid camera of me standing on the nose of the A-6 with the refueling probe between my legs. The A-6 had a unique refueling probe protruding from the nose of the aircraft just in front of the windscreen. The base of the probe was about as long as my leg and came up at an angle. The probe itself that actually plugged into the refueling basket was aligned horizontally, was about twenty inches in diameter and about two feet long. The nose of the probe looked like a huge circumcised penis.

I got up on the nose of the plane with my right leg hiding the base of the probe, my left hand holding the giant penis and showing a great big smile on my face. Roger took the picture and took it back to the Air Force "O" Club that evening.

We spotted the two queen nurses and showed them the picture and said, "Here you are sweetheart, eat your heart out." With that we went, laughing our asses off.

Lieutenant Colonel "Black Tom" Griffin

In the beginning of my tour in Vietnam my squadron commander with VMA (AW) 242 was Lieutenant Colonel Tom (Black Tom) Griffin. Lieutenant Colonel Griffin was a strictly by the book Marine Commander. He was a leader in the sense that he would always take the toughest missions, but to me he was aloof and distant with the men in the squadron or at least with the junior officers. The talk with us was that he would take the tough missions so that he could get a Distinguished Flying Cross award to better his career. He did try at least one time to better the camaraderie with his officers by having a mustache growing contest, which I won, beating him out for first place.

• • •

Lieutenant Colonel Stan Lewis

After about my third or so month in country we had a command change and Lieutenant Colonel Stan Lewis took over from Griffin. He was the finest example of a leader and commanding officer that I had ever served under. He was a very smart guy with probably a genius IQ, a very personable leader who really cared for his men, and he was also the best stick in the squadron.

You might be flying one of our very early two or three AM flights and meet him out on the flight line talking to the plane crew or handing them a wrench or something like that. When a young Marine finished his tour with the squadron, Lewis would write his family and commend him for the job he had done.

Lieutenant Colonel Lewis wasn't the only smart guy in the squadron: we had a bunch of them. Carl Monk was one of the our best BNs and probably had a genius level IQ also. Carl Wydell and Rick Spitz were also very smart guys as were a handful of other guys. Jack Rippy was a lawyer before he became a Marine officer. It was very impressive to be surrounded by so many smart guys.

I was flying Lieutenant Colonel Lewis' wing on a mission down south of Da Nang when we were diverted from our original assigned target for an emergency mission to help some Australian advisers with their South Vietnamese troops who were under heavy attack. When we arrived over target, the airborne FAC told us that the Aussies said that they were on this hilltop outpost, were about to be over run and that the bad guys were inside the perimeter fence. Next thing he said was that the Aussies were getting down in their holes and wanted us to drop on top of them. My heart went up into my throat, and I was very glad that I was with Lieutenant Colonel Lewis because of his skill and experience.

He radioed me, saying that we would lay a string of bombs up one side and over the hill top and said to follow his lead. He made his run and we followed his lead, making our run and placing our five hundred pound bombs up the side of the hill and over the top. My heart was heavy thinking we might be killing our own people. But a soldier on the ground would never call for this extreme action if he had any other option.

It seemed like an eternity passed from the time we released our bombs to when the FAC came up on the radio and said, "The Aussies said bloody good show Yanks, you tore the bad guys up." I don't think that I had ever felt such elation before in my whole life. These guys survived our bombs and survived because of our help. That was awesome.

A6A with bombs in flight

Back in the squadron when we had an AOM (All Officers Meeting), Lieutenant Colonel Lewis initiated The Drink of the Day policy which made the attendance rate and atmosphere much better. It was a pleasure to serve under Stan Lewis: he was the best leader I had served under. At the time he seemed like an older guy, me being twenty-five years old, but he was only about thirty-six years old at the time. Whenever I compare or measure leadership, I use Stan Lewis as the standard.

―――

Cubi Point, Philippines

In October of 1969, I got orders, along with Jack Rippy, Rick Spitz, and Major Coleman, to go to Jungle Survival School—the JEST Course (Jungle Escape and Survival Training)—in the Philippines. Our orders were to stay at Cubi Point Naval Air Station at the edge of the Subic Bay Naval Base. We had a day or so of classroom training and instruction by the Negritos, who were small indigenous people of the Philippines. They were famous jungle fighters of WWII that waged a guerrilla war campaign against the Japanese. The Negritos are an ethnic group that inhabit a number of islands in Southeast Asia. They are a short people and very skilled in the art of living in the jungle and they taught us what we could eat and drink, how to catch our food and what to avoid. After a few days of training, we were dropped off in the jungle to survive for a few days on our own without food or supplies.

I learned to drink water from a vine that grew in the jungle, and eat anything I could catch and kill. However, my buddy Rick Spitz was always looking for an angle to make things better for himself, and most of the time he did just that. So while walking down this jungle road we came upon some of the Marine school personnel with their vehicle stuck in the mud. They asked us for some help to get their vehicle un-stuck.

I would never have thought to take advantage of the situation because after all we were in school to learn to survive in the jungle in case we got shot down and had to do just that. But Rick is

Rick and instantly said that we would help them if they gave us some of those C Rats (C Rations were military field food rations). They said that they could not do that, and that we were there to practice our survival skills. Rick said, "Good luck with your vehicle." They reluctantly said, "OK" and we had food for the next few days while the other guys were catching lizards, snakes and stuff like that.

Time and time again I could always rely on Rick to find an angle, like later on at FAC School on Okinawa when everyone else was staying in the humble BOQ on the Marine Base and he got us into the Air Force BOQ at Kadina AFB. Trust me, the Air Force facilities are always superior to the Marine facilities.

While not in the jungle and back at Cubi Point, after school we got to go check out the night life in the adjoining town of Olongapo. To get to Olongapo from Cubi Point Naval Air Station, we had to cross the bridge over "Shit River." I have no idea what the real name was, we just called it the Shit River because it was basically a sewer. And the thing we all remember about it was the people in boats next to the bridge diving for quarters that we would throw into the river. Just seeing it made me want to take a shower.

The main street in Olongapo was Magsiasia Drive which was said to have more clubs and bars than any other place in the world. (Source: Wikipedia) Olongapo was a kind of an opposite-like Mecca of decadence and the epitome of that was the East Inn Club. You entered the club by going up the stairs into a not very fancy room where the girls came up to your table and asked you to buy them a drink. For a dollar or two they did just about anything and would strip on your table, pick up your beer without using their hands and so forth and so on.

One of our buddies was a very good family guy and read the Bible daily, so Dick and I paid a couple of girls to pay special attention to him. They came up to him and started to strip and then one sat on his lap, all to his animated protest. Well, in the hassle, his chair fell over and he went to the floor with the two semi-naked girls. The two girls then sat on him, one on his mid-section and the other on his face while he was crying out in muffled yells, "Get them off of me, get them off of me." Of course Rick and I were laughing like crazy at the sight of this Marine pilot taken down by two little Filipino girls. He didn't think it was so funny.

You had to be careful in Olongapo and stick with a friend because it could be dangerous. The bouncers outside the clubs were armed with sub-machine guns and would use them, but you could get robbed or worse in a heartbeat.

Transportation was on foot or in a "Jeepney." The Jeepneys were the Filipino version of the jitney. They were made from surplus WWII Jeeps that had been converted into a sort of taxi/mini-bus. They had no doors, just a roof, open sides and bench seats on each side. They were brightly painted, decorated with lights, reflectors, tassels, and beads, small statues of The Blessed Mother or some saint and all kinds of other stuff or glitter. They were a sight to see and ride in. But they too could be dangerous. My brother Lloyd while there in the Navy was riding in one with his arm resting on the back rest going down the crowded street when somebody ripped his wrist watch off his arm and disappeared into the crowd.

Fred Bonati's squadron mate was trying to hire a Jeepney when an argument broke out between two competing drivers; one broke out a pistol and shot the other guy, killing him on the spot. Fred didn't say if his buddy got in the Jeepney or not.

I was riding in one by myself late at night going to some club when the driver turned in the wrong direction and was heading up a dark street. It didn't look good to me so I jumped out while we were still moving and ran my ass off in the other direction.

There was a curfew at midnight and you had to be either off the streets, in a hotel or back across the Shit River Bridge and on base. Fred stayed too late one night and one of the girls took him home with her to her family. He spent the night and they fed him breakfast in the morning and said they were very nice people.

Jack Rippy and I were walking back to the base down the main street which was about five blocks away when I looked at my watch and realized that it was about five minutes to midnight. We started to sprint in order to get across the bridge and onto the base before midnight. The buildings on each side of the streets were lined

Ron Boehm

with clubs, guards and some girls. We were almost to the bridge and at the end of the buildings still running our asses off when from the shadows in between the last two buildings came forth a voice that said, "Psst, hey GI last chance for blow job." Jack and I looked over and to our horror, there was this ugly ass woman with missing teeth and the others grossly stained red from beetlenut standing in the dimly lit space between the two buildings. It was just enough of an adrenaline boost to get us across the bridge in time.

Everybody knows that Naval Aviators go through carrier qualifications in order to land on the aircraft carriers, but "Carrier Quals" in the "O" Clubs and bars took on a different meaning. They came in a few different forms; one was when the guys cleared the bar off, poured beer down it and two guys stood at one end on either side of the bar holding a towel between them. The pilot attempting the "carrier qual" stood at the other end of the bar to get a running start, throw himself on the bar top, slide down the bar on his belly and hope to be stopped or arrested by the towel being held by the two guys at the end of the bar. Again, alcohol was an important factor in this endeavor. This arrestment wasn't always perfect and some guys never made it to the end of the bar, rolling off the deck prematurely incurring possible injury, but the guys that made it to the arresting gear (the towel), using their necks as the tail hook, sometimes didn't fare too well, either.

The "Carrier Quals" at the Cubi Point "O" Club started out being held on a three-foot wide concrete sloped ramp or bannister that ran along the sides of the steps at the club. There, the pilots took chairs with caster rollers from the club and rolled down the ramp. The bottom two feet or so of the ramp turned up from an approximate thirty degree slope to horizontal, so when the guy in the caster-rollered chair reached the bottom he was launched like on a ski jump.

When you have these highly-and expensively-trained pilots on cruises, breaking their arms and incurring other such injuries and then not being able to fly, those were serious problems. So the club or the Navy brass came up with an alternate to the carrier chair launch. They made the bar in the basement break proof with stainless steel mirrors, bar tops, concrete block walls and an ingenious "carrier qual" apparatus. It consisted of a wire cage simulated cockpit set on two rails that ended in a pool of water of about six foot by eight foot by three foot. Just before the pool at the end of the rails was a set of double doors and a step on which was an arresting wire.

You would be propelled down the rails in your cockpit by a couple bottles of compressed nitrogen; there was a handle in the cockpit that you pulled to release the arresting hook in order to engage the arresting wire that stopped you from going into the pool. If you dropped the hook too early you got a hook skip and missed the wire. If you dropped the hook too late you missed the wire and either way you went into the pool. You had to get the timing just right to avoid going into the pool. There were a lot of wet pilots there.

I was there one time with a bunch of Navy aviators from one of the carriers who were with a couple of nurses. There was a lot of drinking going on and somehow they strapped one of the nurses into the cockpit upside down with her legs up in the air and her skirt down around her waist. They fired her down the rails and somebody had to jump in the pool to rescue her from drowning. What a place. Man, when a carrier was in port it was sheer madness.

In 1991, Mt. Pinatubo, a volcano on the Island of Luzon, erupted, covering Olongapo, Subic Bay, Clark AF Base, and the area in ash. Those bases were evacuated just before the big eruption and that spelled the end for those legendary bases which just about any sailor, Marine or Air Force guy who had visited them left with bunch of memories.

Lieutenant Valovich

The squadron plaques from the Cubi Point "O" Club now hang on the walls of the reconstructed club in the Naval Air Museum in Pensacola, Florida. When I visited the Air Museum in August of 2011, I looked for and found my squadron

VMA (AW) 242's plaque from a later time and was pleased to see the squadron commander at that time was Lieutenant Colonel J.M. Valovich. Jim Valovich was a BN and my squadron mate in Vietnam. We were both First Lieutenants at the time and he was a good BN.

VMA (AW) 242 Squadron plaque from Cubi Point "O" Club now on wall of its mock up in the Naval Air Museum in Pensacola, FL.

My favorite memory of Jim Valovich is one when he was about a couple days away from going on R&R to meet his wife in Hawaii. There was a joke at the time about this captain who told his sergeant to tell Private Jones that his father just died. The sergeant called the unit to attention and shouts out, "Private Jones, your father just died." The private was stunned and the captain told the sergeant that he can't just yell that out, he had to be more tactful and sensitive in a situation like that. So then he tells the sergeant to go tell Corporal Smith that his mother just died and to be more tactful this time. So the sergeant calls the unit to attention and says, "Everyone who has a mother that is still alive take one step forward. Not so fast Corporal Smith."

Jim was complaining about being scheduled to fly a night mission over Laos where you usually got shot at when he was only a day or two away from going on R&R. So somebody said, "Yes, I can see it now, the person in charge of greeting the wives in Hawaii saying, 'Everyone who has a husband meeting them on R&R take one step forward—not so fast Mrs. Valovich.'"

Rick Spitz

Back in Da Nang, my then roommate Fred Bonati and his F-4 Squadron VMF 314 moved down to Chu Lai about sixty-five miles south of Da Nang and Rick Spitz moved in with me in our Quonset Hut. On one occasion, Rick came back from a mission and said that they had taken a whole bunch of fire going into a target in Laos. They were on a mission to attack supply trucks coming down from North Vietnam along the Ho Chi Minh Trail. The trails were a number of mud roads through the jungle of Laos that led into South Vietnam. Ever since we had stopped bombing North Vietnam they had moved more and more anti-aircraft guns along the trails.

Rick's mission, along with his BN Carl Monk, was to be a coordinated effort with the F-4s from Chou Li whereby the A-6s would attack the trucks moving along the trail and the F-4s would sit up top and wait for the guns to come up which would fire on the A-6s, then the F-4s would attack the guns to suppress the fire. On this mission, they were assigned a target by the 7th Air Force controller in which they were given the information on the number of trucks, target time (five minutes or so) and direction of attack which corresponded to the direction of the road at that point. The pilot timed the run to the target and descended to attack altitude while the BN set up the computer for the attack and started looking for movers. (Trucks moving more than four miles per hour could be picked up on the Doppler radar.)

The triple A picked up Rick's aircraft early and started heavy fire that looked to Rick as if the bursts were flying formation with them. This was probably because of the ECM gear (Electronics Counter Measures) which gave a false radar image to the attackers' radar and made the aircraft look like it was moved over from its true position.

As I said, Rick and his BN were taking heavy fire and Rick was wondering when the F-4 would attack the guns, but that never happened. Rick continued on the attack, even though they had a computer failure and had to go to a Manual Lay Down using time, heading and altitude to drop the bombs. At about that time, a whole bunch of 37 mm and 23 mm tracers converged on Rick's A-6; some of the guns were actually firing down on him because Rick was running in the valley between the two mountains and the guns were on top of the mountains. The valley floor was about 1230 feet or so and they were running their attack at about three thousand feet AGL (above ground level), the mountains were about five thousand feet on one side of Mu Ghia Pass and about seven thousand on the other side of the pass; the rest of the tops in the area were around thirty-five hundred feet to four thousand feet.

Rick broke hard right and then hard left to avoid the fire. They dropped their bombs and got some secondary explosions. It was about that time he saw what Rick described as the brightest light he had ever seen that left him momentarily blinded.

In his maneuvering to evade the fire and being temporarily blinded by the light from the AAA burst, he glanced at the altimeter and realized that they were in a forty degree dive. He leveled his wings and pulled hard back on the stick and watched in horror as the altimeter bottomed out at about thirteen hundred feet which meant that he had just missed the ground.

Rick was a pretty good athlete and it was his fast reactions that probably saved their lives. As he pulled up he could feel that the aircraft wasn't handling properly and was in a severe yaw condition. He then realized that the two racks of bombs on one side hadn't come off.

They exited the target area, got the thing under control and Rick got the F4 pilot on the phone and asked him where in the hell were they. The pilot said that they lost their radio scrambling capability and aborted the mission. To which Rick probably thought, "Thanks a lot."

Rick said that his hand was shaking so badly when they got back to the base that he could barely fill out the flight de-briefing.

Marine F-4 taxiing in

Rick Spitz and his BN, Carl Monk were awarded the Distinguished Flying Cross for their skill and courage demonstrated on that mission. Rick and Dave Cummings, a Huey Cobra Pilot, were the only two guys that I know of from our Basic School Class of 5/67 to win this highest of flying awards.

Rick Spitz in our hootch relaxed but ready for combat

Ron Boehm

Left My Lights On

Jim Ewing, "They couldn't hit their ass with a baseball bat."

I had a similar but not so heroic a mission as Rick's. We were running a mission in the Mu Ghia Pass area and taking fire from radar-controlled fifty millimeter guns, and we saw the fire walking in on us; then we turned on the ECM equipment and saw the AAA blast walk away for us and seemingly fly formation with us. Getting fired on over the target with the tracers crossing in front of us like a fan spreading out made me think of the rice flying across you from both sides at your wedding on the steps of the church, but much more lethal.

On this mission, I was flying with Jim Ewing as my BN and as we started our descent and run in to the target, we started taking fire from about fifteen miles out. Usually, just a couple of guns would come up over the target and they fired at our sound so the fire was usually behind us. But this time it looked like they had us on radar and the fire was walking towards us. I switched on the ECM and the fire moved away some, but they followed us.

I didn't want to get on our run-in heading too early, but rather I flew a zig-zag course until just before the target. We then turned onto our run-in heading and Jim said we had the target acquired. I pulled the commit trigger as we approached the target and the triple A was all over us. I remember someone telling me that if the fire looks like it is going to hit you, it will most likely go underneath you. If the fire looks like it is going to go over the top of you then that's the one that will get you.

Well, this stuff was in front and above us. It was pretty tense and the last three miles to the target seemed like it took an eternity.

Finally, Jim said, "Bombs off."

I pulled up and to the right, telling Jim, "I'm breaking starboard."

He said in a higher-pitched voice than normal, "Oh shit, don't go this way."

He was looking at muzzle flashes and tracers coming right at us, so I broke to port, and seeing the same thing that Jim saw, I went straight ahead all the while pulling up.

This was taking us right to the North Vietnamese border and a SAM site just on the other side. As we climbed out of the AAA, Jim said in a mocking voice, "Those bastards couldn't hit their ass with a baseball bat." Hell, I was close to peeing in my pants. And before I could respond, the SAM warning light came on and the treat indicator showed it to be coming from straight ahead. The audio warning in my headset was going, "Beep, beep, beep" which meant the acquisition radar was tracking us. I was climbing and turning away from the SAM site while thinking that the last thing I wanted to hear was the beeping sound to go to a steady "beeeeeeeeee" sound, which would mean that they had launched the missile and now the missile's radar would be tracking us.

Finally, the warning light and the treat indicator went off and as I regained some composure I noticed out the corner of my eye that my wing tip lights were still on. "Oh, shit!" I thought to myself and quietly turned them off without telling Jim that I had failed to turn them off.

The navigation lights had a two-position switch, and I mistakenly didn't switch them all the way off, leaving the wingtip lights on. Then I had this image of these North Vietnamese gunners saying to each other, "Nguyen, look at this idiot with his lights on," and blasting away at us.

Flying over Laos at night was always interesting; you and everyone else were flying with their lights off up and down the same route package. The Marine A-6s and the Air Force C-130 gunships worked the Ho Chi Min Trail from Tchepone, which was a hub of activity where several major routes or roads intersected, up to the North Vietnamese border and the two mountain passes, Ban Kari and Mu Gia passes. That's where they really lit you up. And right over the border was a SAM site.

One night, we were in route to our target when Moonbeam told us to be advised that a C-130 was in area also. Just about the same time a dark shadow passed over the top of us. That must have been real close to a mid-air collision.

The Air Force C-130s gunships were flying out of Ubon, Thailand, and that is where we would go from time to time for a three-day mini R&R. Ubon was also the home of the famous 8th Tactical Fighter Wing flying F-4s and headed by the legendary Colonel Robin Olds. Olds was an Ace in WWII with thirteen aircraft shot down to his credit and four kills in Vietnam, one short of Ace status. As far as I know there were only two Aces in Nam, Captain Steve Ritchie, an Air Force F-4 pilot and Commander Randy Cunningham, a Navy F-4 fighter pilot.

Three Day Mini R&R — Ubon, Thailand

After you had been in country about three months, the squadron had a good deal for us flight crews: a three-day mini R&R in Thailand. We would fly our mission with a target time in Laos of about 0600 or 0630 and then continue on to Ubon, Thailand, after our mission was complete. This is where another crew from our squadron would be waiting on the tarmac to take the aircraft back to Da Nang. Then on our third day there we would be the crew waiting on the tarmac at 0730 to take the aircraft back to Da Nang.

When you landed there and had taken care of your aircraft, the first stop was to check into the BOQ, get breakfast and then head to town for shopping and a "hotse bath." The hotse baths were a Thai massage parlor where these pretty young girls would put you in a steam cabinet, wash you, dry you, powder you and massage every muscle in your body. It was a little bit of heaven.

The girls would sit behind a glass window in a room and you could pick the one you wanted by the number on their badge they wore (what we called a VD number). Part of the massage was when these small girls would walk on your back and massage you with their feet. Wow! That was awesome and was one case where I didn't mind women walking all over me.

You spoke to them in broken English; like "Number One" was the best, "Number 10" was the worst. They would say things like, "You number one GI," or "I not like that, number 10."

On my first visit to the hotse bath, I didn't know what to expect except that everybody said that was the number one thing you had to experience in Thailand. So my BN and I headed to town after breakfast to a the massage parlor that was recommended to us. We walked in and were told each to go up to the window and pick out a girl that we wanted to give us a massage. You picked the one you wanted and identified them by the VD number. It was called a VD number because they were given a health inspection weekly and that was their assigned number by the health Department. I picked out this very pretty girl named Nawatee. She was part Thai and part French and probably in her early to mid-twenties. Most of the girls were in their teens.

The first thing she told me was to get undressed and get into this steam cabinet, a mini steam room to open up your pores and make you sweat. After about five minutes in the steam cabinet she told me to get into this tub of hot water. I did that and then she began to wash me. I was a little uncomfortable to say the least since the last time a female had washed me I was about five years old and it was my mother.

Having this pretty female wash my whole body resulted in that natural male response. So there I was sitting in this tub of water and I didn't know what was the most red, my member or my face. The girl could see my embarrassment and said in broken English, "No sweat, OK." She said it with a smile on her face.

After the tub and washing, she dried me off and told me to

Ron Boehm

lie on a table. She then proceeded to massage every muscle in my body, from the ends of my fingers and toes, up my arms, legs to my torso, back and neck. Then she got up on the table and stood with her bare feet on my back and massaged my back with her feet as she leaned against the wall. That was great and I felt like a wet noodle after she was finished.

As I was lying on the table, I heard some girls giggling and looked over as Nawatee motioned these girls over to my table. They were like little girls giggling with a sense of awe showing on their faces. It seems that their awe was inspired by my hairy chest. Oriental men don't have much body hair. So here were these three girls all in their teens being invited by my masseuse to run their fingers through my chest hair. As they did this they would say, "Oh, number one." Of course, I hated every minute of it.

So from that time on I would always ask for Nawatee if she was there. We would get these Ubon flights about every three months or so if you wanted them. It was a great relief from getting your ass shot off or being bored to death. I read someone's account of war as being "Hours of boredom interrupted by moments of sheer terror." That was pretty accurate, I thought.

On one trip, I ran across Nawatee in the village away from the hotse bath as I was having lunch in this restaurant. She recognized me and said, "You Ronniesan GI from (whatever the name of the massage parlor was)" and I said, "Yes, and you are Nawatee." I asked if she would like to have lunch with me. She was very surprised and told me that GIs didn't usually ask girls to have lunch since they mostly only asked the girls to take them to their hotel for sex.

You could rent these girls by the hour, but since I was married that wasn't what I had in mind. Just talking to a female was great since we had very few opportunities to do so and it was nice to see and talk to a pretty woman when you didn't have to worry whether or not she or her boyfriend was a VC who wanted to kill you.

I asked if she went with the guys from the hotse bath and she said very emphatically, "No, I no go GI."

I asked "Why?"

She said, "GI break my heart, I got babysan."

I asked if babysan was from GI.

She said, "What you think? Babysan have blue eyes."

After lunch, Nawatee asked me if I had seen much of the city or the surrounding area.

I said, "No, just the area around the base, the tailor shops, shoe shops, jewelry shops and a couple of bars."

She then said, "You want, I take you to see big Buddha and temple; we go see the city."

"That would be great," I said.

I followed her and she flagged down a sanlo, which was a bicycle taxi, like a rickshaw with a guy peddling a bicycle in front instead of running down the street pulling the taxi carriage. We went to see a giant statue of the Buddha which was about thirty feet tall and covered with gold from little gold leave tablets that looked like cigarette rolling papers and placed on the statue by people as an offering. These were little sheets of gold. Gold was only about thirty-two dollars per ounce back in 1969 and 1970. The statue was covered with gold. It was an awesome sight and then she took me to the temple and that was beautiful also.

As we continued our tour, she said that she would show me where she lived; by now we were out of the city and in the country. It was a tropical or jungle setting with palm trees and bamboo everywhere. When we rode up to her house, I was amazed to see this was an all bamboo structure about twenty feet wide and maybe forty feet long that was about eight feet above ground. The structure was of bamboo with a thatched roof made of palm leaves and the walls and floor was made of woven bamboo strips. She lived with her entire family, parents, child, uncle, aunts and others. There were no rooms for privacy, just one large area off the ground to protect them from water and critters. And they slept on bamboo mats.

The tour was a neat experience that I would never have had if it hadn't been for her. My BN Jim Jerjevich didn't know where I was and was in sort of a panic thinking I was kidnapped or something. He was very relieved when I finally showed up.

Ron Boehm

Shopping in Thailand was a great deal also; tailor-made suits from the Maharaja's were about fifty dollars then, handmade shoes of kangaroo skin or elephant hide were about fifteen dollars and of course there were the beautiful Princess Rings that looked like the crown that the princesses wore.

The Maharaja was an Indian tailor and he and his wife were very nice people. He would invite us to his home in the evening and his wife would cook homemade Indian food for us. It was a great cultural experience and a nice change of pace from being on the military base.

But getting back to the C-130 gunships: my BN and I were in the "O" Club bar having an afternoon drink and talking to the crew of one of the C-130s comparing stories about hunting along the Route Package when the pilot said they were flying that night and if we wanted to check out the action we could come along. I thought that was a great idea and said we would like to do that. But I guess we got involved in "The Ville" and, having had some drinks, we didn't make the flight. The next day we saw the same guys and they said that they had a pretty eventful night the previous night and had come back with a hole in the wing that you could crawl through from AAA fire.

———•——•——

Cartoons in the Ready Room

Our Ready Room was just what it says, the place where you got ready for your mission or a place to wait for your next mission. Guys in their flight suits and flying gear would be sitting around briefing for their flight, playing Acee-Deucee or a game of cards. A cartoon on the wall showed a very gruff Marine with a three-days growth of facial hair, his helmet chin strap hanging down and a rifle in one hand. The caption above the cartoon said,

"Yea though I walk through the Valley of the Shadow of Death, I shall fear no evil for I am the baddest mother fucker in the valley."

There was also a cartoon in the Group Briefing room of two vultures sitting in the dead tree with one saying to the other, "Patience hell! I'm going to kill something." It was amazing how much humor there was in the middle of a war, but I guess that was a way of handling the stress.

Who Will Carry the Mail into the Shau Valley

It seems as if everyone's sense of humor was at it keenest while in combat. It amazed me how people in dire straits or in very stressful situations could come up with some very funny things. I guess it was a coping mechanism to deal with that stress of combat. And there were an abundance of jokes and humorous stories always going around.

One of my favorite jokes or sayings was "Who will carry the mail into the A Shau?" The meaning was who will fly or go into the A Shau Valley which was a bad ass place west of the city of Hue and on the border with Laos. It was a flat valley about twenty five miles long and a mile wide covered with tall elephant grass. It was bordered on either side by densely forested mountains from three to six thousand feet and was a major entry route for the NVA into South Vietnam along the infamous Ho Chi Minh Trail. (Source: Wikipedia)

The joke went like this: "Who will carry the mail into the A Shau?"

"I'll carry the mail into the A Shau."

"But there are lions in the A Shau."

"Fuck the lions."

"You would fuck a lion?"

Ron Boehm

"I'd fuck a lion's mother."

"Why you lion mother-fucker."

The "Docs" — Squadron Flight Surgeons

Our senior squadron officers were for me a likable group; they included Lieutenant Colonel Stan Lewis CO, Major P.J. McCarthy XO, Major "Shooter" Dubeck Ops Officer, and Captain Charlie Carr.

Each squadron had a squadron doctor. Our "Doc" and our sister squadron's "Doc" were some very cool guys probably in their early thirties. It was just like the TV show M*A*S*H with these two guys. Every week on Thursday nights they had movies at their hootch, served drinks or beer and showed porno flicks. Back then porno wasn't like it was now, it wasn't so common and available, and theirs were very much explicit. I have no idea where they got them from, but we had a room full of combat aviators drinking and cheering some flickering image of debauchery being shown on the portable movie screen from a sixteen millimeter projector. Of course, the film would always break or burn showing that brown melting image on the screen right at the best part which would bring on a chorus of boos.

The Docs, since they were flight surgeons, had to get so many flight hours per month just like we did, so they sometimes would go up with us sitting in the right seat. We showed them how to set up the armament panel, handle the radios and we took them on bombing missions. They loved it, but I don't know how that worked out with the Hippocratic Oath and all.

Sea Survival School

In August of 1970, I received orders to go to Sea Survival School in Okinawa. My one vivid memory of Sea Survival School was our parasail training off a landing craft (Papa Boat) fitted with a deck like a small aircraft carrier and wire screen at the back end like a baseball back stop onto which they spread the parasail before the launch.

I was the first guy to be launched off the deck by means of a speedboat with a long rope attached to me and my parasail. The speed boat was just about to take off with me when somebody said, "Look at the size of that son of a bitch!" And everybody ran to the side rail to look.

I said, "What son of a bitch?"

And the reply came back: "A twelve-foot hammerhead shark; that SOB is really big!"

I asked, "Can we move to someplace else before I go?"

So we moved a little bit away from where we were, but not nearly far enough I thought.

When the boat took off and the slack in the tow line was taken up I started to run down the deck, but I was so light—about 135 pounds—that I took only about four steps before I was airborne and rose quickly. The boat ran with me in tow for a while and then I was given the sign to release from the tow line. This was to simulate ejecting from an airplane over water. On the way down you would release the seat pack with the inflatable life raft and a string of other survival gear - flares, signal mirror, water, shark repellant and other stuff all tied to a long line.

All I could think was that a twelve-foot hammerhead shark was following me. I knew it was an impossibility, but I think only the soles of my shoes touched the water when I hit because I was in

Ron Boehm

that life raft so fast it seemed like a blur. I immediately began throwing out shark repellant and had the paddle in hand in case I had to beat the shark off. The name of this school was after all Sea Survival.

We sat out there in the ocean for a while and got familiar with the survival gear and supplies, and then they picked us up and we were put into a large circular rubber raft that was like a kids' lawn pool with a roof.

The best part of these schools was that you got out of Vietnam for a while and back into the real world for a bit.

George Driscoll — Small World

Back in Da Nang with the squadron I got back into the routine of flying, and as usual we were flying a lot of our missions over Laos. One night I had a hop with a 0200 or 0300 target time. We launched out of Da Nang and turned northwest, headed towards our target area along the route package running down from North Vietnam through Laos and into South Vietnam. Over Laos we checked in with the 7th Air Force controlling agency "Moonbeam."

The communication went something like this, "Moonbeam, this is Marine Ringneck fifty-four, angels eighteen with twenty-two delta twos for your pleasure tonight." "Angels eighteen" was eighteen thousand foot altitude and "twenty-two delta twos" referred to twenty-two Mark (82) five hundred pound bombs. We usually carried six bombs on each ejector rack located on four wing stations, except for the two innermost stations on which we carried five bombs to give clearance for the landing gear doors.

Moonbeam would then instruct us to enter a racetrack holding pattern orbit and give us target instructions which would include the target time, run-in heading to coincide with the road's direction at the point of attack and the target location positioned off of a reference point called a Delta Point. The BNs carried an area map with black triangles marked on them as reference points or Delta Points from which to navigate to the assigned target.

The way the system was set up, the Air Force had seismic and audio sensors dropped from the air along the jungle roads (Ho Chi Minh Trail) that would pick up trucks moving along the trail. These sensors looked like an artillery shell with leaf like foliage on top which was an antenna. They would transmit the info back to 7th Air Force command center in Nakhon Phanom, Thailand, which was situated on the Mekong River across from Laos.

Moonbeam would then assign us a target. The target was given to us as a reference off of a "Delta Point" which was a pre-briefed point located on the map from which the BN would locate the target and plug it into our weapons system computer. My BN, having entered this information into the computer, would then send that information to me and it would appear on my VDI (Visual Display Indicator.)

This was instructions to the target drop zone by way of the video screen. It showed as a yellow path, the end of which I would place in a square by maneuvering the aircraft ("Follow the yellow brick road") and the computer would then guide us to the target. If everything went right, the BN would be able to pick up the target (trucks or movers) moving down the road at more than four miles per hour on his radar, lock onto them with his radar cursor hairs and we would then drop our bombs.

It was always a thrill to see secondary explosions.

On this mission as we checked in with Moonbeam, there was an Air Force F-4 up on the same frequency and when I checked in the Air Force pilot said, "Is this Romeo Bravo from Selma, Alabama?" Romeo Bravo referred to my initials R B in the phonetic alphabet and Selma, Alabama is where I went to flight school at Craig Air Force Base. He then identified himself as my buddy George Driscoll who was in my class in flight school and recognized my voice half way around the world, in the middle of the night, two years later in a combat situation. That was awesome. As I had mentioned earlier, in flight school my fellow student pilots used to gather around the radio in the flight shack to listen to me make my position calls with my thick New Orleans accent.

Arlen Handle

Under that same Small World theme, I was back in the MAG 11 "O" Club in Da Nang one day having a drink when I looked down the bar and to my amazement I saw a guy from my Holy Cross High School, Arlen Handle. We looked at each other with a surprised look for an instant or two and I said, "Arlen, what are you doing here?"

He said, "Flying F-4's with VMFA 542 and my brother (another Holy Cross grad) is in the squadron with me."

I had not seen Arlen since we graduated in 1961. He was a state champion wrestler in high school and went to OU on a wrestling scholarship, and now eight years later here we were both in the Marine Corps flying combat half way around the world from our home in New Orleans. What a small world.

Arlen had a close call on one mission. As he rolled in to drop on a target, he and his RIO took some small arms fire and he didn't know they had got hit until they came back to the base. As his crew chief was helping him to get unhooked he noticed that Arlen's parachute harness had been cut by a round that came through the canopy just missing him by inches. If he had had to eject it would have been too bad.

Da Nang, The Big PX

Even though we were stationed at the air base on the outskirts of Da Nang we didn't get into town very often because it was Off Limits for the most part. Occasionally, however, we did get the chance to go into the city. One place we went to was the infamous White Elephant Club and of course a good time was had there. Another place on the list to go was the Big PX at Freedom Hill where you could buy all kinds of stuff that you needed or just wanted. It was like a military Walmart, although I don't think they had Walmarts in 1969, or at least not all over the place like now. That's where you got your stereo, cameras, clothes, food, candy and just about whatever you wanted. And you paid for the stuff in Funny Money (Military Pay Money or MPC.) They paid us in funny money to keep the greenback dollars out of the black market. One thing that I liked to buy at the PX was candy orange slices. I loved them and would stock up when I went there. When I went in the bush with 1/7, I practically lived off them. They were my energy food. Orange slices for candy and Tabasco sauce for spicing up food were staples in my diet.

One day I was walking down the street toward the Big PX when I almost got caught in the middle of an intramural fire fight between some white soldiers and some black soldiers. They were locked and loaded and firing at each other for a little while at about a half block range. Man, I ducked in between two buildings until the fire stopped. I didn't want to be one of those crazy statistics having to do with odd events or "Non-combat action fatality."

In 1969, the racial thing was coming to a head especially with the troops in Vietnam. I could tell that these guys were fresh out of the bush, because of their dirty, shabby dress and just plain unkempt appearance. Somebody said something to someone and somebody gave a finger salute and it escalated from there to a fire

Ron Boehm

fight. Well, at least a few shots were fired from each side. It was just another day at war.

Freedom Hill PX Da Nang

Movies and Steaks at the "O" Club

There wasn't usually a lot to do on the base in Da Nang and I looked forward to flying. If you weren't flying you might be in your hootch reading, writing letters home, playing aceeducee or having a beer at the "O" Club.

The club was no architectural gem, but it had an outdoor patio with tables, chairs and a BBQ pit where you could sit and have a drink outdoors or grill a steak for dinner. In the evening, movies were shown from one of those old reel-to-reel projectors onto a portable screen. The problem was that these movies were shown so many times and had been circulated all over the country so that they quite often broke in the middle of the movie and always at the most critical time. You would be really into the story and then you would see that melting of the film and then everybody would start cursing.

One evening, Jack Rippy and I were watching a movie, drinking a beer with a steak when the missile warning sirens went off. This was our third or fourth time to try to see the entire movie and we just looked at each other, said, "Screw it" and climbed under the table with our beer and continued to watch the movie.

Just about that time, the Vietnamese bar maid came out and said, "No sweat GI, rocket not hit here."

Then Jack said, "Yeah, she should know, her boyfriend is probably the one firing the damn thing."

⚬•••⚬

Toga Night

L ike I said, we had very little to do other than fly, so the squadron would think up all kinds of things to break the monotony and one of those things was "Toga Night." I guess we got the idea from the movie, Animal House. We pulled the sheets off our beds for the toga and made those Roman head wreaths to wear on our heads. There was booze to be had and steaks to be grilled on the outside grill. I don't remember very much other than getting drunk, losing my toga and cooking my steak with Jack Rippy naked until a MP came up and told us we couldn't be out there naked grilling our steaks. That in itself was kind of amazing because Rippy was a pretty straight sane guy. I was probably a bad influence on him.

A-4 Smoke in the Cockpit and Other Strange Arresting Gear Stuff

I t seemed that there was always something unusual happening: after all it was war which by its nature is unusual and unpredictable. For instance, I was on a day time hop and just about to

Ron Boehm

take the active runway when the tower told me to hold there for an emergency in progress. A Marine A-4 reported smoke in the cockpit and was on short straight-in final for an emergency landing. I was listening to the conversation between the tower and the A-4 pilot when the tower asked if he wanted the runway foamed. The A-4 pilot then responded in a slightly excited voice, "Hell, I don't know; this is my first time to do this. You guys are the experts." He made an otherwise uneventful landing and took the midfield arresting gear. The arresting gear was a system of cables at the beginning, middle and end of the runway strung across the runway so that an aircraft's tail hook could catch and stop the aircraft like on an aircraft carrier.

Another time an airliner was landing on the other runway coming in just after an F-4 had taken the midfield arresting gear. They hadn't wound the cable back yet and the airliner, I think it was a 727, engaged the arresting gear and came to an abrupt halt, much to the astonishment of the airline crew and everyone watching.

There was also a story about a Navy A-4 coming in to land at Da Nang with some sort of a problem and was to take the arresting gear at the approach end of the runway. Well, he missed the gear and his plane started to veer off the runway to the point that he thought he was going to leave the runway and he ejected. The A-4 didn't leave the runway but ran into and caught the midfield gear.

I don't know if this is really true, but I heard that the pilot descended in his chute, landed close to the A-4 which was still running while caught in the arresting gear. He supposedly walked up to the A-4, climbed up to the cockpit, reached in and shut the engine down. Pretty embarrassing I would guess, but as they say, "Any landing you walk away from is a good one."

———••••———

Flying in the Middle of the Night

Flying in the middle of the night was always a bit eerie to me. You would do your pre-mission brief and head out to the flight line. Hardly anyone else was around, just the flight crew or two, the duty officer and the ground crew. As you walked out to the flight line area and the steel and concrete revetments where the aircraft were parked, everything was quiet except for an occasional sound of faraway gunfire. As we approached the aircraft my stomach would start getting a little tight and an overall feeling of tension would come over me depending on what and where the mission was. Add to that the fact that this was two, three or four o'clock in the morning and things just seemed a little bit eerie.

One night as we got up to the aircraft, the plane captain met us. We did our walk around and climbed up the ladder to the cockpit. As I reached in to pull the ejection seat safety pins, I looked down and in my seat there were two NATOPS manuals (aircraft manuals) which were each about the size of a major city's telephone book sitting on my seat. Me being the shortest pilot in the squadron, the implications were obvious. I looked down at the plane crew and they were having a big laugh. It relaxed me a bit and was kind of nice because it meant they liked me and knew they could fool around with me. Some officers were asses and too uptight about being officers in relation to the troops. I always wanted to make sure these guys were OK with me, because they kept my aircraft flying and my life depended upon them.

———————

Ron Boehm

Flying Down the Beach

Coming back from our missions in Laos, we would cross just south of the DMZ and reach the South China Sea, referred to as "feet wet." When we did, I loved to head back down to Da Nang by flying down the beach as low as we could get (about ten feet or so above the water).

Most BNs didn't like flying just off the ground like that, nor did they like dropping bombs visually or unusual attitudes (flying upside down or pointing the aircraft down to the ground or up to the sky), but I was a twenty-five-year old jet jock flying this great machine, dropping bombs for a living and I had just dropped bombs on the enemy and survived. Hell yes, I was getting low and fast.

They said that if you got down below ten feet, you could kick up a rooster tail. I can't confirm that since I couldn't see below and behind us. But at that low level you got the aid of ground effect. The air was denser which gave you more lift. Pelicans use this same effect while skimming just off the water's surface. I stopped that practice after we almost had a mid-air with a Huey chopper coming up the beach at the same altitude. Thank God for quick reflexes and good eyesight because the closure rate of two aircraft coming at each other from the opposite direction is pretty fast.

There was talk about a crew that was seeing if they could fly low enough to drop their tail hook in the water (about eight feet) and clean off the grease on the hook thereby proving they had got that low. As the story goes they got too low and skipped off the water like a rock that you would skip on a pond and ejected. As they were sitting in their one man lift rafts, they said, "OK, here is what our story is" on why they had to eject. I can't say if that was true either, but it makes for a good story. But I don't dismiss it either because when you mix a tactical aircraft with youth, a pilot's ego and a derring-do attitude of cheating death for a living, you get some crazy stuff.

Ordinance Disposal

If for some reason you didn't drop your bombs, your mission was canceled or some other reason, we were told not to return with the bombs and were directed to drop them in the South China Sea at a designated drop area which I think was the 075 degree radial off Da Nang at about seventy-five miles out to sea. So, on this one mission, our target as canceled and we headed to the drop zone. But I just hated to see twenty-two perfectly good bombs thrown away, so we armed them and let them go from about one thousand feet. I turned the plane around and rolled it over to watch the explosions. It was an awesome sight with pillows of water shooting skyward and then seeing fish and sharks float up to the surface. It was awesome. Thank God, we didn't see a submarine pop up.

Mustache on Fire

As I said before, there was always something unusual, weird, or just crazy going on, not to mention the circumstances and horrors of war itself. But one of our squadron pilots decided to light up a cigarette in the cockpit while flying a mission. This was considered a bad idea by just about everyone in aviation. They were on a mission over Laos and were either in route to their target or in a holding

Ron Boehm

pattern awaiting a target assignment when the pilot decided to light up. You're in an oxygen environment with an oxygen mask on your face; add to this the oils from your skin and a mustache soaked with both those oils and oxygen. To remove your mask and put a flame close to that mixture—well, you can just imagine what happened next. Of course! His mustache caught on fire and burnt the hell out of his lip. They had to declare an emergency, cancel the mission and return to base.

I can just hear the radio conversation with the controlling agency.

"Moonbeam, we have an emergency and must cancel our mission."

"What is the nature of your emergency, over?"

"Ah, smoke in the cockpit."

"Can you make it back to Da Nang, and do you know what is causing the smoke, over?"

"Ah, yes, we can make it to Da Nang, and yes, the smoke is from my pilot's mustache that caught on fire, over."

Like the saying says, "There are old pilots and there are bold pilots, but there are no old bold pilots."

―――――

Christmas Morning

Time was going by fast and I was averaging about five hops a week, which was great. Sometimes though, I would only get two or three hops and was bored, so I looked forward to flying. It was already getting close to the end of the year and in the early morning hours of Christmas day in 1969 I was flying a mission over Laos when someone came up on the Guard emergency radio frequency which broadcast over all frequencies, and said "Happy Birthday, Son." And a reply came back, "Thanks, Dad." There was humor in every circumstance it seemed.

It was little gems like these that would come time and again in what you would think was a pretty serious situation. It never ceased to amaze me the sense of humor people would display in the most unusual or tense of situations.

———

New Year's Eve

On New Years' eve, 1969, I was on a fifteen-mile final approach to Da Nang at about three minutes to midnight when the tower called me and said, "Ringneck, recommend you secure your landing lights."

I replied, "This is Ringneck, why secure my lights?"

And the tower came back, "Because it's three minutes to midnight and in three minutes everybody with a gun is going to be firing it up in the air and they would just as soon shot at something like an airplane than nothing at all."

"Roger that," I replied and quickly turned off my lights. And, sure enough, at midnight the entire coast lit up with tracers as far as we could see. What a sight. Happy New Year!

———

FAC School — Okinawa, (January 3-17, 1970)

On January 3, 1970, I had orders to Camp Hansen on Okinawa for FAC School or Forward Air Controller School, about a two-week course.

Included on our group orders were my buddies Fred Bonati, Rick Spitz, Carl Widell, Dick Davis, and Doug Burkett. We checked

Ron Boehm

in at the Camp Hansen Marine Base on Okinawa and we were supposed to stay there in the BOQ, but Rick had other ideas. He somehow got us, Rick and myself, into the BOQ at Kadina AFB down the road a bit from the Marine base. All Air Force bases are innately superior in creature comforts to that of Marine bases, plus Kadina had a great happy hour. I don't remember how we got back and forth from Kadina to Camp Hansen, but like I said earlier, Rick had a knack of manipulating the situation for his betterment and worked that out also.

I also don't remember a great deal about FAC School, but a few memories are fresh in my mind. One was of flying in a Huey helicopter, going out to a field exercise when the helicopter pilot learned we were jet jocks. I guess he wanted to make an impression on us by showing us how low to the trees he could fly. Hell, when we landed, I looked at the skids to see if there were any tree branches stuck in them. Then we landed in a field full of ripe pineapples. We didn't have any canteens of water so we ate pineapples, which were, to this day, the sweetest ones I have ever tasted.

The Marine Corps took pilots from the various squadrons with combat flying experience to train as FACs. The idea being that these pilots were familiar with what it took to fly in support of the ground troops and thus would be best at calling in the support from the ground for the rifle companies.

After FAC school I was later assigned as a FAC to 1/7 (1st Battalion 7th Marine Regiment) for a three-month tour in the jungles, mountains and rice paddies of South Vietnam. My official title was Air Liaison Officer, with the "grunts" my radio call sign was the "One Four Actual" and my radio man was just the "One Four."

In the school, we learned how to call in air support for the Marines on the ground, whether it was close air support by directing the planes to drop bombs, calling for helicopter pick-ups, delivery of supplies, medevacs of the wounded or gun-ships for fire support.

One particular function was the use of the radio beacon to get all weather air support from the A-6s which is what I flew. This was a system called RABFAC (Radio Beacon Forward Air Control) which used a transponder to show the position of the FAC on the ground, thus allowing the A-6's electronic weapon system to do off-set bombing in support of the ground troops. It was a very good system which allowed for the first time in the history of air support to be carried out in weather conditions that before would hold up air support until the weather cleared which is what happened in the Battle of the Bulge in WW II. The 101st was hard pressed to hold on against the German assault until the weather cleared and they finally got air support.

The A-6 had one of the most sophisticated aircraft weapon systems at the time with its all weather capability, unlike the F-4s, A-4s and A-7s which had to acquire the target visually in order to attack them. My squadron in Vietnam was VMA (AW) 242. The AW stood for All Weather.

One of my favorite memories from FAC School was when Rick and I went to the Kadina AFB "O" Club for happy hour and we met two other Marine pilots. They were CH-46 helicopter drivers with a whole bunch of combat missions and I think they might have even been shot down a time or two. One of the guys was pretty stressed out and I think they were given some time out of the country for a mini R&R just to recoup a bit.

So anyway, Rick and I and the two other Marine pilots were drinking and telling sea stories when somebody in the club rang a bell and everyone in the place stood up except for us.

An Air Force guy standing next to us said, "Stand up for the returning combat crew coming back from their mission over Vietnam."

We looked at each other and laughed, and either Rick or I said, "Stand up, are you kidding me? These two guys have been flying combat missions multiple times daily getting their asses shot off and Rick and I have been flying over Laos at night getting our asses shot off. We we're not standing up for anybody, especially B-52 guys flying thirty thousand feet over South Vietnam where small arms fire didn't go up more than a thousand feet."

That didn't make us real popular with the Air Force guys. Don't get me wrong, flying in combat is still flying in combat and

Ron Boehm

those guys that flew up North over North Vietnam with the greatest concentration of anti-aircraft fire and SAMS ever were all heroes in my estimation, but this was a different situation. This was 1969 and the U.S. had stopped bombing up North.

Rick and I left to go to dinner or something and we heard later that the really stressed out Marine helicopter pilot got drunk and crazy and they tried to kick him out of the club. This led to a ruckus and the Air Force MPs chased him down the hall and finally up on the roof. The building that the "O" Club was in had a flat roof and was situated up against a hillside so that one end of the roof was about twenty some odd feet off the ground, but the other side was only about six feet off the ground. By luck or by skillful escape and evasion tactics he ran down the roof shouting, "You will never take me alive" and jumped off the roof on the low side. I don't know what happened to him after that. But the guy really did need a break from combat it seemed.

Back with the Squadron in Da Nang

It was a new year, 1970, and we were flying our daytime and night missions on a regular basis. In general, things were a little bit quieter with regards to the war than at the New Year of the Tet Offensive in 1968 when all hell broke out all across South Vietnam. It was called the Tet Offensive because the offensive was launched on the date of the Vietnamese Luna New Year Celebration. It was an unofficial understanding that both sides would observe a cease fire for the Tet festivities, but the communist forces of North Vietnam (NVA) and the Viet Cong (irregular forces of South Vietnam) broke the agreement and launched the offensive in the early morning of January 30, 1968. Approximately eighty thousand communist forces attacked about one hundred towns and cities all over South Vietnam. In most places, they were stopped and beaten back fairly quickly, but in the Battle of Hue the fight lasted for a month and at Khe Sanh the fight went on for several months. (Source: Wikipedia)

All in all it was a big defeat for the communist forces, but the American news media painted a different picture and Walter Cronkite made it look like a defeat for the U.S. and South Vietnamese forces (ARVN).

Most of my TBS (Marine Basic Officers' School) class of 5-'67 were in Vietnam for the Tet Offensive battles as 1st or 2nd lieutenant platoon leaders and company commanders. All of us that went into aviation were in flight school at the time. Ray Smith, who would eventually rise to the rank of Major General, took over as company commander of Alpha Company 1/1 right in the middle of the Battle for Hue against a North Vietnamese brigade size force of about seventy-five hundred. Nick Warr was a platoon commander for Charlie Company, 1st Battalion, 5th Marines and lost most of his platoon in the very beginning of the fight inside the ancient Walled City. His book Phase Line Green is a great account of the Battle for Hue which went down in the annuals of Marine Corps history with other epic Marine Corps battles. (Source: *Boys of '67*, by Charles Jones; *Phase Line Green* by, Nick Warr; Wikipedia)

Les Palm, who like Ray Smith would rise to the rank of Major General, was an artillery officer at Khe Sanh and Hill 881 South with 1/13. On one occasion, the hootch that he used to live in took a direct hit from a mortar round. Thankfully, he wasn't in it.

My good friend in Houston Steve Benckenstein was a CH-46 helicopter pilot and flew into Khe Sanh in the latter part of the battle when things had settled down somewhat and told me it was no fun even then to fly into a place that was subject to constant mortar and artillery bombardment. During the most intense time of the fighting, the Marines were being re-supplied by air, but it became almost impossible for the helicopters and the C-130s to land because the NVA had the runway and entire base targeted and would drop in mortars and artillery rounds whenever a plane landed. It got to where the C-130 would just make a very low fly-over and drop the supplies by parachute.

Lt. Steve Beckenstein coming-back from a mission

The news reports were saying that the Marines could end up like the French at Dien Bien Phu in 1954 with a disastrous defeat. But Marines held on in what was a long and drawn out fight. The Marine air support along with the Navy and Air Force, especially the B-52s, pounded the hell out of the NVA. The B-52s dropped over seventy-five thousand tons of bombs on the NVA positions over a period of about nine weeks. It was the largest payload ever dropped on a tactical target.

The NVA and Viet Cong were on the ropes after they had spent themselves and got decimated by our forces, but thanks to Walter Cronkite, all the anti-war protest and the general public getting tired of the war Americans let the NVA off the hook. The military wanted to finish the job, but the politicians said "No." The military didn't lose a fight in Vietnam; we didn't lose the war, the politicians did.

One account from the Marine Corps' book about the Battle for Khe Sanh which I had mentioned earlier, describes one morning's reveille. It describes the Marines standing up in their fox holes with their helmets and flack vests on saluting the flag then hearing the thumping of enemy mortar rounds leaving the tubes, the Marines getting down for the anticipated incoming barrage and the following explosions. As the dust settled there came from one fox hole a red flag waving back and forth in the air—Maggie's Drawers, which meant you missed the whole target. What a great in your face retort from the Marines under siege and constant attack. I love that story.

At the end of the Tet Offensive, that lasted about five and one half months from January 21 to July 9, 1968, the communist forces were devastated and it took a while for them to rebuild and regroup. At the end of the battle for Khe Sanh, our forces withdrew and closed the base.

Ray Smith got his second Silver Star at Khe Sanh.

One of my buddies from my platoon in OCS and friend in TBS was Dave "Andy" Anderson who was also a fraternity brother of Tom Broderick back at Wisconsin. Andy, like most of the O302 infantry officers of our TBS class, had thirty days leave after graduation and was sent right into the fray of Vietnam. It was learn as you go for these guys and they were in the thick of combat right away.

On December 15, 1967, Andy was a 2nd Lieutenant Platoon leader with the 2nd Platoon of Bravo Company 1/1. They were in the point of a company size ambush against the NVA around Con Thien in Quang Tri Province. His guys sprang the ambush and opened up on several NVA soldiers. Andy went out to search the bodies or the wounded when a NVA soldier jumped up and shot him at close range in the chest. The bullet went through his bullet proof vest, through his chest, lung and exited through his back and the vest again. Lucky the round didn't hit any bone or he would have been dead.

Then all hell broke loose. Andy's company was in the middle of an NVA Regiment and his platoon had lost contact with the other platoons in his company. Andy was lying on the ground spitting up blood when a Corpsman pulled him into a bomb crater. The bad guys were running all over the place and Andy grabbed a grenade and pulled the pin and then thought to himself, "What's the timing on this thing is it seven or ten seconds? Damn, I should have paid more attention in the class."

Ray Smith's Alpha Company 1/1 with tanks in support had to come in and rescue Andy's unit. They put Andy on top of a tank to evacuate him all the while the tank is firing at the NVA. Because of the tank's gun firing so close to Andy, he couldn't hear for several days. He woke in a hospital, looked around and saw several Vietnamese nurses and thought he was a prisoner of war. But thankfully his was in one of our hospitals. He was then transferred to the Hospital Ship "Sanctuary" off shore and his combat tour was over. He was sent home to recoup from his wounds. All this happened while Fred, Tom and I were in flight school.

When he first told his story to our group of OCS platoon mates at our TBS class forty-year reunion in Quantico we were laughing at the bit about him thinking he was prisoner of war, but he was shaking as he told the story.

———•••••———

Feb. 14, 1970 — My Birthday and the USO Valentine's Day Show

There was a much anticipated USO-type show scheduled for Valentine's Day at the MAG 11 "O" Club. The tables for each squadron were arranged ninety degrees to the stage with the attack squadrons lined up to the left side and the fighter squadrons on the right side. These were banquet tables arranged so that they would seat the whole squadron on one long continuous table.

Most everyone had their party flight suits on instead of regular flying flight suits. The suits were of the squadron's colors and had their squadron's insignia and your rank on them. My squadron VMA (AW) 242 had black suits with our gold Navy wings embroidered on the left side and a black bat with red eyes over a yellow lightning bolt on the right side. Under my gold wings was my name, Low Beam. When these suits were worn, it meant that you were ready to party.

The liquor was flowing and bottles of champagne were being passed around. We brought a special surprise to the event—our Beer

Can Bazooka. This was in the old days when beer cans were made out of steel not the flimsy aluminum of today. We took about five beer cans, cut the ends off four of them, cut one end off of the end can and taped them together. We used a beer can opener to punch a hole in the one end of our bazooka. A tennis ball was then loaded into one end and lighter fluid was sprayed into the hole in the other end. It took a team of two to man the bazooka, one holding the tube and the other guy to ignite the lighter fluid with a cigarette lighter. It was awesome, the tennis ball would travel a high rate of speed and go about fifty feet through the air.

So as the party got really going we set up our bazooka and aimed it at the fighter squadron's table on the other side of the room. However, to our surprise, they also had the same idea as we had and matched our technology with their own bazooka. Man, all of a sudden tennis balls were flying all over the place ricocheting off of walls and people. Everybody was diving for the floor and getting under the tables. One senior officer was standing up getting ready to give a toast when a tennis ball almost took him down. He quickly forgot about the toast and hit the deck.

What a great start for an evening of fun and entertainment. It was also a special night for me since it was Valentine's Day and my twenty-seventh birthday.

The first band was from the Philippines and they had all the popular songs of the time down pat except for certain words with "Rs." One song that was one of the most popular at the time was Proud Mary. They were singing "Rolling, rolling, rolling on the river," but it came out as "wolling on the weeever." Well anyway, I thought that was very amusing, but they put on a pretty good show. Hell, we were so starved for entertainment that we would have liked anything.

However, the next band was from Australia and they were also good and had a very pretty girl lead singer. We were all liquored up, having a great time and guys starting sending bottles of champagne up on the stage for the band. It wasn't very long before the band was as drunk as the rest of us. They were supposed to play only so many songs and finish, but they just kept on playing and at one point one guy with an electric guitar was sitting in the rafters playing his guitar even though it wasn't plugged in. Then the pretty singer said, "Will Lieutenant Ron Boehm come up on stage and get his birthday kiss?" Well, everybody, including yours truly, started cheering and some of my squadron mates picked me up and passed me hand to hand over their heads up to the stage and then threw me onto the stage. I stumbled to my feet and walked up to the pretty singer and said, "Lieutenant Ron Boehm reporting as ordered ma'am." She then grabbed me, leaned me over and planted this big, long kiss on my lips, but both of us being drunk she dropped me and I fell on the floor. But I could have cared less; what a great birthday that I'll never forget.

Easter Sunday, 1970

The next holiday was Easter Sunday and I had a middle of the night hop scheduled with a target time of about 3:00 or 4:00 AM over Laos. We were briefed that the area we were going into might have at least one fifty millimeter gun which was usually radar-controlled. Most of the AAA we encountered was twenty-three millimeter and thirty-seven millimeter which were not usually radar aimed and they just threw the stuff up in a barrage type fire or fired at the aircraft's sound which was usually behind us. The barrage type fire was all over the place and you just flew through it as fast and best as you could. Once when we had heavy fire a quick thought came to me that it was like coming out of the church on your wedding with people throwing rice all over you. But of course that was a much nicer experience then flying through the glowing balls of deadly AAA fire.

The radar controlled guns would track you and you could see the AAA burst walking in towards you. We had a pretty good

ECM system (Electronic Counter Measures) and we put that baby on, dumped chaff (strips of aluminum foil) that would, we hoped, fool the guns' radar and it would lock up on the chaff instead of your aircraft. The ECM gear would electronically give a false reading to the radar and in essence made the radar image of your aircraft look as if it was moved over away from where you actually were. And when you put it on you would actually see (fingers crossed) the AAA burst move away from you and sometimes fly in formation with you off to the side.

So on this early Easter morning as my BN and I left the ready room and headed out to the flight line the thought of the fifty millimeter gun and the mission was on my mind and the closer I got to the aircraft parked in the covered revetment the tighter my stomach got. The procedure was that as you walked up to the aircraft you were greeted by the plane captain and maybe another ground crewman. The pilot and BN would do a walk around pre-flight of the aircraft, check the bombs and pull the safety wires, climb into the plane, go through the procedures to start the aircraft. After getting all the various systems up and running, we would then contact the tower for taxi instructions.

The ground crew helped you get in the plane and strapped in, get it started and on your way. As you left, the plane captain would salute you and you were on your way taxiing out to the runway.

On this particular night as we walked up to the plane to begin our preflight, I noticed that the ground crew had these big grins on their faces and then when I looked at the bombs attached to the racks hanging from the wings my BN and both broke out in a huge laugh for they had painted all the bombs like Easter Eggs. That was awesome and a welcomed laugh that helped to take the edge off. All I could say was, "You guys have too much time on your hands."

Ron Boehm

R&R

In June of 1970 I got my very welcomed orders to go on R&R. Two weeks in Hawaii. The married guys mostly went to Hawaii to meet their wives and most of the bachelors went to Australia where the local Australian girls seemed to like the American GIs pretty good, probably because they knew these guys had two weeks to spend a bunch of money on them.

I got on a flight to Honolulu and met my wife Eileen there for the two-week vacation. She was waiting for me when I arrived at the airport and it was so great to see her. It was a funny thing, when you were "In country" (Vietnam) that was your world, but as soon as you went out of country to the real world then that was now reality and the two didn't seem to mix. They were just two very different worlds.

Eileen had given birth to our daughter Laura only eight days before I left for Vietnam so it had been quite a while since we had a chance to make love and so we did a lot of catching up so to speak. We did manage to get out of the hotel room for some sightseeing and catch Don Ho's show at a club.

We were not very impressed with Honolulu and Waikiki Beach so we only stayed there for two days. We then made arrangements to fly to the Island of Kauai. It was the very essence of what we thought Hawaii was, absolutely beautiful. It was where they filmed the movie "South Pacific." In 1969 the island was scarcely populated, the beaches were wonderful and there was a canyon that was a scenic wonder. It was truly an island paradise.

One night Eileen and I decided to take a bottle of wine and go down from the hotel to the beach at night for a romantic evening and maybe go skinny dipping. We set up a blanket on the sand, opened up a bottle of wine and began our romantic evening. The moon was beautiful and bright with the moonlight shining off the magnificent white-topped waves rolling onto the shore, but Eileen wasn't getting into the mood like I was and seemed uptight for some reason.

After some hugs and kissing didn't seem to work in getting her into the mood I asked her, "What's wrong?"

She said that she was afraid of the bears.

"Bears? There are no bears in Hawaii," I said.

And in her very Eileen-like manner said, "You have never been here before. You don't know that for sure."

So the skinny dipping was out and any other ambitious ideas I had for a deserted beach. But the trip to Kauai was wonderful as was seeing my wife for the first time in six months.

It was over all too fast and we said good-bye at the airport as she got on a plane back to the States and I back to Nam. It was tough to say good-bye because it would be another six months before we saw each other again.

———•◦•———

FACing with 1/7

Shortly after getting back from R&R, I was called into the Ops Officer's office along with Rick Spitz and Carl Widell. The CO said that Carl and I were going out with the grunts on a three month FAC tour and that Rick was going to Group headquarters (Marine Air Group 11). The CO also added that one of us was going to 1/7 (1st Battalion 7th Marine Regiment) at LZ Baldy (Landing Zone Baldy) and the other to the ROKs (Republic of Korea Marine Unit). I did not want that assignment at all and then Carl who was a Princeton graduate, spoke several languages and majored in South-east Asian Culture, spoke up and said that he would love to go to the ROKs. He said that it would be a great opportunity to learn another language and learn about their culture. And I chimed in by saying, "You are right, Carl, that would be a great experience for you."

I learned later that my buddy Fred Bonati was also chosen to go FACing. Throughout our Marine Corps careers Fred and I quite often ended up on the same orders, our being names right next to one other's since Basic School.

So in March I caught a helicopter ride down to LZ Baldy about thirty-seven miles south of Da Nang, the headquarters of 1/7 and reported in for my new duty as one of the Battalion's Air Liaison Officers. There were three of us, a Major who was the Battalion 1-4 and two of us Lieutenants who would be out in the bush with the rifle companies, radio call sign "1-4 actual." I reported into Lieutenant Colonel Cooper, the commanding officer of the 1st Battalion. He was a no-nonsense Marine infantry officer and a very good commander.

My duties were to coordinate air support operation for the company or battalion with helicopter and fixed wing aircraft support. This could be in scheduling and arranging for helicopter transportation, emergency medevacs, calling for air support from Marine or other service support like Army helicopter gunships, Marine fighter/attack aircraft, Air Force "Spooky" AC-130, and "Puff the Magic Dragoon" AC 47 gunships. I sometimes worked in the Battalion Fire Direction Center along with the Artillery Officer coordinating artillery fire and the aircraft passing through our area.

Mostly I dealt with the helicopters, CH-46s, CH-53s and Hueys. I was a few months senior to another 1st Lieutenant FAC so I took over for the Major when he went on R&R and worked with Lieutenant Colonel Cooper who wanted to tour the AO (Area of Operation) on a regular basis. So I arranged for the helicopters and accompanied him to visit the troops in Alpha, Bravo, Charlie and Delta Companies. When the Major was there I would go out into the "bush" for a couple weeks at a time, usually with Alpha or Bravo Companies and return to the battalion HQs. The other FAC officer pretty much stayed out in the field with Charlie and Delta Companies.

Marine CH-46 coming
into the LZ

Ron Ambort

On my first combat ground patrol, I was with a squad size unit led by 1st Lieutenant Ron Ambort who was the Bravo Company Commander. Ron was under investigation for an incident that happened shortly before I got there in which a small patrol from his company rounded up a bunch of villagers and killed them. It was another patrol from his company that discovered the dead villagers and reported it. This was the Marine Corps Mi Lai incident and the Marine Corps was going to make sure there was not any cover up like what happened with the Army's Mi Lai incident.

The village in which this happened was believed by the men of Bravo Company to be full of bad guys and often when a patrol went near that village they would come under attack. So somebody or some guys decided to take matters into their own hands and take retribution on the villagers. The investigation of Ron Ambort was to determine whether Ron ordered the action or had knowledge of it.

Bravo Company had the reputation as being a very aggressive unit under 1st Lieutenant Ambort and had the highest kill numbers of the four companies in the battalion. I thought from my own conversations with Ron he showed he did not like the Vietnamese at all and didn't trust them. In a war were you could not know who was the enemy or who was friendly, I thought Ron just considered them all to be the enemy or potential enemy.

On this particular patrol my radio man, a Lance Corporal named Hank, and I were at the back of the patrol. We had just finished a lunch break where I was talking to a Marine with a scout dog. Ron called for everyone to mount up and called for the scout dog and his handler to go up to point at the front of the patrol. We were following the worn path around the edge of an elevated farm field that had been freshly tilled. It was all mud and little vegetation. As Hank and I came up to turn the corner of the field we heard a loud explosion and Ron shouted for me to get a medevac immediately. I rushed up to the front of the patrol and there were several Marines, a Vietnamese scout, the kid I had just been talking to minutes before, and his scout dog on the ground. The scout dog had tripped a Claymore mine booby trap and it got just about everybody in the front of the patrol. I got on the radio and called for a medevac helicopter.

Everybody was either setting up a defensive perimeter or trying to render first aid to the wounded. I went up to the young Marine with the scout dog; he was sitting up staring straight ahead. He had blood coming from several wounds. I opened his shirt and saw a couple small red holes in his chest, one in his forehead and one in his neck that was spurting out blood. I didn't know what do, so I stuck my finger into the hole in his neck to stop the bleeding. As I did, his eyes rolled up in his head and he fell over dead. I checked for a pulse and there was none. At that point I almost lost my lunch and I remember thinking, "Come on Ron, get a grip, you're a Marine officer." It was the first person I had seen die.

My next thought was about bringing the medevac helicopter into the adjacent field. I thought to myself that if they set up a booby trap on the trail they would expect us to bring a helicopter into the adjacent field, and it occurred to me that they may have mined the field also. So my radioman and I started carefully walking the field looking for mines, probing suspicious patches of dirt with our bayonets just as I had been taught in Basic School. I was very nervous and I just had that fear of stepping on a land mine. Thank God there was none and we got the copter in OK. We loaded the dead and wounded into the chopper to be taken to the hospital.

Zippo Attack on the Village

Once we got the situation under control and the wounded taken care of, Ron Ambort got the remainder of the patrol mounted up, turned us around and headed back to the village we had come by earlier. Ron was pissed off and in my estimation he was going to make someone pay for this attack on his men. When we got back to the village, most of the people had cleared out already, but the ones that were left were pulled out of the huts and the troops searched the village for weapons.

Ron then took out his Zippo cigarette lighter and started to set fire to the bamboo and thatched roof huts. It was like the scene in the movie Platoon that came out after the Vietnam war where they burned the village down. When I saw that movie I immediately thought of this incident at this village. At that time, I had the fear that he was going to start shooting people, and I told Ron to remember that he was already under investigation for the patrol from his company that killed people from the other village of Son Thang. I don't know whether or not it had any bearing on his actions, but I just wanted him to think before his anger got him in any more trouble.

Ron Ambort, in my estimation, was a damn good officer, combat leader and a fine company commander just based on the short time I knew and worked with him. When I left 1/7, the investigation was still on going and I didn't hear what the results were or what happened to him until years later.

According to excerpts from an article published in the Michigan Law Review and the book "Son Thang: An American War Crime" by Gary Solis, a former Marine combat officer and judge advocate for eighteen years in the Marine Corps, 1st Lieutenant Louis R. Ambort (Ron Ambort), company commander of Bravo Company, 1st Battalion 7th Marine Regiment, sent out a fire team size (five member) "Killer Teams" to search for the Viet Cong, weapon and food caches. On February 19, 1970, one of these killer teams went to the small hamlet of Son Thang, found no men in the village, but rounded up sixteen women and children in three huts or as we called them "hootches," and shot and killed them. This was similar to the Army's My Lai Massacre which happened on March 16, 1968, which was in the same area as Son Thang, about twenty-five miles away, but unlike My Lai there wasn't a cover up involved and an investigation into the killings was started the next day by the Battalion Ops Officer Major Theer.

The investigation resulted in four general court-martials with one team member given immunity for his testimony in the trials. One Private was convicted of pre-meditated murder and given a life sentence which was reduced later, one PFC was convicted of unpremeditated murder and given five years in prison which was later reduced, one PFC was acquitted, and the fourth team member, Lance Corporal Harrod, was also acquitted.

A couple of interesting side notes regarding Lance Corporal Harrod; he was put up earlier for a Silver Star and his defense team was aided by Lieutenant Oliver North who credited Harrod for saving his own life months earlier.

First Lieutenant Ron Ambort was charged with failure to obey a division order to report an incident thought to be a war crime, dereliction of duty for failing to take effective measures to minimize noncombatant casualties, not insuring that his men were aware of the rules of engagement, and making a false official statement regarding the killer team's actions.

He received non-judicial punishment for making a false official statement and received a letter of reprimand rather than face a trial by general court-martial on the theory that he was Company Commander of the killer team and bore responsibility for their actions at Son Thang. (Source: *Michigan Law Review*, Vol. 96, No. 6; Reviewed by Robinson O. Everett, Prof. of Law, Duke University in Song Thang; *An American War Crime,* by Gary Solis)

———•••———

Life in the Bush

Life in the bush was a little different than what we guys in the Wing experienced. Back at the air base in Da Nang we lived in luxury compared to how the "Grunts" lived. Out in the bush, you tried to keep yourself and your men as clean and shaved as best as you could. That meant washing and shaving out of your metal helmet. I remembered that an instructor back in Basic School told us to keep our men clean, shaven as best as possible and make sure that they ate with a fork and knife. At the time I thought to myself, "Why?" He went on to say the troops were mostly eighteen- and nineteen-year olds and that civilization was a very thin veneer and they would go animal on you in a heartbeat.

———•••———

PFC with Ear Necklace

This became very clear to me when I was as out with the rifle companies. One time I went out to one of the platoons' encampment which had been out in the bush for weeks. It seemed that most of the guys were without shirts, which was OK, after all it was 103 degrees. But I spotted one young Marine with a

Ron Boehm

necklace made of leather string and two human ears. I called him over and asked what that was all about. He said, "Gooner ears, Sir." I jumped all over him and asked if he had his Geneva Convention Card on him? The Geneva Convention Card listed the Rules of Warfare and we all were instructed on them in training. I told him that he was in violation of those rules and he had better go bury those ears now and if I ever saw him do anything like that again I'd have him court-martialed. He didn't think it was a big deal until I called him on it. Like the instructor at TBS said, "Keep them clean as best as you can, make them eat with a fork and knife or they will go animal on you. Civilization really is a thin veneer on an eighteen-year old."

Alley Cat

On one occasion I went out on a night ambush with a small group of Marines on what they called an Alley Cat. I don't know if the Battalion CO would have approved it, but Ron Ambort said that I should see what the real action was like, so I went out with the fire team size Alley Cat. We stayed out all night and then just around daybreak all hell broke loose with sounds of a lot of gunfire and tracers going out. We had set up the ambush on this well-traveled trail through the high elephant grass. When the firing stopped, I rushed over to the scene and saw two dead NVA and blood trails which the troops were following.

I continued on with two of my guys and we came upon another wounded enemy soldier. This guy was a Viet Cong dressed in the typical black pajamas that they wore. He was lying in the tall grass bandaging his wounds when we came upon him and we had our guns aimed at him. I could tell this was a combat trooper for he was physically fit and looked to be hard as nails. I didn't see as much fear in his face as pain. One Marine checked him for weapons and tied him up.

I heard a commotion coming from another area just fifty feet or so away, so I went to see what that was all about. There was a wounded NVA nurse who two of the troops had stripped naked below the waist and they were about to shove a pop-up flare up her vagina. Pop ups were flares that you would hold with one hand and hit the base with the other hand and that would send a bright luminous flare up about one hundred feet or so.

I said, "What the fuck are you doing?"

They then looked at me with a question on their faces and said, "Come on Lieutenant, she's just a fucking gook."

And for a guilty micro-second that thought went through my mind, "Yea, she's just a gook."

But I immediately erased that thought, put my hand on my pistol and said, "She is a wounded prisoner and you will take care of her according to the rules. Now put her clothes on, bandage her wounds and tie her up. We need to get both prisoners back to the company CP."

One of the dead enemy was a pay master who had a bunch of money on him, some of it U.S. dollars, some Vietnamese money, and some U.S. military funny money.

It really came home to me again about what a thin veneer civilization was when you were in war and taught to kill the enemy. Religion and society had taught you, "Thou shalt not kill," but that is what your job was, so in order to do that and for your mind to handle the contradiction, you had to de-humanize the enemy. You did that by changing their name to "Jap" or "Nazi" or "Gook" or "Gooner" and so on. They were somehow less than human and therefore you could kill them.

It seemed like your mind couldn't put both worlds together: you were "In country or In the Nam;" then when you left Vietnam even for a day, you were back in "The real world."

Back before you got in combat, John Wayne and all that hero stuff in the movies and the "High diddle diddle straight up the

Ron Boehm

middle" was glamorous, but "War is Hell" and for the men that went through it, some of them went through hell. And some could never get over it.

———•··•———

Meal Time in the Bush

Meal time was an experience also; everyone sat around and we broke out our "C Rats" (C Rations) which consisted of a box containing such things as a can of meat, can of beans, can of fruit, bread or pound cake in a can, a chocolate bar, fork, spoon, toilet paper, a pack of five cigarettes, sugar, instant coffee, dairy creamer and heating tabs. There were various combinations of the items and, by and large, the food, I thought, was pretty good.

The technique we used to heat up the food was to take an empty can, punch holes in the bottom for air, drop a heat tab in it and light it. This was your stove; you set the can of food you wanted to heat with the top still on, folded, to make a handle on top of your stove. If you didn't have heating tabs, you could use a pinch of C-4 explosive as a heat source. Just don't try to stamp out a lit piece of C-4.

When they broke open a case of C Rats, the guy distributing these delicious cuisines asked, "Who wants turkey loaf?" or "Who wants corned beef?" and so forth and so on. The least favorite it seemed was ham and lima beans, but they were called something else. The call was, "Who wants ham and mother fuckers?" That was because those things would make you fart and then somebody would say "mother fucker" referring to the smell. That just tore me up every time I heard it. Of course you always had a bottle of Louisiana Hot Sauce with you because that stuff covered up the taste of almost anything.

Fruit cocktail was a big favorite, and guys traded off one thing for another. I didn't smoke so I traded my cigarettes for peaches or fruit cocktail.

My favorite dessert was to take my canteen cup, add in some broken up pound cake, a pack of dairy creamer, and a can of peaches. God! It was like a peach cobbler and I loved it.

Sleeping, or the attempt to get sleep, was quite an endeavor, especially during the monsoon season when it just rained or drizzled all the time for about two to three months straight. In order to get off the hard ground, I had my "rubber whore," a blow-up air mattress, but those little valleys in between the air-filled rolls funneled the rain water right to the lowest point, which was my ass. So there I was in a slight foxhole (the Marine Corps call them "fighting holes") with a poncho for cover lying on my rubber whore that was funneling the water to my ass, holding my weapon, trying to sleep. Not too good. Us fly boys had it good back at Da Nang.

Radio Men Talking All Night

Another thing that happened in the middle of the night was that the radio men carried on all night conversations with each other. I guess it was the equivalent of teenagers talking for hours on the phone. Everyone else was trying to sleep except for the people on guard duty.

1-4 Radiomen in
the bush with 1/7

Ron Boehm

I heard this constant whispering, so I asked Hank, my radio guy, what was up.

He said, "Oh, they are just bull shitting."

I said, "They are jamming up the net when there might be important transmissions coming in."

"It's no big deal Lieutenant; that's just their little bit of relief from boredom."

I finally agreed and didn't worry about it again.

———————

Tiger Bait

One of the more interesting events that I got to encounter was when I flew with the CO to visit one of our small combat outposts to the west of LZ Baldy. They were set up along the infiltration route through the Que Son Mountains and Que Son Valley.

The Battalion Commander Lieutenant Colonel Cooper was very big on visiting his troops out in the field on a regular basis to keep up with the fluid situation. Very often I accompanied him on these visits. Being an Air Liaison Officer, I worked with the Major who was the Battalion Air Liaison Officer to set up the helicopters, most often a CH-46, to pick us up at battalion headquarters and make the trip to one or more units out in the field.

On this one early morning, we dropped in on a Marine unit out in the bush and everyone was a-buzz about something, so I asked what was going on. A Lance Corporal told me that earlier that morning a tiger tried to bite a Marine's head while he was sleeping in his foxhole. Lucky for the Marine, he had his helmet on and the tiger tried to bite the steel pot and drag him out of his foxhole. I asked what happened next and he said there was a lot of screaming and hollering and a bunch of rounds fired as the tiger got frightened off and the Marine probably had to change his shorts. Now that is not your average morning in the bush.

Three Kids with Homemade Coolers

On one patrol in the middle of the friggen jungle, miles from the closest village as far as I knew, we were approached by three kids with homemade Styrofoam coolers strapped to their shoulders. They'd made the coolers from packing material that was taped together. They were selling Cokes and popsicles, which were pretty attractive to the troops in the jungle with 103 degree temperatures and one hundred percent humidity. But you didn't know what the popsicles were made of and I was worried about dysentery or something worse, so I told one of the troops to tell the kids to "de de" which meant scram or get out of here. But the kids paid no attention to him. So I said in a very firm and very officer-like voice, "De de mow" which translated loosely to, "Get the fuck out of here." They took off running and went about fifteen feet; then they turned in unison and all three gave me the middle finger and said, "Fuck you lifer" in very understandable English. I wonder who they learned those words from. The troops referred to officers and senior NCOs as "lifers."

Gunny and the Scout Dog

There was a Gunnery Sergeant with one of the companies who was a Marine's Marine and the classic hard nose Gunny. I remember on one occasion, we were taking some light in-

Ron Boehm

coming fire so I got down, but I saw him standing up with flack vest opened, holding onto a green towel hanging around his neck looking for where the fire was coming from. He seemed invincible with that pose and all the troops respected him and didn't give him any crap if they knew what was good for them.

As an officer you made the decisions, but it was a good idea to get the Gunny's thoughts on the matter also.

There was a Marine with his scout dog attached to the unit who considered himself somewhat independent and had words with the Gunny over some matter. As I said, the Gunny didn't take any crap and grabbed the Marine by the collar and got right in his face at which point the German shepherd scout dog lunged at the Gunny. The Gunny punched the dog and then the scout Marine, knocking him out with a right. Order was restored and the dog and the Marine both learned who was boss.

I learned later on after I had left 1/7 that the Gunny had been killed. A good man lost.

Marine Sniper

One day out in the bush with the Battalion CP we had a sniper with us. Frank, my buddy the artie (artillery) officer, and I had noticed for several evenings in a row these three to five "farmers" walking in a military-like spaced formation with their rice hats and black pajamas carrying hoes like you would carry a rifle. They were at the other side of a large rice field area about a "klick" (one kilometer, one thousand meters or .62 miles) away. This was a free fire zone, so we told the sniper about it and he said, "They're bad guys, do you want me to take care of them?"

We asked if he could get them at that distance and he said, "No problem, that's what they pay me for."

That evening sure as hell, there were these three men walking across the rice field down that same path in formation just like we'd noticed. The sniper set up a shot and dropped one of the guys and the other two dove for cover and then got out of there. Nice shot.

On another occasion, Frank and I were looking out over the same area and looking at about the same situation of three or four enemy troops walking across the rice paddies and Frank said, "Let's call in an "arti-mission on them" and asked if I would like to call the mission.

I said, "Well, it has been two years since Basic School when last I called in an artillery mission, but I'll give it a try."

We had no friendlies in the area so what the hell. I studied the map and looked out over the area with Frank's binoculars where the bad guys were walking and called in the fire mission back to the fire base. We got the word from the fire base that the rounds were on the way. We saw no splash (the resulting explosion), and I called for the guns to drop five hundred—still no sight of the splash.

Frank took back his binoculars and said, "Here, let me show you how to do it" and then he said something about pilots missing targets.

—————

Que Son Mountains

The 7th Marines TAOR at the time that I was with them in March through May of 1970 was an area south of Da Nang in Quang Nam Province. It lay south of the Republic of Korea Marines (ROKs) TAOR and their base at Hoi An near the coast ran west to the Que Son Mountains, Antenna Valley and north to the Song Tinh Yen River and the 5th Marines position and their base at An Hoa. To the south was the Army's Americal Division.

The Regiment had three continuously occupied bases: LZ Baldy which was the Regimental HQ located at the intersection of

Ron Boehm

Route 535 and QL 1 and about twenty miles south of Da Nang, Fire Support Base Ross which covered the Que Son Valley, and Fire Support Base Ryder which covered the Que Son Valley and Antenna Valley.

From the coastal planes and rice paddies the land rises to the west and southeast of An Hoa into the Que Son Mountains. This was a major NVA and Viet Cong stronghold along the infiltration routes from the Ho Chi Min Trail that had numerous base camps, headquarters and hospitals. The Marines were in there to conduct search and destroy missions, to destroy supplies of weapons and food, to deny the enemy the use of these base camps and to block the infiltration to the coastal areas. (Source: Marine Corps History 7th Marines in Vietnam)

The 7th Marines rotated their battalions around the various areas and these three bases. At this time, my Battalion 1/7 was at LZ Baldy protecting the Regimental HQ and surrounding areas. On one of these operations we had set up a base camp for 1/7 on a hill overlooking the river which ran down to the coast of the South China Sea. From our vantage point on the hill, we could see all the way to Hoi An on the coast and over most of the Que Son Valley.

Lieutenant Colonel Cooper had a set of a pair of ship's binoculars on a base stand to look over the area. I spent some time looking through the binoculars and noticed that almost every evening a small boat came down the river and pulled into this area of large cane growth. It looked very suspicious and I told the CO. The next day he sent out a unit to check out the area and they found a pretty good size arms cache including AK-47s, RPGs (rocket propelled grenade), ammo and other supplies.

I went down to check out the captured cache of weapons and it was my first time actually to handle an AK-47 and RPG. So these were the infamous weapons that the enemy used to shoot at us. The AK was a very good assault rifle and the RPG was very simple but very effective.

They tried to burn down the cane field along the river but with little success. So the CO asked me if I could arrange for an air strike on the area. I said that I would love to since I hadn't had much opportunity to work with fixed wing support and had mostly worked only with the helicopters. I called in the request to the DASC for a napalm strike on the enemy storage site. The DASC set it up for the next day.

The next morning, my radio man and I were monitoring the radio, waiting for a call from the airborne FAC who would coordinate with the F-4 to strike on this enemy cane patch. Soon the radio came alive with a call for the OV-10 spotter plane which was on station. I told him that this was the 1-4 actual and gave him the mission and coordinates. He said that he could see the smoke from our attempt to burn the cane and asked if he was "cleared" to mark the target with "Willy Peter" (white phosphorus rocket). I said that he was cleared and we all watched from on top of the hill as the OV-10 rolled in and fired off a rocket which struck right in the center of the cane field. The white smoke from the phosphorus rose from the site and AO asked if that was the correct target and that he had an F-4 Phantom circling overhead ready to light up the place with napalm. I said, "Roger that; you got a bull's eye on the target, my troops are clear of the area and he is cleared hot."

I looked up and could see the signature black smoke trailing from behind the F-4 who appeared to be up about three thousand feet. We then watched as the Phantom rolled in hot in a low angle dive towards the target. Napalm was dropped at a low dive angle with the bomb tumbling so that it would strike the ground and spread over a large area causing maximum damage and the high drag tumbling bomb allowed the fighter or attack plane to avoid its own bomb's explosion. I could see the two napalm canisters leave the F-4 as the plane pulled up out of his dive. The napalm hit near to some of the cane patch and fired it up for a while, but when the smoke cleared, there was the cane patch still there, just a little blacker. The CO looked at me and said, "Well that didn't do very much; do you have any other ideas, Lieutenant?"

"Well, Sir, the CH-53 helicopter guys say they have a very effective system to handle targets like this," I said. "They hook up a

Ron Boehm

cargo net under the chopper with fifty-five gallon drums of napalm, and when over the target they release one side of the net dropping the drums on the target. They have some kind of a make-shift aiming device like a bolt sticking out in front of the windscreen or something like that. When the drums hit the ground they are ignited by the door gunners or a gunship firing a couple of rockets."

The CO told me to set it up, so I called DASC and they put me in touch with a CH-53 Squadron at Marble Mountain. I told them what the situation was and that I heard that they had this napalm weapon system that sounded ideal for our situation. They told me that what I said was correct and that they could do it. I gave them our location and all the pertinent information, my name and how to get in touch with me. Then I asked them when they could do the mission. They said they needed several days to get it cleared and to set it up and would get back with me.

In a couple of days, the squadron's Ops officer got back to me and said everything was "go" and said that the CH-53 would be on station at such and such date and time.

War isn't always excitement and things can get very boring at times so everybody in our unit on top of the ridge overlooking the river was keyed up in anticipation of the big show. Hell, everybody loves to see a good explosion as long as it's not aimed at you.

So the fateful day arrived and I was in communication with the CH-53 as they and a Huey gunship approached our position. I directed the chopper to the target and after verification told them that they were cleared in "hot." I said that so that the helicopter guys could feel like real attack pilots on a bombing mission.

The chopper made his run on the target at about two hundred feet or so, released one end of the cargo net and the drums full of napalm dropped towards the cane patch; however, only one or two of the drums hit the edge of the cane field and the other ones went in the river just off the bank. I responded with an "Aw-shit" and to my disbelief the Huey was right in behind the 53, firing its guns at the drums of napalm. Well, they all ignited and the cane patch was on fire, but so was half the damn river. I looked at Hank my radio man and he gave me that "I can't fucking believe it" look. Meanwhile, the troops with us up on the ridge were cheering, jumping up and down and pointing like someone had just scored a touchdown or something.

I tried to avoid making eye contact with the CO, but cringed a bit when I heard him sarcastically say, "Very effective weapons system, Lieutenant. The air wing has saved the day again."

I told Hank, "I hope that shit burns out before it floats down to the coast and burns down Hoi An." As Desi used to tell Lucy, "You got some 'splaining to do."

AC 130 "Spooky" Gunship, More Entertainment

Afew days later, in an area not too far from the cane patch, we had a squad take some sniper fire from this small hamlet. It was close to sunset and they called in some artillery support but that didn't suppress the fire. As I was talking with Frank our arti officer, I told him that we had an AC-130 gunship in the area looking for a target and he said, "Shit, let's use them."

So I told the CO and he said the same thing, "Let's use them."

I got on the horn and was told that "Spooky" would be on station in about ten minutes.

It was soon night we could hear the droning of the AC-130's engines overhead and soon after that I was on the radio with the Spooky gunship. I gave him the target info and the pilot said that he would illuminate the target with a spotlight and told me to adjust his spot onto the target. At the same time, we were in communications with the squad leader that was taking fire and told him what the situation was and that he was to give the OK when the spot light was on target.

Ron Boehm

The pilot then said, "What kind of fire would you like for us to put on the target?"

I said, "What do you have?"

And he responded with, "We have twenty mike-mike Vulcan cannon, 7.62 mini-guns and forty millimeter pom-pom guns."

I said, "How about a little of everything?"

"Roger that," the pilot said. "You got it."

Then out of the black night sky came this beam of light, and I adjusted the spotlight onto the target with help of the squad leader and told Spooky he was cleared hot. All of a sudden out of the darkness came this red waterfall of tracers arcing down from about two thousand feet or so and just destroying everything in its path. It was an awesome display of firepower and all the troops were hopping and hollering and saying, "Do it again, Lieutenant!"

I told the AC-130 pilot, "Great job Spooky, target destroyed." That went a lot better than the CH-53 napalm for sure.

Hank, My Radioman

My radioman, as I mentioned, was a Lance Corporal named Hank, and he was quite a character. He was about twenty-one years old, about five foot, ten inches tall, slender and with a smiling face and a kind of cavalier attitude. I really liked the guy, and I don't know if I believed half of the things he would tell me, but they were always very interesting. For example, once we were camped out in the Que Son Mountains on the south side of the river that runs into the Song Thu Bon River which runs down to the coast of the South China Sea and the ancient town of Hoi An. We were with the battalion CP when he told me that he knew of a cave nearby that was a VC/NVA hospital and that he was going to see if he could get an SKS (an enemy) rifle. The SKS was not an automatic rifle like the AK-47 and could be kept as a souvenir; AKs had to be turned in.

I said to Hank, "Exactly how were you going to do that?"

He said that he might find a VC or NVA sleeping in the cave, kill him and take his rifle.

"Well that sounds simple enough, Hank," I said in a sarcastic way and didn't think much of it; after all he did have some interesting stories. The next day he had a SKS. Now, he may have had found it and hidden it somewhere earlier or that was my assumption anyway, but it wasn't out of the realm of possibility when it came to Hank that he did what he said he did.

So when I saw him and the rifle, I asked how many "gooners" he killed to get the rifle.

He said, "Just one."

So then I asked how many kills he had.

He responded, "Here or in New York?" So I just dropped it there.

Another time he invited me to go with him to get some whores in the village that he said he had set up earlier. I told him, "No thanks. There are diseases in Vietnam that they don't even have names for yet, and you have to be crazy to get with a whore in Vietnam. If her VC boyfriend doesn't kill you then a disease will." Then I added, "Hank, how do you find the time or means to come up with all this crap?"

He said, "War is hell and you have to make the best of it."

As I said, I really liked the guy, and I knew that he had my back. Another time we were with a squad size patrol in the evening time crossing some rice paddies walking along the paddy dykes and talking to an OV-10 spotter aircraft overhead when we stopped in the middle of the rice paddy. Snipers look for antennas, guys wearing pistols or shiny bars on their collars. So here we were in the middle of this rice paddy with Hank carrying the PRC 25 radio and its antenna and me with a .45 on my hip and talking on the radio which indicated that I was an officer.

While we were talking on the radio, the squad had moved on past the paddy into the tree line up ahead. All of a sudden I heard a

Ron Boehm

shot and the crack of a round hitting the paddy dyke in front of us. We both jumped behind the dyke for cover and a few more shots hit the dyke which was only about one and one-half foot to two feet high. I had this uncomfortable thought go through my mind that my ass was sticking up above the dyke and I would take one in the butt which was not the good way to get a Purple Heart. Of course there is no good way to get a Purple Heart. I also thought that each round hitting the dyke would wear it down exposing my ass even more.

Hank said, "Lieutenant, let's make a run for it."

I said, "Screw you, call somebody on the radio and get some rounds in that tree line where the shots were coming from."

I had been shot at in the air but they were shooting at my airplane, this was the first time that someone was shooting at me, personally. So we did get the squad to give us some covering fire and Hank and I hi-tailed it to catch up with the rest of the squad.

Go to the Mama-San's for Dinner

One evening we were just settling down and I was about to break out my c-rats for dinner when Hank came to me and asked if I wanted to go with him to the mama-san's hut in this little hamlet out in the middle of nowhere to have dinner. We were camped nearby and I have no idea how he came up with some kind of an arrangement like that but after eating c-rats for weeks on end it sounded like it might be interesting. I asked him how he had pulled this off and he said that he was swapping the mama-san a case of c-rats for her cooked dinner. I then asked what we were having for dinner, and he said it was a surprise and I probably didn't want to know anyways. So we hiked over to the mama-san's hut which was a simple one room bamboo structure with thatched roof and walls and a mud floor which the mama-san was sweeping as we got there. It struck me as a bit odd that someone would sweep a mud floor, but this was a fairly primitive lifestyle.

The Vietnamese were very resourceful and would use discarded ammo boxes, pieces of metal, Styrofoam and anything else they could find to make something useful for them. I mentioned earlier that the kids had made Styrofoam ice chests out of waste materials. A lot of the people wore rubber sandals made from tire treads and straps made of strips of rubber inner tubes. As long as you don't have hair on the top of your foot they were ok, but for me the rubber straps would pull on the hair on my foot.

The mama-san's dinner was surprisingly good with vegetables, rice and some meat which I thought was duck, or I hope was duck, and of course nuoc mam, a Vietnamese fish sauce made from fermented fish. Nuoc mam is to the Vietnamese as olive oil is to the Italians. However, I had to pass on the nuoc mam, I couldn't get past the smell, but the mama-san assured me it was "number one." In the broken English and pieces of Vietnamese words that we communicated with each other "number one" was the best, "number ten" was the worst.

We sat on a straw mat that was on the floor and ate our dinner. It was a nice experience and another Hank event that never ceased to amaze me.

Mama-San's hootch

Ron Boehm

Recon Marines Hanging from Rope Ladders

One of the strangest sights I encountered while out in the bush as a FAC was that of a CH-46 flying across the sky with three or four Marines hanging from a rope ladder. At first I thought how odd, then I realized that it was Recon Marines being extracted from a hot zone and probably with the bad guys hot on their tails. Force Recon are the elite of the Corps and their mission was reconnaissance, unlike the Navy Seals, who were often on a covert offensive mission. The Recon guys operated in the enemy's hip pocket right up next to the NVA and Viet Cong. When I was in the Fire Direction Center at LZ Baldy with Frank the Arti-Officer we would listen in on their net (frequency) and they would be speaking in whispers because they were so close to the enemy. These guys train with the Seals and a cut above the rest of us.

Often when they were in trouble or just ready to be extracted from an area, they were on the run with the bad guys chasing them. They were in awesome condition, outrunning Charlie with fifty-pound packs on their backs. The choppers would come in with the rope ladder or lanyard hanging and rather than the chopper landing in a hot zone, the Recon guys would run up and hook C-clamp and lanyard onto the ladder and be hoisted away probably within a shower of AK-47 rounds. Those guys were heroes with big ones.

Phil Vannoy — Back at LZ Baldy

After being in the field for about two weeks I was called back to Battalion headquarters at LZ Baldy; the Major who was the Battalion Air Liaison Officer was going on R&R and I was to fill in for him while he was gone.

One night I went to the little "O" club bar there to have a drink and to my great surprise I ran into a buddy from OCS and TBS, 1st Lieutenant Phil Vannoy who had just taken over as Company Commander of Hotel Company 2/7. We drank some beers and chewed the fat a bit, but it wasn't until our TBS Class reunion forty-five years later that I found out the circumstances involved with his taking over as Hotel's CO. There had been a "fragging" incident (a term used to describe a fragmentation grenade tossed into a hootch or enclosure to injure or kill someone) in which the Company commander was wounded and a senior NCO was killed. This was in 1970, right in the middle of all the racial strife going on in the U.S. and it was very much in play in the war in Vietnam. Black and white soldiers and Marines would sometimes be on different sides of a big racial divide.

In this case the CO and NCO were white and it was thought that those responsible for the fragging were black.

I had almost been in the middle of an intramural fire fight in the street by the Da Nang PX when black and white Army troops opened up on each other at about a half of a block apart. I ducked in between two buildings to get out of the line of fire. It only lasted for a few rounds as they both retreated in opposite directions. This was also the time of the Black Power and other racially-charged situations. So I could appreciate Phil's dilemma with having to deal with a racial situation and very little experience with that type of matter.

Phil, who was from Michigan, said that he had only known two blacks up to that point in his life, one in high school in Michigan

Ron Boehm

and the other a fellow officer from OCS, Richard Jessie. Jessie, as far as I know, was the only black officer in our OCS and TBS class. But here Phil was sent in to calm down this explosive situation where the black Marines were all holed up together in a tent and not taking orders. I asked him how he slept at night and he said, "Not very well."

David Noyes and "The Satchel Charge"

Another riveting story that came out of our TBS reunion, of which there were so many that you could fill volumes of books, was that of David Noyes, a friend of Phil's who was a Lieutenant with 3/7 in Vietnam, but was there a year earlier than Phil and me.

He had been in Vietnam about three weeks and with his platoon for about two and one-half weeks. They had been on a Bald Eagle mission as a reactionary force for the division. They had returned to their normal position (Hill 25) which was a platoon-size outpost about eight klicks from their company and another eight klicks from the battalion battery position. It was in an area where "Charlie" (The Viet Cong or phonically "Victor Charlie") would come down the Ho Chi Min trail from North Vietnam through Laos, cross over the mountains, called by us "Charlie Ridge" and mass in the Go Noi and Arizona areas right before the Tet offensive in 1968. Dave said that they were seeing a lot of action and the VC had determined that they needed to be eliminated.

He said that he had about thirty-five Marines and that the enemy hit them with about twenty mortar rounds and then with bandoliers to blow the wire. It was a sapper company estimated to be one hundred fifty VC.

Dave said, "I ran out of our CP tent to see what the fuck was going on. It was very dark and the only way to determine Marine from the sappers was the flash of light from an explosion. When I got over next to the wire I saw someone moving but I wasn't sure if it was a Marine until I saw a flash and saw that it was a sapper with a satchel charge. All I had was my .45 caliber pistol and he was only about five feet from me. I fired but realized that I had not chambered a round. I think he had thought I was one of his unit until he heard the click and he froze for a second while I chambered a round and fired."

By then the VC were on the hill and it was mass confusion and hand to hand in some cases. Dave ran back to the CP tent to call in for fire support and get his M-16. His platoon sergeant and radioman had already moved to a covered bunker. He got there and on the radio to call in for illumination and the on- call fire and found that the gunny already was calling for fire support. The enemy had a well-planned attack and had hit all the positions within the battalion TAOR with small probing action before they hit Dave's unit so the battery was busy supporting them.

While he was on the radio he heard someone say, "honcho-honcho" (what the Vietnamese called officers) and, knowing they had no Vietnamese on their hill, realized that they were after him. They fired and threw in grenades and Dave moved back to the outside of the tent behind the sand bags and was firing back with his M-16.

They then were moving on both sides of the tent to envelop him.

"I saw firing from a squad bunker close by and ran over there yelling 'coming over.' The Marines said that I was within a hair of being shot by them. We set up outside the bunker and waited for them to hit us which they did and we killed four or five right in front of us."

By then he was worried that they would get the radio in the CP tent so he tried to pin the VC down. It had been set up that if they were overrun, as a last resort, they would call fire on top of themselves with a green flare signal. The gunny on the radio set out the flare and everyone left dove for a covered bunker.

"They hit us with VT fused artillery (Variable Time) that went off about ten meters above ground for maximum damage to the VC.

Ron Boehm

Two Marines were lost when a round went into their bunker. Of the enemy dead, one was a Chinese major and some of the men swore that they saw either a Russian or an American with the enemy."

"The shelling got the VC off the hill and then the gunny got the fire fly and they did more damage."

"The VC had set up an ambush in case our company tried to react. We lost ten Marines and another ten seriously wounded. We got out our dead and wounded and the reaction force finally reached us about at daylight that morning; the battle had started about 0200 on November 2nd," Dave said.

Like most battles over there it was determined that the position they held was not that important and was disbanded shortly thereafter.

David Noyes received a Silver Star for his actions in Vietnam. Our TBS class earned twenty-nine Silver Stars, six Navy Crosses and two Distinguished Flying Crosses. We lost thirty-nine officers killed in Vietnam out of our class of 516.

Dave's story wasn't the exception to the rule. There were so many heroes with so many stories of courage and sacrifice over there. But when you talked to those guys, you see they never considered themselves heroes. I agreed with Dave when he said that most of us consider the guys that didn't make it as heroes. It was like I said earlier, their stories would fill volumes.

Back with 1/7 — Evening Heat Casualties

It was quite often over one hundred degrees and about one hundred percent humidity in Vietnam and it seemed like the heat casualties would always come on in the evening time when we would stop to settle in for the night and prepare to eat dinner. On one occasion we had been humping the rice paddies and coastal plain area around LZ Baldy in one hundred degree heat and humidity, carrying heavy packs, weapons and equipment all day.

You had to really monitor your men and keep them hydrated because heat exhaustion and heat stroke were very serious problems in Vietnam and caused a bunch of casualties.

One evening while I was with Alpha Company, we had just stopped for the evening when the Company Commander called me to get a medevac helicopter to pick up one of the troops whose temperature was soaring above 103 degrees. I called DASC (Direct Air Support Center) for a Medevac, but they did not have a Marine chopper available, so I had Hank call the Army to see if they could help us out. It was getting close to sunset and I wanted to get them in before it got dark.

The Army said they would get something out to us ASAP. I told them thanks and that this kid was getting worse and had to be taken to an aid station "ricky tic." We had moved out of the rice paddies and were in the tree line now which was a tall double canopy wooded area. I was looking for a good clearing for the helicopter to land in when I heard a chopper coming, but it wasn't a Huey as I had expected. You could always tell the distinctive Huey two bladed "woop woop" sound. Then all of a sudden, here came a LOC (Light Observation Helicopter) that was a small sperm looking two-seated bird flying underneath the trees. He landed right in front of us and I ran over to the chopper and asked this young soldier where the pilot was. He said, "I am the pilot, Sir." He looked like he was eighteen or nineteen years old and didn't shave yet. He was a gutsy young Warrant Officer that had this new hot rod to fly instead of his hot rod car back home to drive, or that's what I imagined. He told us to load the Marine into the left seat and he would drop him off at the nearest aid station.

The Army used the LOCs for observation as their name would indicate, but also in their Air Cav's (1st. Air Cavalry Division) Red, White and Blue operations where they used them as bait. They would fly the small choppers low to see if they could draw fire and if they did, then they returned fire with a M-60 machine gun hanging by a bungee cord from the co-pilot's door and/or drop hand grenades on the bad guys. That was the Red team. They would then

Ron Boehm

call in the White team made up of Cobra gunships to hammer the enemy and then finally, if the situation called for it, they called in the Blue team. The Blue team was the Air Cav's soldiers that they landed to destroy the rest of the bad guys. The Air Cavalry was some very good soldiers.

———•••••———

The Shower and the Tower

After about two weeks out in the bush I was called back to Battalion HQ. Lieutenant Colonel Copper, our CO, told me that he had a a an observation tower that he wanted to have moved from Alpha Company's area to our HQ's hill at LZ Baldy. I said that I thought that we could get an Army Sky Crane to do the job, so he told me to get it set up.

I went through the necessary channels and put in a request for the big Sikorsky helicopter which was like a CH-53 with a cockpit but no cabin. It was great for carrying cargo underneath where the normal helicopter body would have been. I was told that the winds coming down from spinning blades could be 125 miles per hour. The people that I made the request to said that it would probably be several days to get the chopper to us, so I informed Lieutenant Colonel Cooper and he said, "Good, the sooner the better."

In the meantime, it was good to be back at LZ Baldy where I had a roof over my head, a mess hall to eat in and a shower. Well, when I say shower I really mean a fifty-five gallon drum on top of a wood structure in the open area of a saddle between the two hills that made up LZ Baldy. There was no shower stall, just open air. The shower procedure was to fill a Gerry can with water, haul it up to the hill, climb the ladder, and pour the water into the fifty-five gallon drum; then you'd get underneath and pull the chain to release the cold shower water. Don't get me wrong, it was better than a helmet full of water and a washcloth in the field, but being naked with no cover on a hill with a cool night breeze blowing on your wet body and thinking about what a great target for a sniper I would make was not my idea of the ideal shower. "I felt so naked."

On the day that we had set up for the tower transfer, I was coordinating the operation and talking with the sky crane pilot. We had dug deep holes to set the four tower telephone pole main supports into and everything was ready to go. I tried to think of everything to the smallest detail to make sure the project went well, because it was my deal, my responsibility and the CO would be looking at the job that I did.

The chopper arrived and everyone on the base was watching this huge thirty foot tower suspended under the big Sky Crane helicopter being moved into place to drop into the holes. It took some finessing, but the crew on the ground and the helicopter crew got the tower into the holes and when the chopper released the tower it stood erect and solid. Everyone cheered. That was the good part, for as I had mentioned, the chopper's blades created a down draft force of about 125 miles per hour. Well, the CO's shitter was close to where the tower was being placed and the down draft winds blew the CO's outhouse over.

Someone told me that the CO was in the shitter at the time, but I think he just wanted to pull my chain. It was bad enough that my operation didn't go off perfectly well without the CO being in the shitter at the time. Things like that can reflect on your fitness report.

—◆•◆—

Back to Da Nang for a Flight — Low Pass Over LZ Baldy

I had been at LZ Baldy and out in the bush for a couple of months, and I needed to get some flight time so I asked the CO if I could go back to my squadron in Da Nang over the weekend and get

Ron Boehm

a flight. He said that would be OK, and I caught a ride on a CH-46 out of LZ Baldy with brief stop to drop off some stuff to some troops out in the field; then we flew on to Da Nang. As we were coming into the LZ, we took some small arms fire that hit a hydraulic line and we came down hard from about twenty feet up. I guess we could say that we were technically shot down, but it amounted to a hard landing. We scrambled out of the chopper and took cover. There was no more fire. But we had to wait a while for another chopper to pick us up.

This was the second time riding in a chopper that ground fire brought us down. The first time we were lifting out of the zone and took some rounds that hit a hydraulic line that sent us back down from about fifteen feet for another hard landing.

In my 124 combat missions flying an A-6 I never took a hit, close, but never a hit. But there I was riding in helicopters and I got knocked down twice. I had a great admiration for the chopper jocks because they took fire and hits on a regular basis. We fixed-wing guys made fun of them and said things like, "Having rotary wing time on your flight record is like having VD on your health record" or "If your wings are going faster than your fuselage then you must be in a helicopter," but they were very good at what they did and were an integral part of the Marine Corps' infantry, air and sea team.

I had an uncomfortable feeling riding in choppers and I always sat on my "bullet bouncer" (flax vest) because I thought that I would rather take one in the chest or head than have a round take out my manly equipment or take one in the ass. The fire came from the ground, so it made sense to me to protect my bottom.

It was an unnerving situation to see a sudden pencil-like beam of light come through the thin aluminum skin of the chopper and realize that a bullet had just passed through and made that hole where none was before.

I finally got to Da Nang late that day and got to my old hootch with Rick Spitz and slept in my rack that was still mine since no one had moved in with Rick in the time I had been gone. I made it to the "O" Club, had some drinks and shared some grunt tales with my squadron buddies.

I saw my good buddy Jack Rippy and he told me that he laughed at the letter I had sent him while out in the bush where I described how I was with one of the rifle companies and we were taking some fire one night. That was actually the first time that I had been fired at on the ground and I was reluctant to stand up and see where the fire was coming from. There were these green and white tracers zipping in over our heads and red tracers going out from our guys. Someone told me that the green ones were Chi-Com and the white was Czech or vice-versa.

As evening passed into night, my radio man and I had taken cover in this moat-like earthen structure which had a round mound in the center and a depression around it.

I asked my radio man what was this thing.

He said, "A grave."

"Oh great," I thought. "I'm getting fired at and I'm already in a grave. This could be a grave situation." I'm sorry, I couldn't resist the pun.

Well anyway, I wrote to Jack that "I was lying very deep in a shallow hole." Rippy loved that line.

While my radio man and I were in the grave's moat talking to the air support people to get some flares to light up the area, artillery flare rounds started to pop right above us. Then all of a sudden I heard this "woop," "woop," "woop" sound over our heads and the sound of something hitting the ground right next to us. It was the base plates for the flares raining down on us.

In the middle of the action, the company commander, a captain, called me to come over to him, so I ran over to him in a low crouch as intermittent tracer rounds flew overhead. He had this combat vet smile on his face and said, "I told you I would get you a combat action ribbon, Ron."

I said, "Thanks Captain, I appreciate it," feeling embarrassed by my rookie fear of being shot.

The next day in Da Nang, I arranged with the Ops Officer to get a hop with an early morning target time that was just about at sunrise and it happened to be down south of Da Nang. We flew the

Ron Boehm

mission and were returning when I thought that it would be cool to fly over LZ Baldy on the way back. I told my BN that I wanted to fly over LZ Baldy and show him where I was located with 1/7. He said great. We got to LZ Blady about 0700 and I descended to about two hundred feet or so in a slow descent while aiming for the saddle between the two hills and doing about three hundred knots airspeed. We came across the hills right at eye level with the observation house on top of the tower that we had just set in place. As we flew past the tower I pulled up and did a roll, thinking I wanted to give the troops a real show.

Later, when I got back to LZ Baldy, the Marine who was in the tower at the time told me that he almost shit on himself and that he could see me in the cockpit as we flew by at his eye level.

The CO asked if that was me flying over the base on Sunday morning and I reluctantly said, "Yes, Sir." He then said that he thought it was incoming and dove in his bunker and didn't see the low pass. He didn't seem to appreciate the aeronautic display very much.

Airborne Assault

I was just back a short time when the Battalion 1-4 called me in to brief me on an upcoming operation that would be a company-size airborne assault on a bad guy position build-up in the Que Son Mountains. One company of 1/7 would make the airborne attack while another company would be in the ready as a reaction force. I helped the Major with some of the coordination with the helicopters. We had both CH-46s and CH-53s set up for the operation. This was my first air assault and my radio man and I were going in with a squad from one of the platoons. This was classic "vertical envelopment" as developed by the Marine Corps and the forte of the

Air Cav in Vietnam. This was helicopters swooping in on the bad guys for some ass kicking.

We started loading up the helicopters at "O dark thirty" and my excitement level began rising by the minute. I tried to look cool, like an officer that has been there and done that, but this wasn't going to be just some rounds going over head; this could be a big ass fight with the NVA.

Finally we were off, and inside the big CH-53 I went over some coordination details with my radio man and in no time we were going into the drop zone. Before the rear wheels touched down, the ramp was open and the squad of Marines was pouring out of the chopper. My radio man and I were the last to get off the bird which had set us down in a wet rice field. Thinking I was John Wayne or something like that I ran down the ramp with my .45 in my hand ready for combat. I was just getting off the ramp when the chopper started to take off and I landed face first in the mud of the rice paddy. I quickly looked to see if anyone had seen my combat face plant, but thank God no one saw me; they were too busy with their own situations. Damn! I thought, that didn't look very Marine officer professional.

It turned out that there wasn't much action, the bad guys must have got word and "de-deed."

———•••••———

Dan DeBlanc Flies Through LZ Baldy AO

A little while later and back at LZ Baldy, I was sitting in the Fire Direction Center next to my buddy Frank the artillery officer, who like myself was a 1st Lieutenant, when I heard the Marine helicopter calling in for clearance through our AO. The pilot on the radio had a very thick New Orleans accent that I picked up on immediately and radioed back, "Who is this and is that a New Orleans accent?"

Ron Boehm

"Roger that, Lieutenant Dan De Blanc Marine Cobra gunship -----" came the reply.

"Dan, this is Ronnie Boehm, I'm down here at LZ Baldy as the 1-4 for 1/7."

"Hell Ronnie, I'll come down, land and visit you next time through your AO."

"I'll look forward to it Dan; give me a ride when you come back."

"Roger that, I'll give you a ride in the front seat and let you fire the guns; we'll blow up some trees just like back at SLC with the dynamite."

Dan was my friend back at Southeastern Louisiana College in Hammond, Louisiana. He was in my OCS class but not my TBS class. Back in college, he was a bull rider on the weekends, traveling around to rodeos. His crew in college or the guys he lived with and my roommates hung out together and one of our things was to go out in the woods and blow stuff up with dynamite that we would get from the local hardware store. That was before all the domestic terrorism stuff, back when farmers would go to the hardware store to get dynamite to blow up tree stumps. We would also throw a stick of dynamite in the river to catch fish to eat. So I guess blowing up stuff was a natural thing to us.

We never got to do the give-me-a-ride-and-blow-up-stuff, but later when I was back in Da Nang, Dan kicked open the door of my hootch in the middle of the night with a bottle of wine in his hand and yelled out, "Ronnie, let's party." Shit, I almost shot him. I had just come back from out in the bush where I slept with my pistol on my chest. Dan didn't remember it that way, but that is how I remembered it and it makes for a good story.

Dan won a Silver Star for his heroic actions on March 17, 1969, while flying as co-pilot in a UH-1E Huey gunship with VMO-2 in support of a Marine company that was engaged with a large NVA force near An Hoa in Quang Nam Province southwest of Da Nang. The Marines were pinned down in a rice paddy by heavy automatic weapons fire and had taken several casualties. The enemy was in fortified positions and the wounded were too close to the NVA to use either artillery or fixed wing air support.

To paraphrase Dan's Silver Star Citation: with deteriorating weather conditions and the heavy volume of automatic weapons fire directed at them, Dan and his pilot made numerous rocket and strafing runs over a four-hour period to suppress the enemy fire but it was not enough for the Marines to recover their wounded. The Huey pilot then decided to land their chopper to evacuate the wounded. While exposed to heavy enemy fire, they landed and loaded a wounded Marine into their helicopter while Dan was providing covering fire from his side of the Huey with his rifle. They took one wounded man to An Hoa Combat Base and returned on three more occasions to land and evacuate wounded men, all the while taking fire and with Dan helping the pilot and providing covering fire with his M-16 directed at the NVA gun emplacements.

Their Huey took extensive damage in this engagement, and Dan has a piece of the aluminum skin from the chopper with a big .50 caliber hole in it mounted on the wall of his restaurant in Slidell, Louisiana.

Dan also had the dubious distinction of flying the first Cobra to be shot down in Vietnam (September 1969 near An Hoa). He took three fifty caliber rounds to the transmission. Shortly after being shot down, he was sent to Da Nang DASC as the Marine Helicopter Director. Dan said, "I think my CO was pissed that I fucked up his chopper."

Dan's restaurant in Slidell is called the Southside Café and the walls are covered with Marine Corps memorabilia that has been given to him by the scores of Marines who have visited his place. Rich in history would be an understatement.

Dave Cummings "Dave's Ride"

Of all the stories involving my friends in Vietnam, few can match the story of my friend Dave Cummings, a fellow squad mate in the 1st Platoon of Mike Company at The Basic School.

Dave was just a very nice guy and talented Marine, or as my buddy and fellow M/1 squad-mate Fred Bonati said, "Dave was just a natural at everything he did." Dave was just like most of my TBS classmates of 5/67 in that he was a grunt 2nd Lieutenant infantry officer sent off to Vietnam just after finishing up at TBS. He was seriously wounded in a fire fight and was evacuated to the States to recuperate. While recuperating, and since he had always wanted to fly, he applied for Naval Flight School and was accepted.

After earning his "Wings of Gold" he returned to Vietnam at the same time that I got there in September 1969, as a helicopter pilot. He was also a squadron mate in VMO-2 with Dan DeBlanc. Tom Broderick was also in our M/1 squad along with Dave and Fred. When talking to Tom about Dave's heroic story, he said, "We refer to it as Dave's Ride." And when I asked Dan DeBlanc about it, he said, "Oh you mean when Dave rode the rocket pod."

Even I had heard of the story from someone I can't remember back in Da Nang. The story is almost folklore in the Marine Corps, especially in the helicopter part of Marine Corps aviation.

It starts out in December of 1969 where a remote Marine observation team had set up a defensive perimeter atop Hill 845 about forty miles southwest of Da Nang in the Que Son Mountains. The team's perimeter was being probed by elements of a battalion-size unit of Viet Cong and they had called for some air support. Responding to that call for close air support was a Marine OV-10 "Bronco" piloted by Captain Dennis Herbert.

It was the middle of the monsoon season and the cloud-base was rapidly deteriorating when the Bronco made contract with a ground-based forward air controller (FAC). After getting his target information, Captain Herbert made his attack run aimed at a shallow ravine leading up the mountain to the outpost. Captain Herbert fired off two Zuni rockets and followed them visually to the ravine where they exploded; he then pulled up hard to avoid the debris from the explosion and the thickly forested mountain and then punched up through the clouds on top. The FAC reported the mission a success and reported also that they had a very seriously wounded Marine who had tripped off an enemy bobby trap. He was bleeding profusely and was going into shock and the FAC asked the Bronco to relay a request for an immediate medevac.

Here's an account of what happened after the request for a medevac was relayed by the Bronco pilot.

"Meanwhile, at Landing Zone Baldy, Cobra pilot First Lieutenant David Cummings and his aircraft commander, Captain Roger Henry, were standing by on routine medevac escort alert in their AH-1G gunship. The rear cockpit seat of the Cobra, normally flown by the pilot in command, would today be flown by the copilot, Lieutenant Cummings, as part of his aircraft commander check ride. When the call came to escort medevac helicopters, the pilots launched with another Cobra to marry up with two CH-46 Sea Knight transport helicopters as part of a constituted medevac (medical evacuation) package. After a smooth join up, the flight headed 40 miles southwest of Da Nang into the Que Son Mountains in Quanq Nam Province where they rendezvoused with the Bronco for a mission brief.

The weather at Hill 845 had deteriorated badly. Rain and lowering cloud bases made it virtually impossible for the larger Sea Knights to get into the area for the pick up. Despite persistent maneuvering, the rescue flight finally retired to the edge of the weather mass where they loitered to wait for another opportunity to come in and pick up the wounded Marine.

After obtaining approval from the medevac mission commander, the agile Cobra flown by Captain Henry and Lieutenant Cummings

Ron Boehm

proceeded to scout the landing zone in order to facilitate a more expeditious evacuation. The worsening weather, however, prompted Captain Henry, positioned in the higher visibility front gunner's seat, to assume control of the aircraft's more difficult-to-use side console forward cockpit flight controls. Visibility was now practically zero.

In those days, there was a variation of a popular song theme that 'only mad dogs and Englishmen ventured into noonday monsoons!' Undaunted, Captain Henry and Lieutenant Cummings pressed on despite harrowing weather conditions. The two Marines worked their Cobra up the mountain-side amidst severe turbulence generated up and down gnarled mountain slopes. Scraping tree tops at airspeeds that often dipped below 30 knots, or required holding in perilous zero-visibility hovers, the flyers anxiously waited for a call from the outpost giving them either a visual or sound cue that they were above the elusive, ill-defined landing zone. After three hours and five different attempts (with refueling runs interjected in-between), the aviators finally found their mark.

Sporadic radio reports confirmed to Captain Henry and Lieutenant Cummings their worst fear that the injured Marine was succumbing to his wounds. Guiding the Cobra down through tall trees, Captain Henry landed the aircraft on the edge of a bomb crater in a skillful display of airmanship. The helicopter settled to the ground amid swirling debris. The tightness of the landing zone was such that only the front half of the aircraft's skids rested on the rocky outer lip of the bomb crater. While the Cobra loitered in this precarious teeter-totter position, Lieutenant Cummings climbed out of the aircraft to investigate the situation."

Dave saw that the wounded marine was in bad shape and probably close to death, so he ordered the casualty lifted into the Cobra. Then after strapping the semiconscious Marine into the back seat, Dave fastened the canopy shut and as the grunts looked on in amazement climbed atop the starboard stub wing rocket pod. Straddling the pod and facing aft, Dave banged his fist on the wing to get Captain Henry's attention before giving him the thumbs up. With that, Captain Henry nodded and took off while Dave flashed the

"V" for victory sign to the grunts remaining in the zone as they cheered.

The Cobra disappeared into the clouds and they leveled off at four thousand feet and increased speed to about one hundred knots to improve maneuverability. The wind, rain, extreme cold at altitude and the vibrations of the aircraft all added to a very hard and tenuous situation. Dave could hold on only by squeezing his thighs tightly against the rocket pod wing mount. To make matters worse, the wind grabbed the back of his helmet pushing it forward thereby causing the chin strap to choke him.

After about a twenty-five minute flight through the weather, the gunship descended through the clouds into the clear over a navigation point and headed for the medical facility. After landing, the wounded Marine was whisked into the medical facility for stabilization and the Navy Corpsmen helped Dave to defrost himself off the rocket pod. A short time later, a CH-46 arrived to fly the wounded Marine to Marble Mountain for emergency surgery. Captain Henry and Dave Cummings flew escort for the CH-46 to make sure their rescued Marine made it safely to the more sophisticated medical facility.

It was said that some more senior aviators "in-country" talked about censure and a court-martial for the rocket pod affair which they thought was grandstanding regardless of the fact that the young Marine would have died had he not received medical attention as soon as he did. But after Captain Henry and Dave were invited each personally by the Commanding General of the First Marine Division to dine as his special guests in his quarters, the issue was dropped.

For their action, Captain Henry and First Lieutenant Cummings were each awarded the Distinguished Flying Cross. The word Heroes is appropriate. (Source: *A Marine Hero—Rescue at HIll 845*, by Greg Johnson (retired USMC CH-46 helicopter pilot who flew many medevac missions)

Ron Boehm

Tom Broderick

Another buddy of mine from TBS was Tom Broderick. He was also in my squad in M-1 along with Fred Bonati, Dave Cummings, Pete Barber and Bob Bracken. Tom was also a good friend and fraternity brother of Dave "Andy" Anderson who was in my platoon in OCS.

Tom, like Fred, Pete and I, went to flight school after TBS and became a pilot. Fred and Pete got F-4s, I went to A-6s and Tom got to be a Huey gunship pilot. Tom had a near life-ending experience in Vietnam when his UA-1 Huey lost power over Da Nang Bay and went into the drink

I don't know if it was that crash or another one of Tom's several unplanned returns to the earth, but he told the story of losing his bottom teeth in a crash and having a tough time pronouncing some words, two of which being "Peach Bush" the call sign of HMM 263 a CH-46 helicopter squadron. He would say something like "Peech Buuss." His squadron mates in turn called him "Fang."

Cheating death seemed to run in Tom's family; not only did Tom survive several aircraft crashes, but his older brother who was a Navy A-1 Skyraider pilot, lost power on takeoff from an aircraft carrier and went into the drink. He got out of the aircraft only to see this huge aircraft carrier's bow coming straight at him. The ship actually ran over him; the propellers were stopped but this several-football-field long ship ran over him. He could feel himself bouncing along the bottom of the ship, and miraculously, he resurfaced again after the ship passed, but he was pretty much written off by the crew on the carrier. A destroyer doing a search spotted him and rescued him.

So Tom Broderick, his brother and his good friend Dave Anderson all narrowly escaped death and can thank God for their survival. I guess God wasn't ready for them to come home just yet.

End of My FAC Tour

At the end of May, 1969, my three months FAC tour with 1/7 was up and I was anxious to return to my squadron in Da Nang and resume flying. The CO shook my hand and they gave me a wood plaque with the 1st Marine Division insignia of a number 1 with the word "Guadalcanal" on it and the 1st Battalion 7th Marines banner over it. I still cherish it and it brings back so many memories every time I look at it.

Flying an attack jet in combat was an awesome experience, but it was a different experience of war than what the grunts on the ground experienced. So I was grateful for the opportunity of seeing what the war was like for the troops on the ground. They were the war and we the aviators were the supporting cast. But one thing that really stood out in my mind about that experience was seeing the relationship of a young 2nd Lieutenant Platoon Commander with his men. Here was a twenty-two-year old brand new officer in charge of forty-five Marines, forty-four of whom were eighteen or nineteen years old and a Staff or Gunnery Sergeant who was about twenty-five years old.

If the Lieutenant was respected by his troops, they had this love, respect and protective attitude for him that was like "Don't screw with my Lieutenant, he is my Lieutenant, our leader." A good relationship between the Platoon Commander and his Platoon Sergeant was that of mutual respect and cooperation. That respect within the platoon really impressed me and is one of the basic foundations of the Marine Corps.

Ron Boehm

Back with My Squadron VMA (AW) 242

Antenna check, Grumman Film Crew, Carl Widell and the ROKS

Finally I was back with my squadron VMA (AW) 242, as was Carl Widell who had gone with the ROKS (Republic of Korea) as a FAC. That must have been a really unique experience. He told me about one of the disciplinary methods they used: the top sergeant would beat the troops who screwed up with a baseball bat and there was a very strict adherence with respect to rank between the officers of one grade and another and the same for the enlisted ranks.

We had heard stories about how the South Vietnamese, the "friendlies" on our side, had surrounded a U.S. truck that supposedly hit a child or someone and held it for ransom and that cash had to be paid to the "injured party" before the truck was allowed to leave. Well, that wasn't a problem for the ROKS, for when they came through a village, the locals got the hell out of the way and were thankful that the ROKS didn't kill everyone and burn down the village. That was the reputation the ROKS had. They were bad asses and didn't cut the Vietnamese, North or South, any slack.

Carl also said that they had crappy equipment in Vietnam, because they sent all the good equipment that we gave them back to South Korea to deal with their number one enemy, North Korea.

Antenna Check

Since I hadn't flown much in the last three months, the operations people got me some daytime hops in country and in support of the ground troops to get me up to speed. Some of it was visual drops, or system ordinance drops that became visual because of computer equipment failure. The pilots loved to drop visually like the F-4s and A-4s did, but the BNs hated it. Hurling this advanced electronic computerized weapon system that the A-6 was at the ground at four hundred knots and a thirty-degree dive angle using a bombsight wasn't their cup of tea. But having been on the ground with the troops calling in the air support, I had an appreciation for what the grunts felt when they saw a jet coming in and dropping bombs on the enemy in support of them. There would be cheering on the ground and then often the troops on the ground would ask for an "antenna check," which was a very low pass over their position—the lower the better. But some pilots got themselves in trouble doing this and either crashed or damn near crashed.

The problem was that a bomb run was right out of the book; there was a chart for a certain dive angle, airspeed, release altitude and making mental adjustments as you roll in on the target. However, an "antenna check" was just eyeballing it, winging it. I learned very quickly that the technique to use was to get down low and easy first, being more or less level before you got to their position and then pulling up as you went over their position and tipping your wings in a wave or if it was to really be "Shit Hot," a roll, but only if you had the airspeed and plenty of altitude and in a climb. The roll wasn't part of my repertoire. The A-6 didn't roll very fast.

Ron Boehm

Grumman Film Crew

I hadn't been back very long when the XO asked me if I would like to escort a film crew from the Grumman Aircraft Company around for a couple weeks while they made a film about the A-6 Intruder All Weather Attack System. I jumped at the chance and it turned out to be fun. It was a chance to do something different and watch them make a thirty-minute sixteen-millimeter film showing the A-6 dropping bombs in the weather and at night using its sophisticated weapon systems and the Rab-Fac Beacon when most other fighter bombers had to rely on clear weather to drop visually.

The film began with images from the Battle of the Bulge when the American troops were under attack and surrounded by the Germans. The soldiers from the 101 Airborne Division couldn't get air support or supplies from the air because the weather had them socked in. The film showed that that wouldn't happen now (1970) because we had the A-6 Intruder for air support in any weather or condition.

I got to be in several shots in the film as did my squadron mates and guys from our sister squadron VMA (AW) 225. I was the pilot in a couple of shots where the cameraman did his filming from the right seat of my A-6 filming another A-6 dropping bombs while we were flying in formation. It was pretty cool to see up close an A-6 dropping twenty-two bombs as I flew next to it at about forty feet away in loose formation. You couldn't tell it was me flying in the pilot's seat since I had on a helmet with dark visor and oxygen mask. In another shot, I was in the ready room playing acee-deucee with my BN, waiting for our flight.

In one shot, they filmed several pilots and BNs sitting around a table in the mess hall talking about flying and the funny thing I noticed was that it was the BNs using their hands to indicate aircraft positions, and not the pilots. That just struck me as funny. Aviators always seem to talk with their hands.

When the filming was complete, I made sure to ask the Grumman Tech-Rep to get me a copy of the film, which he did and I still have it in the original sixteen millimeter reel.

A-6s Taxiing Out

AF O-2 Cessna Push-Pull FAC — Flight of B-52s

One of my memorable missions started out as a support mission south of Da Nang, but when our target was canceled, we called DASC to report that though we had been canceled, we had plenty of time, fuel and twenty-two Mark 82 five hundred pound bombs if they had another mission for us.

DASC said that they did and sent us over to an Air Force airborne FAC flying in an O-2 Push-Pull Cessna Skymaster. This was the aircraft that Danny Glover flew in the movie Bat 21 in his effort to rescue Gene Hackman, based on the true story of the rescue of Lieutenant Colonel Iceal Hambleton, whose EB-66 was shot down behind enemy lines. There was an O-2B version equipped with loud speakers for psychological warfare that they called the BS Bomber. (Source: Warbird Alley, www.warbirdalley.com)

Ron Boehm

We checked in with the Air Force FAC on the frequency given to us, reporting in, "This is Marine Ringneck 54 an Alpha-6 with 22 Mark 82s looking for a target, over."

The FAC came back with "This is a flight of B52s, over?"

"Negative," I responded. "We are one Alpha-6 with 22 Mark 82s here for your pleasure today."

The "flight of B-52s" was his little joke since they were not used to working with A-6s. We usually had missions that required systems drops and we didn't do a lot of visual work. We also carried more bombs than the F-4s, A-7s and A-4s that they were used to working with.

He replied, "Shit hot, we are going to have some fun today. I've got a squad-size unit of bad guys that crossed the river and are hiding on the island in the middle of the river."

He gave the target coordinates and said that he was orbiting the target area at one thousand feet.

We told him we were on our way and our ETA was oh-five minutes at Angels five (five thousand feet).

He said, "Roger that, report on station" and he would mark the target with "Willy Peter" (white phosphorus rocket).

We got to the target area and reported that we were on station and holding at five thousand feet.

The FAC said, "Roger that," then went silent.

We tried several times to reach him but got no response.

Finally, after about five minutes, the FAC came back up and said, "Sorry about that" and that he had lost his head set out the window and had to use the pilot's head set. Then he said that they were rolling in to mark the target with willy-pete.

I said, "Roger that, we are ready to make two runs with twelve bombs on the first and ten bombs on the second run if the FAC wanted it." I reported that we saw his smoke on the island.

He said, "Roger that, you are cleared hot and we are clear of the target."

I rolled the A-6 Intruder over on its back, pulled hard and got the smoke in my bomb sight, then rolled upright in a thirty-degree dive while watching the target track down towards the center of my bomb sight. At about three thousand feet, I pickled the bombs and pulled up hard, bottoming out at about fifteen hundred feet and came around to position us for a second run if necessary. I was in a turn to port and watched as our string of twelve bombs tore through the little island in the river.

The FAC came up and said, "Great shooting, how about a second run to make sure."

I said, "You got it; I don't want to take these home."

The second run was just like the first, with a string of ten bombs tearing up the island and denuding it of trees. The FAC again said that it was a good run and that if there were any bad guys hiding there they were in the hurt locker now, but he didn't see any bodies. He then gave us our BDA (Bomb Damage Assessment); one hundred meters of tree line destroyed and a stream cut. How in the hell do you cut a stream?

Napalm Run on the Side of the Mountain

On another visual drop mission working with an airborne FAC and in support of some troops on the ground, this time we were carrying "snake and nape" ("snake eye" five hundred pound bomb with high drag tail fins and incendiary napalm bombs) instead of the regular conventional fin five hundred pound bombs. Both of these weapons were dropped at a low altitude and at low dive angles. The purpose of the high drag tail fins was to slow the bombs down so that the aircraft dropping them wouldn't be damaged by the same bombs that they dropped. It also made for better close air support accuracy, allowing the aircraft to get in lower and closer.

Napalm was a different story; made from jet fuel or gasoline and petroleum jelly, the bombs had no tail fins and that caused them to tumble when dropped which in turn helped to spread the flames

Ron Boehm

when they exploded upon contact. The napalm burned with intense heat for about three to fifteen minutes and, being a jelly-like substance, it stuck to whatever it touched.

On this mission, as we arrived on station, we made contact with the airborne FAC who told us that he had about ten NVA troops on the run and they were heading up to a draw between two fingers on side of the mountain, a dead end. We got a visual on the OV-10 FAC and he made a run marking the enemy with a "willy-pete" rocket. We were right behind him and cleared hot. I came in low and at about a fifteen- degree dive angle; the BN had set up the armament panel to drop two napalm bombs. As we rolled in to initiate our run, I could see the NVA running up into this dead end draw. It was the first time I had ever seen people on the ground as my target—mostly you just saw smoke or a target area, but I released the bombs and pulled up out of the low angle dive and banked to the left to see the bombs exploding. The fire filled the small valley between the mountain fingers that the NVA troops were running into. The flames covered the entire draw; I couldn't see how anyone would escape from that. That made a lasting impression. Like I said, as a pilot of a fighter/ bomber or attack jet I usually don't see the people I am bombing.

Getting Short

I was getting to be a short-timer; my year's tour in Vietnam was coming to an end. The Ops officer, Major Shooter Dubeck, told me that I would be part of a ferry flight of three aircraft to transpac across the Pacific Ocean to Whidbey Island Naval Air Station in Washington then across country to deliver the three Intruders to the Air Rework Facility at NAS Norfolk, Virginia. Upon signing the A-6s over to the Air Rework Facility, our tour in Vietnam would be over, and we would be on thirty days leave.

Several things would be in order before I would be on my way home; for one thing, I had to get a practice in-flight refueling hop which I had not done since Cherry Point, two years prior. We were to island hop across the Pacific Ocean and on one leg of the flight between Barber's Point, Hawaii and Whidbey Island we had a six-hour flight and, therefore, we would have to refuel in-flight. Second, my last real combat flight was approaching; that usually happened about two weeks before you were to leave Vietnam. After my last real combat flight, most likely in Laos along the Ho Chi Min Trail, I might have several flights in country that were not very dangerous. But before my last flight—and they never told you when that was until you landed and the fire trucks pulled up and hosed you down—I would have my last mission over Laos and then on to the Air Force Base at Ubon, Thailand. There I would pick up all my stuff that I had bought, tailor-made suits, handmade shoes, wood carvings, jewelry and of course one last trip to the "Hotse Baths" for a rub and scrub.

I was scheduled for a couple in-flight refueling hops, but on the first one the C-130 refueling aircraft was down for maintenance reasons and then I was scheduled for another refueling hop and the weather was too bad to refuel. The bottom line was that I never got to practice in-flight refueling before my trans-pac. This meant that I would get to experience the pressure of attempting to refuel in-flight in the middle of the ocean when I had to do it or fall out of the sky into the ocean and I hadn't done it in two years.

Last Trip to Thailand

As I had said, it was SOP that when you were about a couple of weeks from the from the end of your tour in Nam you would get one of the early morning Laos missions to drop

Ron Boehm

your bombs in Laos and proceed west to the Air Force base in Ubon, Thailand, for the last time.

So it was on this my last flight to Thailand that we completed our mission in Laos, took some light AAA fire and then landed at the Air Force Base in Ubon at about 0730 hours. As we taxied up to the ramp, there were the two crew members from the previous Thailand flight waiting on the tarmac to climb in our A-6 and fly it back to Da Nang. In turn, on our third day, there we would be the crew waiting on the tarmac to take the flight back to Da Nang.

The procedure was that you would shut down one engine, climb out of the aircraft one at a time, and the other crew would climb in, get clearance, take off and, officially, we were not there.

The first thing we did was go to breakfast; then we checked into the BOQ. We relaxed a bit at the BOQ; then we went to town. Our first stop when we got to town was the hotse bath for a massage. Wow, what a nice feeling after a combat mission and having been up since about 0400. First was the steam cabinet, then the bath tub, dry off, powder and then the wonderful massage. I just felt like a wet noodle after the massage, every muscle was relaxed. Of course, it didn't hurt that the girls giving the massage were all young and pretty and, if I remember correctly, the price was only about three dollars an hour.

After that, we went to a bar for a drink or two and then on to the shops to pick up the stuff we had ordered on earlier trips. The tailor shop that most of the guys in the squadron went to was The Maharaja's Tailor Shop. He and his wife were Indian and very nice people. He did pretty well with all the GI clients either stationed in Ubon or with transients like us. We told him that this was our last trip to Ubon and we were picking up our tailor made suits. He said that he very much appreciated our business and invited us to his home for a homemade authentic Indian dinner cooked by his wife. I don't remember what we had for dinner other than the curry rice, but it was delicious. After dinner my BN and I went to a bar or two and in the process of going from one bar to another we ran into two girls from the hotse bath. One of the girls was the one that my unmarried BN favored and we stopped to talk to them and ask where there was a good bar to go to. As we were talking to the girls on the street a bicycle taxi called a "sanlo" came by; then it stopped just past us. Another girl from the massage parlor that I usually got my massage from, Nawate, got out and in a very angry voice said, "You number one butterfly, you som-ma-ma-bitch." A butterfly flies from flower to flower and a "number one butterfly" of course was the best at doing that. Thai women were known for their jealous temperament. I tried to explain in broken English to her that we were not with these girls who took off, but just on our way to another bar. But she just kept shouting "You number one butterfly" while shaking her fist at me. Then I realized as I caught the glimmer of the street light reflecting off the blade that she had a knife in her hand and was shaking it in a stabbing like manner at me. And I thought to myself, "Oh, this is great! I just completed a hundred and some odd combat missions in Vietnam without a scratch and this girl is going to stab me in a mistaken jealous rage."

Finally she settled down and got back into the "sanlo" and took off. My BN made the understatement of the day, "Wow! She was pissed."

We made it back to the base and on the third day we were ready on the tarmac with all our booty to fly back to Da Nang.

Rick Spitz's Last Flight to Thailand

My buddy and roommate Rick Spitz's last fling to Thailand was also a memorable one. He and Doug Burkett, his BN, were literally the last A-6 flight to Ubon. They flew their mission over Laos and then continued on to Ubon where the previous crew met them and flew the aircraft back to Da Nang. Rick and Doug were then to catch a C-130 back to Da Nang on their

Ron Boehm

third day thus ending his little mini — R&R set up since the A-6 squadrons were leaving country soon thereafter.

Well, like I pointed out earlier, Rick kind of thought that he should make his own rules and since he and Doug were having such a good time in Ubon which was a lot better than getting rockets fired at you in Da Nang or guns fired at you over Laos, they decided to stay a while longer. He had met some good-looking Thai girl with a beautiful face and big tits and that added to the attraction of staying.

So on the third day he called back to the squadron and told the Ops officer Shooter Dubeck that they had missed the daily C-130 flight but would catch the one tomorrow. When tomorrow came, they had another excuse and same for the next day on until the ninth day when finally Major Dubeck told them that he was sending two OV-10s, one for him and one for his worthless BN to pick them up and take them back and that they better be on them.

Rick was a story waiting to happen, and there are a bunch of them. That is why I loved to be with him; he was and still is a great friend.

My Last Combat Flight

We had just returned from a supposed piece-of-cake TPQ mission in country up north towards the DMZ and the Laotian border where we were to drop our ordinance on a suspected enemy position. In a TPQ mission, we were directed by an on-the-ground controller who guided us to the target via radar and we would pickle our bombs in level flight at six or eight thousand feet or so, well out of the range of enemy small arms fire. However, on this mission the target was cancelled and we jettisoned our bombs over the water at a designated drop zone. It was an uneventful hop other than cancellation and I didn't think of anything other than getting back, taxiing into our revetment area, shutting down the aircraft and filling out the end of mission paper work. But as we were pulling up to our ramp area, a fire truck followed us and as we came to a stop, they started to hose us down. We shut down the engines, turned off all the equipment and I climbed out of the aircraft. Then they hosed me down and as I stood there, dripping, with my helmet bag and knee pad, Major P.J. McCarthy walked up to me and presented me with a bottle of champagne. He said, "Congratulations, Ron, this was your final in country hop - you did a good job."

After my last combat flight

So this was it, August 15, 1970, my last combat flight in Vietnam, number one hundred and twenty four. I made it and survived without a scratch. I was a lot luckier than a whole bunch of other guys that shed their blood or lost their lives in this war. Many guys carried scars within them that others could not see, but I had none and I was proud to be a Marine and serve my country in combat. I wasn't a hero, but I knew a bunch of them. I just did my job as best as I could. Actually, it was the greatest thrill of my life.

My actual last flight in Vietnam, later on August 27 was with Wally Siller, my BN, and we were to go up and practice air refueling, but the weather was bad and we couldn't tank as I explained earlier. That was a bad deal for me since I would now have to trans-pac and not have air refueled in well over a year.

CHAPTER 5

Coming Home

Trans-Pac

On September 1, 1970, I was one of a flight of three A-6s to leave Da Nang in route to Cubi Point, Philippines, our first leg of the trans-pac ferry flight and an epic journey of two weeks that was full of memorable moments.

Jim Jurjevich was my BN on this half-way around the world flight going back home after one year in Vietnam.

We were to ferry three A-6s from Da Nang, island hop across the Pacific to Whidbey Island, Washington State, and then continue across country to NAS Norfolk, Virginia. The flight from Da Nang to Cubi Point Naval Air Station at Subic Bay took about two hours and was non-eventful. We landed, taxied in to the transit flight area, shut down our birds, did all the paper work and went to meet with our ferry flight leader from the Navy's Ferry Squadron.

The three crews included Lieutenant Ted Lyons and his BN in the lead plane, which had the only good and complete navigation equipment. The other two birds were less than complete system-wise since VMA 242's maintenance department kept the other two aircrafts' good systems for the aircraft that remained in Da Nang. Lieutenant John Halleran was the pilot and Lieutenant Carl Monk, his BN, were in the number two plane, and Lieutenant Jim Jurjevich and I were in the number three plane. Our aircraft was the worst of the bunch, having a degraded navigation system with basically only a wet compass for navigation, plus no auto pilot. This meant I had to hand fly my aircraft the whole way which wasn't usually a problem since our flights were normally about three hours long. But this would become a problem later on our five and a half hour leg from Hawaii to Whidbey Island when I had to fight to stay awake.

We meet up with the Navy crew from the Ferry Squadron that would lead us on the trans-pac flight. They would take over the bird that Ted Lyons and his BN flew to Cubi Point and Ted and his BN would then catch a C-130 back to Da Nang. The entire squadron would leave in another few weeks, but these three birds had to be delivered to the air rework facility in Norfolk, Virginia, on a certain date and before the squadron was to leave Vietnam.

That Navy Ferry Crew consisted of Commander Diz Laird and his BN, a Navy Lieutenant whose name I can't remember. Commander Laird was a legendary Navy fighter pilot who was an ACE in World War II and the only Navy pilot to shoot down both a German aircraft in the North Atlantic and a Japanese aircraft in the Pacific theater.

Commander Laird flew the Brewster Buffalo, then the F4F Wildcat and the F6F Hellcat in WW II. In the Korean War, he flew the Phantom 1 Banshee and the F-86 in the Air Force Exchange Program.

Commander Laird had retired, but the Navy brought him back to active service to fly these ferry flights during Vietnam. He flew seventy-two trans-pac flights leading F-8 Crusaders and A-6 Intruders across the Pacific Ocean. Diz Laird was said to be type-rated in ninety-nine different aircraft and was lead pilot of the Japanese Naval Fleet of converted T-6s and BT-13s in the Movie Tora Tora Tora.

Commander Laird was a hell of a fighter pilot and also one hell of a character who drank us young Lieutenants under the table in the bar at night after each leg of the flight. (Source: Golden Gate Wing — Prop Talk — Guest speaker article.)

When we arrived in Cubi Point on September 1, 1970, there was a typhoon heading towards the Philippines and this would cause us a couple of days delay waiting for the storm to pass. Then when it did, I had a mechanical problem with my A-6. The Rat Generator (Ram Air Turbine) was bad and had to be replaced. This, we were told, would take several more days to get one from Da Nang.

Ron Boehm

As I was at my plane getting something out of the cockpit, I noticed a Navy mechanic working on a Navy A-6 parked nearby on the ramp. I asked what was wrong with the Navy bird and he said it had an engine problem and a light went on in my head.

I said, "We have been waiting to leave for a few days and we have to deliver these three Intruders to Norfolk, Virginia."

I then asked him if I could swap my bad Rat generator for the one in the Navy A-6 since it was down anyway. He said he'd see what he could do. Then later he said he would swap them out and my bird would be ready to go by the following day. I thanked him and gave him twenty dollars.

So finally after waiting in Cubi Point for three days for the storm to pass and my aircraft to get fixed, we were ready to go on September 5, but Commander Laird had a policy that he wouldn't take off with crews that he had not flown with before unless it was VFR (Visual Flight Rules) conditions. That morning we went to the operations room, briefed our mission, filed our flight plan, went out to our aircraft and loaded all our stuff into the "bird cages" of the A-6s. The bird cage was a platform that could be lowered down from the fuselage for access to the electronic equipment, but also a place where we could stow our clothing bags and any other stuff you wanted to carry on a flight. In this case it was all the goodies that we had bought in Thailand, Vietnam and the Philippines.

The Trans-Pac
BNs at Cubi Point

After our pre-flight inspection, we climbed into our aircraft, went through our pre-start procedures, started our engines and then waited for the weather to clear up and turn VFR. We waited on the ramp for about an hour, but the weather wasn't getting any better, so finally Commander Laird called it off, told us to shut them down and said we would try it again the next day.

The next day, September 6, we went through the same procedure, got into our aircraft, cranked up and waited for the weather to break. Finally, after an hour's wait, we started to see the clouds break up a little, so we called the tower and got clearance to taxi to and hold short of the runway. Just as we anticipated clearance onto the runway for a takeoff, we saw a flight of A-7s from one of the aircraft carriers that was coming into the Port of Subic Bay doing touch and goes. One after another they came in touched down and took off again from the opposite end of the runway, the direction that we were to take off.

So here we were having waited for five days to take off and now the clouds closing in again as we had to wait for these A-7s to do their repeated touch and goes. Commander Laird called the tower and demanded clearance onto the runway and permission to take off, only to have the tower tell us to hold short.

We waited a little while longer and then Commander Laird taxied onto the runway without clearance. John Halleran in the number two bird looked over to Jim and me, lifted his hands and shrugged his shoulders as if to say, "Oh well" and followed the lead onto the runway. I looked at Jim and said, "This isn't good," and followed number two onto the runway. Then the lead started to roll, followed by number two and then Jim and me.

We were rolling down the runway headed right at the A-7s coming in for a landing in the opposite direction. It looked like some kind of weird air show as the A-7s broke hard to avoid us headed right at them. As we got airborne with gear up we followed lead climbing out and on a course that took us right through Clark Air

Ron Boehm

Force Base's restricted area without clearance. We got only to about three thousand feet when John Halleran said that he was having difficulty with his flight controls. So Commander Laird said, "Let's head back to Cubi Point." We turned around and headed back to Cubi, landed and as we were taxiing in, a Follow Me truck and Shore Patrol jeep came up and said to follow them. As we shut down and climbed out of our aircraft, the SPs told us to follow them to the Base Operations Officer's Office.

We were escorted up to the Base Ops Officer's office and as soon as we entered his office he lit into us with some very harsh verbiage, "You son-of-a-bitches went onto the runway and took off without clearance and then violated Clark's airspace. You almost caused a mid-air disaster flying into the A-7s who were landing. I'll have your wings and you will never fly again. You will be Lieutenants for the rest of your service life and you're lucky I don't put you in the brig." This was the best ass chewing I had ever received, better than OCS, even better than the Marine Major Ops Officer with 1/7 that grabbed me by the collar at LZ Baldy.

Just then, as the five of us were standing at attention and getting a major ass chewing from this Navy Captain, Commander Laird walked in. The Base Ops Officer looked at him and said, "Diz, are these your guys?"

"Yeah," Commander Laird replied. "What's the problem?"

The Ops Officer said, "You guys are dismissed. Commander Laird and I need to talk."

As it turned out, Diz Laird and the Base Ops Officer were old friends and former squadron and shipmates.

Commander Laird took care of that situation and Halleran's aircraft troubles turned out to be that they had stuffed too much crap in the bird cage. The clothing bags were pressing up against the horizontal stabilizer bar that ran down through the fuselage to the horizontal stabilizer in the tail causing the difficulty in moving the control stick and the vertical movement of the aircraft.

Guam

The next day, September 7, we were back on the flight line and ready to go with VFR weather conditions and our flight plan to Guam in the Marianas Islands. As we took off and got gear up somebody came over the air and said "Hurrah" and that summed up everyone's feelings and I'm sure the people at NAS Cubi Point, too.

Finally we were on our way after all that waiting at Cubi, the storm, my aircraft's rat generator problem, the takeoff comedy of errors, flight violation and Halleran and Monk's over-stuffed bird cage. We climbed out on a beautiful day, heading east. We leveled off at about thirty-one thousand feet in a loose cruise flight formation and finally relaxed and enjoyed the flight over the large expanse of beautiful Pacific Ocean.

After a three and one-half hour flight, we landed in Guam at NAS Agana which was built originally by the Japanese in 1943 and then captured by the US in 1944. It was used by the US 7th Air Force flying B24 Liberator bombers until they moved to Okinawa. Then it was used by long range reconnaissance aircraft and also as a fighter base. It was turned over to and operated by the US Navy in 1947 until it was closed in 1993. (Source: Wikipedia)

The flight to NAS Agana was uneventful, and after shutting down our birds and checking into the BOQ, we all relaxed a bit and then met in the Officer's Club for dinner and drinks. True to his style, Commander Diz Laird asked the bartender for the dice and another round of Ship, Captain and Crew was begun, along with the shots of whisky and Afterburners. All us younger guys, being twenty-five to maybe twenty-eight years old were getting out done by this WWII veteran fighter pilot who was probably about fifty-five at the time. To us he was an old man,

Ron Boehm

but none of us could match him in flying or drinking. He was a legend to us even then.

It seems like through that whole trans-Pacific flight we started off each morning hung over and looking forward to putting our oxygen mask on.

A funny thing to watch at Agana was the gooney birds (albatrosses) lining up and taking off on the runway. I guess they thought they were airplanes; actually they have very long wing spans made for gliding and it took them a long run to get off the ground so what better place to take off than a runway. As you can imagine, they could be a problem for aircraft operations. Birds and jet intakes don't mix very well. Bird strikes to a windscreen or up an intake can be disastrous. But we had no problems with them.

Wake Island

The next day, September 8, we had breakfast, filed our flight plan and headed out to our aircraft for our next leg to Wake Island. The flight to Wake was about three hours, cruising at an altitude of about thirty-one thousand feet over a very large and beautiful Pacific Ocean.

Wake Island is actually a triangle-shaped coral atoll consisting of three islands. It was discovered in 1568 by a Spanish explorer and later named for Captain William Wake of the British trading schooner Prince William Henry who visited the island in 1796.

The island was annexed by the United States on January 17, 1899. Pan Am Airways used it as a stopover for its flights to China and in 1941 in a military buildup in WW II the U.S. Navy constructed a military base there. The base was garrisoned by elements of the 1st Marine Defense Battalion consisting of 449 officers and men.

The Battle of Wake started with Japanese bombers attacking the island on December 8, the same day as the attack on Pearl Harbor, which was on the other side of the International Date Line. Twelve F4F Wildcat fighters of VMF 211 were on the ground. The island defenders repulsed the first amphibious assault on December 11 but the greatly outnumbered defenders were overwhelmed on December 23. U.S. casualties were numbered at fifty-two Navy and Marines and seventy-two civilians. The Japanese lost seven hundred to one thousand dead, two destroyers and one submarine sunk plus twenty-four aircraft shot down.

The Marines took the island back on September 4, 1945. (Source: Wikipedia)

The flight to Wake Island was almost uneventful except for one thing. As our three-plane flight was in loose cruise formation over the blue ocean below and the almost cloudless sky above, the lead aircraft radioed for us, the other two birds, to come in tighter. As I pulled in closer on the starboard side of Commander Laird's A-6, I saw Commander Laird, the pilot, with his mask off waving at me from the BN's right side seat.

I told Jim, my BN, to look over at the other aircraft, and asked, "Is that Commander Laird?"

"Oh shit, they changed seats in midair" was Jim's response.

I then came up on our frequency and said some smart ass remark like "I hope you know how to fly that thing," or something like that.

The A-6 has a big cockpit, but how in the hell they could swap seats in flight was pretty amazing, but then Diz Laird was pretty amazing. The whole trans-pac flight was one amazing or crazy thing after another.

After landing and securing our aircraft, and checking into the BOQ, I took a walk down the beach and visited two small memorials, one for the American defenders and the other for the Japanese soldiers who fought and died in the battle for Wake. After that, I did a little snorkeling in the crystal clear water of the lagoon.

Ron Boehm

Later on in the "O" Club, we were laughing about the trading of places with more drinks and Ship, Captain and Crew dice rolling.

Johnston Island

The next morning, September 9, I was slightly hungover again as we filed our flight plan for our next 3.1 hour leg to Johnston Island.

Johnston Island is part of Johnston Atoll and is about seven hundred fifty miles west of Hawaii. It is only about 1.03 square miles in size. I was told that it was operated by the U.S. Atomic Energy Agency at that time. The runway filled most of the island which ran from one end of the island to the other and it looked like if you ran off the end of the runway you were in the ocean.

The Island was used as an airbase during WWII and nuclear weapons test site in the 1950s and '60s then as an airbase and as a Naval refueling station later on.

The island was discovered when the U.S. brig Sally ran aground on a shoal near it in September 1796, but was not officially named until Captain Charles J. Johnston of the Royal Navy ship HMS Cornwallis sighted the islands on December 14, 1807. (Source: Wikipedia)

So as we began this beautiful Pacific day on the tarmac at Wake Island, we cranked up our Intruders, got our taxi clearance to the end of the runway and watched briefly as a couple Gooney birds made their takeoff run down the runway and took off before us. Then it was our turn, following our now normal procedure of number one taxiing onto the runway centerline, number two on the port side of number one, and Jim and I in the number three aircraft to the starboard side. Then we were rolling down the runway and lifting off into the blue Pacific sky.

I never got tired of that feeling of taxiing onto a runway, pushing the throttle forward and seeing the center strips passing underneath the nose, and then climbing up into the heavens; it just thrills me every time.

We climbed out and leveled off at our cruising altitude and spread out again into a loose cruise formation. Since I didn't have a working autopilot, I trimmed the aircraft up as best as I could so I could relax a bit. As I had said earlier, our A-6 had very little navigation equipment; all the good electronics black boxes were left behind with the squadron in Vietnam, since these planes were going to be overhauled at the rework facility in Norfolk, Virginia. I had a wet compass and just the basic flight instruments. The lead aircraft had a fully operational system and would provide the navigation for the flight.

About a little more than halfway to Johnston Island we crossed the International Dateline and it became September 8 again. As we approached Johnston Island, we started our let down from our cruising altitude, but with Commander Laird it wasn't "pull the throttle back and coast down." No, he just pushed the nose down for a high speed let down. I was just off of his starboard wing, not in real tight, but with about twenty foot separation between the aircraft and I was watching the compression wave cloud forming over his canopy and wings. We were smoking hot for an A-6 anyway.

As the Island came into sight, we were lined up for a straight in approach to the runway. We pulled the throttles back, lowered our flaps and dropped our landing gear. But then lead said that he didn't have a down and locked indication for his right main gear, so I pulled underneath his aircraft to do a visual inspection and confirmed that his right main gear was not fully down and locked. Commander Laird did an up and down porpoise-like motion with the A-6 to get the gear down, but to no avail. He then tried to blow the gear down with the pneumatic system, but that didn't work either. He then told us, Number two and Number three to land and he would follow after burning and dumping some fuel.

We did as instructed and landed our aircraft and waited for him to land. By this time all the thirty or so people on the island

Ron Boehm

including some crewmen from a Navy Seagoing tug had heard of the emergency going on and had come out to watch. There wasn't a lot of excitement on Johnston Island I guess, so this was the big event at the time.

I was already very impressed with Commander Laird's flying skills and this event confirmed that. As he came in for a landing with his right main gear visibly not fully down and locked, he rolled the aircraft slightly to the port side and bounced the A-6 on its left main gear once, then twice and the right gear popped down and locked. He then set the right gear onto the runway and rolled out to the end of the runway which was very close to the ocean's edge. They turned around and taxied back to the ramp where we were waiting. As he and his BN taxied in with their canopy open all the people who had watched this great demonstration of flying skill were cheering and clapping like it was a parade or something. Matter of fact, so were we cheering; John, Carl, Jim and I were cheering and waving our arms. It was a great show. Diz Laird was our hero and he acted like it was just another day at the office. That's what heroes do.

Stopover To Refuel and on to Hawaii

Johnston Island was to be just a stopover to refuel and then we were on our way to NAS Barber's Point, Hawaii. We were all concerned about the right landing gear on Commander Cmdr. Laird's bird and how it would operate when we tried to land in Hawaii, but there was no fixing it here on Johnston Island. It had operated OK up to that landing on Johnston, so Cmdr. Commander Laird said we would proceed to Barber's Point.

We went off to get a bite to eat at the mess hall, then planned for the flight for our next leg. While we were being refueled, we got in a conversation with some of the crew of a Navy tug that was stopping over on its way to the U.S. mainland. The crew member asked us how long our flight was to the mainland and I told him it was about a couple of hours to Hawaii and then a long six-hour hop from Hawaii to Whidbey Island. He then said he wished he could go with us for it would take his boat two weeks to get to San Diego.

On to Hawaii

As we climbed into our aircraft again and began the routine of our preflight procedures for our next leg to NAS Barber's Point on the Island of Oahu, I had the thought that we were better than half way home to the U.S. mainland.

The flight to Barber's Point was short, only about 1.7 hours and uneventful. We had good weather and Commander Laird's landing gear worked OK upon our approach and landing at Barber's Point. It was just another glorious day of flying over the beautiful Pacific Ocean.

When we landed in Hawaii we were officially in the U.S. now, so we had to go through customs and get our aircraft sprayed to kill any bugs we might be carrying from Vietnam or the various islands where we had stopped.

It was going to be a nice three day stopover near beautiful Honolulu and Waikiki Beach because we were not to leave until September 11 for our flight to Whidbey Island in Washington State. We had to get Commander Laird's landing gear inspected and fixed. It turned out that the problem was caused by a slightly tapered bushing in the landing gear mechanism that was installed backwards and caused the gear to bind up upon extension.

We spent a leisurely two days in Hawaii, dined at the "O" Club and of course had some drinks and rolled the dice at the bar. I went to the beach one day and tried to body surf in the ten-foot waves. Some surf guy loaned me one of his flippers and convinced me to try to body surf in what I thought were huge waves. After almost drowning—not really but it seemed like it—I just went back and lay on the beach. As I watched the ocean and the people on the beach, it hit me when I saw a pretty Hawaiian girl walking on the beach, that I was back in the "real world" and this was the first "round eye" (non-Asian) woman I'd seen in about half a year. Well, except for the two fat Air Force Nurses Roger De Jean and I sparred with at the Air Force "O" Club in Da Nang, but I didn't count them. Man, it was great to be almost home. I had thoughts of seeing Eileen and my new daughter Laura Lee.

Flight to Whidbey Island — In-Flight Refuel and Take a Piss

On September 11, we repeated our now familiar routine of checking the weather, filing our flight plan, pre-flighting our aircraft, starting up, getting our clearance and taxiing out to the runway. But this leg of our trip half around the world would be different from the previous legs. For one thing, it was a lot longer, about six hours, twice as long as the other legs of the trip, and we would have to aerial refuel. As I had mentioned earlier I had not done that in over a year and had missed two opportunities to practice back in Da Nang.

We took off and climbed out to our cruising altitude, passing in and out of the clouds and had to adjust our heading to get around some thunderstorms. It was such an awesome sight to fly right next to the edge of one of these huge thunderstorms and witness the cloud mass boiling and growing ever bigger and higher. You feel so small and weak compared to this monstrous but beautiful cumulus nimbus cloud.

I remember one time flying under the anvil of a mature thunderstorm and being pelted with hail even though we were quite some distance away from the storm. They can be very dangerous and can tear the wings off a plane or stall out engines. I had heard a story about an F-8 pilot who had punched out in a thunder storm and spent about a half of an hour being circulated up and down in the storm and seeing his parachute open, then collapse, only to open again. He survived, but he was beaten up pretty badly.

USMC Lieutenant Colonel William Rankin told his amazing story about ejecting at 47,000 feet in a thunderstrom in his book, The man Who rode Thunder.

In telling this story it reminded me of verse from a poem that I wrote while on a flight to Costa Rica and flying past one of these beautiful clouds.

"Now thunderous clouds boiling as they rise to great height,
Displaying their power and grandiose might.
We soar along within their view,
Passersby, passing through."

After about two and a half hours into our flight we made contact with our refueling tanker, an A-3 Skywarrior, nicknamed "The Whale." The A-3 was a large carrier-based aircraft that was originally designed for the Navy as a strategic bomber and came into service in the mid-1950s then retired in 1991. Used as an air refueling tanker, it utilized the Navy's system of a long hose coming from the tanker aircraft with a circular basket at the end.

The refueling procedure was to fly up to the basket, momentarily stop with the A-6 refueling probe about three feet in back of the basket, then edge forward, pushing the probe into the basket and making the connection. You would then take on fuel you needed. After you received fuel, you backed out and the next plane in the formation would then plug in.

Our flight descended to a lower altitude and joined up with the A-3. The lead plane was first to tank, then John Halleran was

Ron Boehm

next. After they both tanked, it was my turn to plug in. I moved over into a position just behind the basket which was oscillating about three feet up and down. The trick is to time the oscillation and put the probe in the basket. I moved the throttle forward a bit and the refueling probe went just under the basket. "Damn, a miss." So I backed off and got into position behind the basket again, pushed the throttle forward a bit and this time the probe went over the basket. Two misses. Did I mention that we were out in the middle of the Pacific Ocean with no hope of landing anywhere as we ran out of fuel?

So I backed off again and went through the same procedure. I pushed the throttle forward and the probe once again bounced off of the basket, miss number three. My asshole was now getting a little tight and Jim, my BN, was looking at me with that "Come on Ron, get it in there" look on his face. Then I heard Commander Laird, his BN, and the number two crew mocking me.

Someone said, "Just picture hair around it; that should help you to put it in."

They were laughing, but I wasn't seeing the humor right then. I thought about the two missed opportunities to practice refueling back in Da Nang and how much I wished I would have done it.

I thought to myself, "OK, let's get back to the basics: fly formation on the aircraft, not the basket. Don't chase the basket: get into position about three feet behind and move forward slowly." So I did that and hallelujah the refueling probe went straight into the basket. I pushed it forward a bit, turned on the refueling switch and told the A-3 guys I was ready to take on fuel. My ass relaxed a bit as I heard clapping and cheering over the radio coming from the other guys.

I've Got to Take a Leak

So now we had enough fuel to make it to Whidbey Island; we had passed the point of no return and it was now on to the U.S. mainland. After about four hours into the flight we were back up at altitude of about thirty-one thousand feet and in the clouds so I pulled into a tighter formation on the starboard side of the lead plane. But now I had to go to the bathroom. I tried holding but finally I had to piss so bad that I told Jim that I was going to use the relief tube for my first time ever.

The A-6 was one of the only fighter/attack type aircraft to have a relief tube, but I had never used it before. The relief tube is a funnel with a trigger that is attached on the end of a hose which is stored under the instrument panel. Using it is easier said than done. I didn't have an auto pilot, so I had to fly the plane holding the control stick in my right hand and hold the funnel in my left hand with my finger on the trigger that emptied the tube. But first you had to get your dick out of your Jockey shorts, your flight suit, past your G-suit and torso harness which tended to choke your private equipment. Then after you got your little man out, cold air was blowing directly on him from the air vent tending to shrink him up even more, plus there is a guy sitting next to you, laughing. This was almost as much pressure as the aerial refueling deal. Oh yes, and we were flying formation in the clouds at the time. Damn, I really had to go bad, and so being in the clouds flying in a tight formation with the other aircraft I decided to get some separation. I took a thirty degree heading change away from our course heading for one minute to clear us from the flight than turned back onto our original heading. I told the flight leader what I was going to do and that I was going to take a leak. I couldn't get the little man out sitting down so I un-hooked my parachute harness straps from the ejection seat and

Ron Boehm

stood up in the cockpit. Being only five feet, six, I think I was the only guy in the squadron that could accomplish this feat of standing up in the cockpit; maybe Roger DeJean or Dave Clary could also. But being short did have its advantages this time.

So now I was standing up in the cockpit holding the stick with one hand, the relief tube and my little guy with the other hand, while trying to fly, using the instruments in the clouds. I finally got my pissing equipment going but it was very difficult to fly instruments while standing up and taking a piss.

Jim told me we were in a thirty degree bank, but I just said, "OK" and continued relieving myself. The flow was going good and I wasn't about to stop now.

Jim then said, "We're losing altitude," with a slight concern in his voice.

I said, "I'll be finished in a bit," and continued with my task in hand. Pardon the pun.

Jim then said with much concern this time, "We're going through twenty-five thousand feet."

I said, "Let me know when we get to fifteen thousand feet," and continued peeing.

I had my finger pulling the trigger on the funnel which opened the relief tube and created a vacuum effect that just sucked the piss out of you.

Jim was now getting panicky but I leveled off at about eighteen thousand feet. However, now we had lost the flight, and were in the clouds, thirteen thousand feet below them and without our sophisticated navigation gear. So we now had to find the rest of the flight.

I called the lead plane to give me a radio transmission which would make the radio direction finder needle point to the transmission source. I then took that heading while climbing back up to altitude. I did this several times until we finally got the flight in sight and joined up. That is the most memorable piss I have ever taken.

One hour Out, Can't Stay Awake

This was a long flight by our normal standards and about one hour out from Whidbey Island I had trouble keeping my eyes open. You know the feeling while driving when your head bobs and you catch yourself nodding off. But in this case I couldn't pull over to the side of the road and catch a wink or two; I was flying an airplane over the ocean with no auto pilot. Even though I had the A-6 trimmed up good, the plane wasn't going to hold heading and altitude by itself for long.

Normally, with a good operating system and auto pilot, the BN could maintain heading and altitude by using his computer, but of course, we didn't have either one of those. Finally, I told Jim that I just had to close my eyes for a few minutes and asked him to reach over and fly the aircraft with his left hand. We did this for about five minutes or so and then I opened my eyes and took control of the aircraft again. Jim informed me that we were only about a few hundred miles out from Whidbey and soon we picked up the Whidbey area TACAN navigation station and then Whidbey's approach control. We were then getting steering to the airfield.

This woke me up and we were in communication with the air controller. As we approached NAS Whidbey Island we set up to enter the break instead of a mundane straight-in approach. It was great to get sight of the airfield because this meant we were home in the U.S. of A. We came in smoking hot over the end of the runway and lead started his break followed by Number two and then Jim and me. I was in a ninety degree bank pulling hard, throttling back, lowering flaps and landing gear then turning final and lining up for touchdown. I didn't drive it into the runway like a good Navy landing but greased my A6A onto the runway, then rolled out and followed lead and Number two to the parking area. As we were taxiing

Ron Boehm

in, I reached over to Jim and gave him a high five. Wow! We were in the U.S. after a year away in combat and having the adventure of a lifetime. We had made it, one year in combat and over one hundred combat missions. What a great feeling to be back in the U.S.A.

We shut down our birds and climbed out, and as I put my feet on the ground, I literally got down on my hands and knees and kissed the ground, thankful for making it.

NAS Whidbey Island is near Oak Harbor, Washington, in the Puget Sound and was the center for the Navy's A6 training and operations on the West Coast. It was also a seaplane base until the late 1960s and the legendary PBY Catalina flying boats operated out of there during WWII.

We checked into the BOQ, got cleaned up, went to dinner and then celebrated our trans-Pacific crossing at the "O" Club with more dice and more shots. I think we had at least one round of "Afterburners" which was a shot of some high octane alcohol that is set afire and tossed down while still burning. You had to be careful if you had a mustache like me; it could set it on fire or burn your nose hairs.

The next day, September 12, 1970, was the last leg of our trans-pac flight. We would be flying from Whidbey to NAS Norfolk, Virginia, where we would turn over our A6s to the Air Rework Facility. When we got the aircraft signed over to the facility, we were officially finished with our tour in Vietnam and on leave.

After the previous day's long and arduous flight from Hawaii to Whidbey Island, I was mentally drained, and on this the last leg of our journey we all decided to break up into individual flights and not fly as a three plane flight. We were all carrying two drop tanks under our wings for extra fuel and greater distance so the other two crews decided they were going to go non-stop across country to Norfolk, approximately a five-hour flight, but I didn't want to go through another day like yesterday. However, Jim really had "get home-ictus" and wanted to go no-stop so I finally acquiesced and said that if we had a certain amount of fuel when we reached St. Louis, which was about halfway, we would continue on to Norfolk, but if not, then we would land and refuel at St. Louis.

So we all launched off separately, but were fairly close to each other in time and distance as we crossed the western part of the country. As Jim and I approached St. Louis, I checked our fuel status and we had enough fuel to make it to Norfolk so we pushed on. Somewhere over Kentucky or West Virginia the Flight Control Center came up on the radio and said that he had two other flights of A6As all going to NAS Norfolk (NGU) and asked if he could join us up as he directed us on to Norfolk. We all said "Roger that" and got joined up for the final part of our flight.

As we were getting close to Norfolk over the West Virginia / Virginia border we got into some weather and requested to get vectored around some thunderstorms but ended up running right through one and got bumped around pretty much. At one point, the clouds were so thick that I pulled in very tight to the leads' wingtip and all I could see was his green wingtip light, but it was very rough and bumpy so I told the other crews that I was going underneath lead to the rear and began flying off of his tail pipes. Finally we broke out of the clouds and after that Halleran told us he was very low on fuel and Commander Laird declared a low fuel emergency. Atlanta Center handed us off to Norfolk Approach Control and they said they acknowledged our fuel situation and would bring us straight in to final approach.

On final approach, Commander Laird told Halleran to take the lead and we would follow. We got some separation and John crossed the end of the runway and touched down and we all gave a sigh of relief. Commander Laird then touched down and finally Jim and I landed and rolled out. As we turned off the runway onto the taxiway, we saw Hallaeran and Monk parked on the side of the taxiway waving to us as we passed by; they had flamed out taxiing in. Out of fuel and barely off the runway, how close was that.

We continued to taxi and got directions to the Air Rework Facility's ramp, parked our aircraft and went inside. We signed our aircraft over to the facility and were officially on leave and our one year tour of duty in Vietnam was over.

Now I was in a rush to make a flight at the commercial airport to New Orleans. I changed out of my flight suit into my uniform in the rest room and caught a cab to the airport. I had to pinch myself to make sure it was real.

About a month after my three-plane flight left Da Nang, Vietnam for our trans-pac flight back to the U.S. the last two A6 squadrons VMA (AW) 242 and VMA (AW) 225 ended combat air operations and departed for home in the U.S.A.

VMA (AW) 242's last combat mission in Vietnam

VMA (AW) 225 our sister squadron end of Vietnam Tour photos

Back Home with Eileen and My Daughter Laura

I arrived home in New Orleans and Eileen, along with my "new" baby daughter, Laura, who was only seven days old when I left for Vietnam, picked me up at the airport. Now she was one year old and looked at me like "Who is this strange man?" But that would change and Laura and I would become very close and she would become, like most little girls, "daddy's little girl."

I had thirty days leave and soon got used to the leisure time and being with my family again. My orders read thirty days leave and then I was to report to VT-7 at NAS Meridian in Mississippi to train to be a flight instructor in the T-2 Buckeye, which was the Navy's primary jet trainer then. I was looking forward to this billet because even though I had one year's combat flying experience I knew that I still had a lot to learn to become a really good pilot. We were so green when we were sent to Vietnam that for all practical purposes we had learned to fly there in combat. It was in being a flight instructor that you also learned to be a better pilot by practicing and demonstrating your skills every day.

About two weeks into my leave, I got a telegram on September 23, 1970, from CG Third MAW (Marine Air Wing) informing me that I was to report to MCAS EL Toro in Orange County, California, to rejoin my squadron VMA (AW) 242. It was supposed to be disbanded, but they changed their minds and reformed it as part of MAG 13 (Marine Air Group) in California. El Toro was a great duty station, but as I said, I was looking forward to being an instructor.

When my leave was up, Eileen and I packed up our household belongings for the moving company to haul them to El Toro and then we packed the rest of our stuff into our 1965 Volvo and headed off to California.

This was our first time to go to California and we planned our trip to go through and visit along the way Abilene, Albuquerque, the Petrified Forest, Flagstaff, and The Grand Canyon, then cross over into California at Needles and finally to Santa Ana, California. I reported to MCAS El Toro on October 19, 1970.

We stayed with a bachelor friend and squadron mate, Ken Paulsen, for a couple of weeks until we could get our own place in base housing. Our base housing rent house was quite nice and had plenty enough space for the three of us. It was on the edge of the hills on the base and about five minutes away from our squadron's hangar.

Santa Ana in Orange County back in 1970 was not as crowded as it is now and was covered with citrus orchards. During the spring-time a drive through the orchards would overwhelm you with the fragrance of the lemon and grapefruit blossoms. It was like going into a perfume shop and smelling the wonderful fragrance of the blossoms.

At that time just about all of the squadron's aircraft were being refurbished at the rework facility after being in combat conditions for so long, so I think that we didn't fly very much for about four or five months. We tried to keep busy, but things were pretty slow and Eileen and I took advantage of the time and did a lot of sightseeing with our infant daughter Laura in tow.

Eileen was a big McDonald's hamburger fan and that was passed on to Laura who loved their French fries. If we just passed by a McDonald's and she saw the Golden Arches she would start saying "yum, yum, yum," smacking her lips as if she were eating fries. Too cute.

One Week's Training at NAS Whidbey Island

At that time, the Marine Corps, and for that matter all the U.S. forces in Vietnam, were drawing down. As for our Squadron VMA (AW) 242, Vietnam was over and now we were going to prepare for a different mission, that of nuclear delivery. A number of us were sent up to NAS Whidbey Island for A-6 training in the delivery of nuclear weapons. This was different from our standard mission of low level interdiction missions to attack an enemy target with five hundred to two thousand pound bombs. This was to deliver a nuke in a manner that gave us a chance to escape the bomb blast after releasing the weapon. It was called LABS IP.

The LABS IP maneuver was an over-the-top technique for delivering a nuke and getting away as fast and as far as possible in the opposite direction from which you had released the bomb. In this procedure, you came low to the ground to stay under the radar, pulled up as if starting a loop as you approached the target and released the bomb at a certain point in your pull up to loft it high and down range. The idea was to strike the target while you did an Immelman-type aerobatic maneuver and headed in the opposite direction before the nuke exploded.

If nothing else, it was fun to practice with our little blue practice bombs. As you can image, accuracy wasn't the biggest thing in the world when it came to dropping a nuke. "Close" is good enough I would think when you are dropping a nuke on somebody. As the training proceeded we were told that we would be assigned target cities in China to be pre-assigned in case of the U.S. going to war with China.

Just considering the math, I figured that those missions were a bend over and kiss your ass good-by operation; you were not coming home. But then you probably would not have a home to come home to if we got into a nuclear war with China or Russia.

On this particular occasion, the squadron had deployed to Fallon, Nevada, for practice in the Chocolate Mountain Bombing Range. Here we practiced our deliveries which included low level flights across the desert into the target range and then practiced our LABS IP delivery, throwing the blue practice bombs down range hopefully on to the target. The range control tower would then score your hits. We were supposed to make our runs five hundred feet above the ground, but if five hundred feet was OK, then fifty

Ron Boehm

feet was a lot more fun. So here we were screaming across the desert floor at just above cactus height making our target runs and doing this about six times a day.

I was the Duty Officer one afternoon when the telephone rang and I picked up the phone to hear a rancher on the other end screaming at me about the noise from the jets flying over his ranch and that his horse was so frightened that it had kicked down the barn door, injured itself and he had to put it down. Then right in the middle of the conversation he shouts, "Here the son-of-a-bitch comes again," and all you could hear was this very, very loud aircraft roaring overhead. It was deafening over the phone so I can image how it must have sounded to the poor rancher and his horse. All I could say was that I would pass it on to the Ops Officer and some-one would get back with him.

I couldn't help but remember when we had deployed to Roo-sevelt Roads in Puerto Rico before going to Vietnam and Jack Rippy had napalmed a farmer's goat and the squadron had to pay the farm-er for it. I don't remember how this particular incident worked out, but it made for some insensitive laughs at the "O" Club that night. Of course it wasn't at all funny to the rancher.

Fallon, Nevada, was about an hour's drive to Reno so some of us made the trip to the casinos, but I never had much money for gambling so my stint at the casinos was short and I would rather spend my money at the bar than in a slot machine. For some of the bachelors, they decided to make a trip to the infamous Mustang Ranch which was in Fallon. I felt rather naive when some of the guys spoke of it and I asked what kind of a ranch it was. I had never heard of it before. It was like when some of the guys in Vietnam were mak-ing a big deal about buying a Rolex Watch at a bargain price in Thai-land. I had never heard of a Rolex watch before. I was from a meager background and no one in my family probably heard of one either.

T-28

Having gone through the Air Force Flight School, my only prop time at that time was in the Cessna 172, but the guys that went through Pensacola and the helicopter pipeline got to fly the radial engine T-28. So at NAS Fallon I came across a pilot of a T-28 spotter plane and he invited me to go up with him on one of his spotter missions and I gladly accepted the offer. It was fun flying something different, especially a propeller plane. That was a pretty big prop plane with a big ass engine and a bunch of torque when you gave it the throttle.

It reminded me of the story about a student pilot in Pensacola flying the T-28 who had inadvertently rolled the aircraft on takeoff due to the torque but recovered, barely missing a crash and going into the Flight Ops Officer's office and turned in his wings. The Ops Officer said, "Anyone who would get himself into a situation like that, should DOR (Drop On Request), but anyone who could get himself out of that situation should continue to fly."

Ken Ptack (Our Milo Minderbinder) — Whidbey Island Pick Up

Ken Ptack was our squadron's embarkation officer for leaving Vietnam. He was also our squadron's own Milo Minderbinder, Joseph Heller's fictional character in his novel Catch-22. 1st Lieutenant Milo Minderbinder was the Mess Officer in Yossarian's squadron and was a genius as an entrepreneur. He was a wheeler—dealer and cornered the Egyptian cotton market only to find he couldn't unload the cotton. He even coated the cotton with chocolate to try to market it. (Source: Wikipedia)

Ken Ptack, while we were in Vietnam, was always trying to make some sort of deal, like trading a Naval leather flight jacket to some Air Force guy for an AK-47, which you could not bring back home to the U.S. because it was an automatic weapon. But Ken was always figuring a deal.

When we got back from Vietnam to the MCAS El Toro in California, on one occasion I had a flight to NAS Whidbey Island to pick up some A-6 parts and bring them back to El Toro. Ken heard that I was flying up there and asked me to pick up a flight bag with some of his stuff that a Navy pilot friend of his had brought back from Nam.

When I arrived at Whidbey Island, I asked at Flight Ops if there was something to pick up for Captain Ptack and I was handed a flight bag. As I picked it up, the bag made a clank sound and it felt like a bag of rifles, but I didn't open it up because I didn't want to know what was in it. I just thought Milo was at work again.

On the way back from Whidbey Island we flew down from Washington state through Oregon and northern California, and as we did we passed over a number of the snow-capped high mountains in the Cascade Range of the Pacific Northwest. We flew past Mount Rainier at 14,410 feet just outside of Tacoma, then past Mount St. Helens in south Washington which was 9,677 feet before it blew up on May 18, 1980, on to Mount Hood at 11,235 feet east of Portland, Oregon, the Three Sisters (North 10,085 feet, Middle 10,063 feet, and South 10,354 feet) and on down to Mount Shasta in northern California at 14,162 feet. (Source: *Rand McNally US Road Atlas 1973*)

In flight school, we were warned to be wary of lenticular-shaped clouds or mountain-wave clouds that form over the peaks of mountains. They are called lenticular because they are shaped like a lens. They look smooth and harmless but are caused by the wind rushing over the mountain top much like the pressure wave over the wing or canopy of an aircraft. They are very dangerous and can tear apart an aircraft if it gets too close.

As we flew over Mt. Shasta at about twenty-five thousand feet, I had just commented to my BN about the fact that that was a lenticular cloud or mountain—wave cloud over the mountain just like what we heard about in flight school. And then we experienced a rather strong and quick movement to the aircraft, like some giant hand had grabbed it and gave the A-6 a strong shake. Wow! I looked at my BN and all he could say was, "Son-of-a-bitch." I was a true believer after that. Never fly low over a mountain, especially if it has a smooth cloud sitting on top of it.

As we were coming back to El Toro and approaching Los Angeles, night had fallen and I thought to myself, we haven't heard from LA Center in a while and I gave them a call. I could tell from his response that he had forgotten about us.

He then came back and said, "Marine Alpha 6 can you be at eleven thousand feet by such and such intersection?"

We were currently level at about thirty- thousand feet and the intersection the controller was talking about was only a few air miles away.

I replied, "Roger that" and put my Intruder over on its back and did Split S maneuver pulling some serious Gs, rolled out at eleven thousand feet, keyed the mike and said, "Level 1-1 thousand."

The controller replied with a surprised sound in his voice, "Good job Alpha-6." We were then handed off to El Toro Approach Control for a straight-in approach to the airport.

When you flew down the coast of California from San Francisco to LA it looked like one continuous city of lights set next to the blackness of the ocean, very pretty.

The next day I handed the flight bag of "stuff" to Ken Ptack and told him that I didn't know what was in the bag and I didn't want to know even if it looked like and sounded like a bag of guns.

Ron Boehm

Twentynine Palms Air — Ground Combat Center

Ed Kenney Killed

In continuation of our regular mission of supporting the ground forces with close air support, the squadron was doing Air/Ground coordination exercises at the Marine Base at Twentynine Palms, California. We were running several missions a day for about a week in support of the grunts: we were running both systems drops and even got in some visual bomb drops.

One of the things probably every pilot did at least once in Vietnam was to give the troops on the ground an "antenna check" after making a successful bombing mission. In this show-off maneuver, the pilot would come back over the troops at a very low height i.e. "antenna check" pull up and he might even do a victory roll to the thrill of the grunts.

Captain Ed Kenney was a pilot just back from Vietnam like most of the guys in the squadron and had just completed an Air/Ground support mission and came back at the request of the ALO (Air Liaison Officer) on the ground for an "antenna check" which they did. However, he mis-judged his descent and as he pulled up and started a banking turn, his wing tip caught the ground and the A-6 cart wheeled and exploded into a ball of flames, killing Ed and his BN.

It was a pretty sad day for everyone. I don't remember if any of the troops on the ground were injured or killed, but it was a real tragedy. But I had learned back in Nam that if you were doing any hot dog stuff like that you had better make sure you are on the way up as you come over the site and had plenty of clearance before you make a turn or a roll. When you made a bomb run, it was according to the charts as for dive angle, airspeed, roll-in altitude and release altitude. When you did a hot dog maneuver it was by visual judgment or seat of the pants and since it wasn't something you did everyday it was subject to errors in judgment, and those errors were deadly.

It was a very sad mistake for Ed and his BN.

Party on My Friend's Boat

Back at El Toro, I had met a fellow Marine pilot around the area who was a CH-46 helicopter driver and was stationed just up the road a MCAS Santa Ana. He had a sailboat and asked me if I would like to go sailing sometime. I said that I had always wanted to sail and I would jump at the chance to go with him. We became friends and I did go sailing with him several times.

On one occasion, my friend asked me if I would like to try sailing in foul weather and I said, "Hell, yes." We set out from Newport Beach harbor, sailed out into the Pacific in the rain and wind and were soon sailing in foul weather on a Pacific Ocean that was not very peaceful. We had ten-foot waves breaking over the bowl, rain pouring down on us and the boat leaning over from the strong wind. My buddy asked me what I thought of sailing in that kind of weather and I said without a thought, "I love it." It was an adrenalin rush. After you had flown aircraft in combat, few things could match that sort of rush, but that activity was good.

After we were finished sailing one day my friend said that he was having a small party later on and asked me if I wanted to stay for it. I said, "OK, I'll stay for a while." There were about a dozen people on the boat in his slip at Newport Beach and we were making homemade sangria wine. Every time I hear Jimmy Buffet's song Sangria Wine I think of that party.

I was standing next to an attractive young girl in her early twenties and she asked me if I were a Marine. It was pretty obvious,

I thought, since I had the Marine's high and tight haircut with skin on the side of my head.

I told her, "Yes, I was a Marine pilot."

She then asked me if I had served in Vietnam.

And I again replied in the affirmative that I had just got back from Vietnam.

She then asked me if I had killed anyone.

I told her that I had dropped over one million pounds of bombs and that I hope to hell that I had killed somebody.

She looked me in the eye and said, "You are a criminal and you disgust me."

The words were like a knife piercing my heart. I thought to myself, "This girl never faced the draft or had to go to war. No, her daddy sent her to college and everything was easy for her."

But I didn't say a word. I just turned around and left without say good bye or anything to anyone. It really hurt me, but I was like many other returning Vietnam vets who all had their own negative encounters with an unsympathetic public. Some guys were spit upon, others cursed and others called "baby killers." Many guys didn't wear their uniforms while traveling so as not to draw attention.

I was very proud to be a Marine and to have served my country. I was very proud to be an officer and a pilot and although not a hero, I did my job and I faced fire and death with courage and honor. And now this girl was calling me a criminal. This conflict of being proud of the job I did in combat and what the public and media said about the Vietnam War would come to the surface ten years later as it did for many vets. I would get it resolved for me one evening sitting in a bar in Houston by writing a poem in which I laid out my emotions and feeling about the war in a poem called "Young Men to War."

Young Men to War

This poem is dedicated to my comrades who fought, and especially to those who died, in the Vietnam War.

The young knight on his charger, indestructible.
The Captain in his fighter, invincible.
The Lieutenant in lead of his platoon, unbeatable.
Young men off to war,
Visions of glory,
Tales of valor,
Dreams of adventure,
An ancient ritual into manhood.

A wounded steed!
A shattered cockpit!
The chaos of an ambush.
Instincts of the warrior carry him through.

Look at the blood!
He was my friend,
So were we all, the best they could send.
The few that rule, the many that die,
A few in the multitude think to ask why.

"He fought through, though his mount be dead."
"He nursed his battered craft back to safety."

Ron Boehm

"Though nearly overrun, he pulled his men through."
With 20% KIA, 40% WIA and the others will carry the scars.

Gallant men them all,
Those standing and those that fall.
But I made it through,
And my friend is the hero,
God rest his soul.

© Ronald H. Boehm — 11/20/78 (*One of The Boys of '67*)

Air Medal Awards Ceremony

I think it was about March of 1971 that we had a squadron formation for presenting awards and promotions. When the squadron
formation was called to attention, the CO or XO began reading
the awards which all sounded very heroic and some like a Medal
of Honor from the way it was worded. This one particular award
the speaker started reading with, "The President of the United
States takes pleasure in presenting the Air Medal (Bronze Star
for the First Award)." I was thinking to myself "Who is this hero
going to be?"

The citation read: "For heroic achievement in aerial flight
while serving with Marine All Weather Attack Squadron 242, Marine Aircraft Group Eleven, First Marine Aircraft Wing in connection with combat operation against the enemy in the Republic
of Vietnam. On the night of 4 February, 1970, First Lieutenant
Boehm launched as Pilot aboard an A-6 Intruder aircraft assigned
an interdiction mission along a heavily defended enemy supply
route."

"Holy shit, that's me," I thought to myself.

I didn't even know that I was ever written up for an award.

And as the reader continued with the description of the event the guy standing at attention next to me said, "Isn't that the one when you left your lights on?"

And I realized to my embarrassment that was the mission that Jim Ewing and I got our asses hosed down by about a dozen guns while flying through the Mu Gia Pass on the infamous Ho Chi Minh Trail. As we pulled off the target I noticed that my wing tip lights still were on, but I never told Jim and I guess he wrote us up for the award.

I can still remember that flight every clearly, the red glowing thirty-seven millimeter anti-aircraft rounds arching up towards us in five round burst and the twenty-three mm looking like a garden hose pouring tracers into the sky around us. It was barrage fire and all you could do was just fly through it and hope for the best. It was all around us. Then as we approached the North Vietnam border, the missile warning light and horn came on notifying us that a SAM missile site was tracking us. It was pretty tense and my ass didn't stop puckering until we pulled off target, turning back away from the border and climbing out of gun range at about twenty thousand feet.

Jim made some smart-ass remark as I had mentioned before, like "Those guys couldn't hit their ass with a baseball bat," breaking the tension a little bit. Sometimes heroics are simply a matter of dumb luck.

MAG 13 Maintenance and Headquarters Formation

Sometime around February of 1971, I received temporary duty orders for Maintenance Officers School at NAS Memphis in Millington, Tennessee. It was a several-month school and when I returned to El Toro it wasn't long thereafter that I was being transferred to Group (Marine Air Group 13) for duty as a maintenance officer.

After my transfer I became the Groups Maintenance Officer and by rank, I had made Captain in December of 1970, I was third in command behind the CO, a Lieutenant Colonel and the Major who was the XO.

We had a Headquarters Squadron formation scheduled at a time when the CO was to be on leave and the XO was off for some other reason, which left me as a Captain to be the acting squadron commander at the time that we were to have a Squadron Formation. The formation was to be held in the morning in the parking lot in front of Squadron Headquarters. The procedure was set up that the whole Squadron was to be in formation standing "at ease" when I would enter the parking lot and walk towards the formation; at that time the "Top," the Sergeant Major would call the formation to attention, I would walk up and we would salute and then proceed to inspect the troops.

Eileen, my wife, who had a caustic sense of humor was to drop me off at the edge of the parking lot and then I would proceed to the formation. I had been really pumped up for this and had spit-shined my shoes, the brim of my cover (hat) and shined my belt buckle. I was squared away as we say in the Corps. I reviewed my every step in my mind and even practiced my salute at home to Eileen's amusement.

So the big day came and Eileen dropped me off at the edge of the parking lot and as I got to about half way across the lot and all the formation was called to attention, Eileen blew the horn in our Volvo and with the whole world watching, shot me the bird out of the driver's window. I couldn't believe it. She had a propensity of doing shit like that at the most inopportune time and mostly to me. I guess it was her way of keeping me humble.

Well, as the Top and I made it through the formation and I would step in front of each Marine and exchanged salutes they were having a tough time hiding their smirks and smiles. She was a very big hit with the troops though.

The next day when I would see one of the troops, he would say, "Captain, you wife is really cool."

"Yeah," I responded. "At my expense."

———————

Getting Short

My friend Fred Bonati and I were both getting short coming to the end of our time in the Corps and I was debating whether to stay in and re-up for another four years or get out. Flying time was hard to come by and that had a bearing on my decision, but I loved the Corps. I think Eileen was ready to get out and that had a big part in my decision making.

Just about that same time my CO called me into his office and asked me if I was going to stay in. I told him I had not made up my mind yet, but I was leaning towards getting out. He told me that I was a fine officer and he would like to see me stay in and if I did he could get me an assignment to the new AV-8 Harriers. They were the so called Jump Jets or vertical takeoff attack aircraft that were just coming into use by the Marine Corps.

This was an enticing offer and I thought about it a whole lot but finally came to the conclusion that another career as a civilian was the way to go. Now, when I look back, my feelings are that I wish I would have stayed in at least a little bit longer and flown some more airplanes.

But for my buddy Fred, getting short was also getting salty. His hair cut looked more like the Navy pilot than that of a Marine and his attitude was, I guess from hearing him tell about it, less than ideal. This came into focus when a senior officer told him to shape up and get a haircut or that it would reflect on his fitness report. Fred then told the officer, a Major as I remember, that the only way he could hurt him with that fitness report was to wrap it around a brick and hit him in the head with it. Now that is salty, but not very good for your career. But, of course, Fred was getting out in a few months.

My other buddy Rick Spitz had a similar attitude, but he wasn't a short timer. He was a flight instructor in the Navy training command. He also had a haircut problem and a less than desirable attitude. It seemed like his duties were interfering with his time on the base softball team. Rick was a very good athlete. His senior Marine Officer told him also to get a haircut and he had just come back from the barber. It must have been a Navy barber I guess. Rick had a bunch of run-ins with his senior officers and as you can imagine, he wasn't going to make general and he got out a few years later than Fred and I and went on to fly for the airlines.

Not Much Flying Time, Close to Getting Out

I finally made up my mind to get out of the Corps and started looking around for a job when I got out. Just before getting out I was offered a job with a freight forwarding company as salesman in Houston, Texas, which I accepted.

On November 15, 1972, I was released from active duty and transferred to the United States Marine Corps Reserve.

So ended a wonderful and most eventful episode in my life so far. I am very proud to have been a Marine, an officer, combat pilot, and to have had the opportunity to serve my country. I am also very happy for the great friendships I made while in the military; many of them are still friends today.

Several years ago we had our fortieth reunion of my Marine Corps Basic School Class of 5/67. The wonderful feelings I had in seeing these guys again after such a long time and hearing the stories of their experience in combat, plus the feeling of pride I had in being part of such an incredible group and that of being a Marine was overwhelming. It inspired me to write another poem, this one about the pride of the United States Marine Corps. The poem is called Always Faithful which is the Marine Corps motto, "Semper Fidelis."

Always Faithful

They called for the best of us.
They called for the best from us.
They called us to every war and every conflict, to every battle that
    had to be won;
And to every situation that had to be handled.
They called us to desert sands, to far away islands and to frozen
    grounds.
We went by land, sea and air.
We fought on beaches, in forests and in rice paddies, in every clime.
They called us since 1775 and we answered—always faithful.
They will call us for a long time to come, whenever freedom is to be
    protected.
They called us fathers and sons, generation to generation.
They called us warriors and heroes.
They called us Leathernecks and Devil Dogs, the very best.
They call us MARINES.
Ron Boehm, Capt. USMCR '67 - '72.

Ron Boehm

The Boys on Cherry Street
(Young Men of the Vietnam Generation)

These are some of my friends who served in Vietnam, the guys that played such a big part in my life and who helped to make my life so rich with such fine memories. And to the many more that are not mentioned here I say thanks for being a part of my life:

From the Lakeview Neighborhood of New Orleans:

- Charlie de Gruy — Captain USN Retired, Flew combat in Vietnam as a F-4J pilot, VF 96, Air Medal, Navy Commendation w Combat V, CO (F-14) VF-211, CO (F-4) VF 101, XO USS America CV 66, CO USS Austin (LPD4), CO USS Saipan (LHA2), US Navy Test Pilot School, US Navy Test Pilot, Chief of Staff — Naval Doctrine Command.

Classmates from Holy Cross High School:

- Dr. Tom Crais — Major US Army, Walter Reed Hospital, William Beaumont Army Hospital, 279th Station Hospital Berlin, Germany, Flight Surgeon.
- Arlan Hanle — Captain USMC, Pilot F-4 VMFA 542. 182 combat missions, 12 Air Medals, Forward Air Controller 2nd Battalion 4th Marines.

- Danny Phillips — Lieutenant Commander USN, Radar Intercept Officer F-4, VA 33, USS America CV 66. 160 Combat missions, 9 Air Medals, (2) Navy Commendation Medal.

From Southeastern Louisiana University:

My Roommates:
- Pat Reith — Owner of an Oil Field Supply Business.
- Malcolm Bech — Life long career in the Oil Field.
- Jerry Leblanc "Seagull" — Major USAF Retired. Flew in Vietnam as a pilot in EC-121, C-141 aircraft. 186 Combat Missions, Air Medal, Air Force Commendation Medal, pilot in the 89th Military Airlift Squadron, Deceased.
- Ronnie Radelat — Tax Lawyer, died way too early.
- Richie Cerise "Leg" — Accountant, Deceased.
- Corky Barris — Owner of a printing company.

Friends:
- Dan DeBlanc — Captain USMC, Pilot UH-1E Hueys, AH-1G Cobras, VMO-2. 575 Combat missions, Silver Star, Navy Commendation, 23 Air Medals, 3 Single Mission Air Medals, Pilot Air America. Owner — South Side Cafe, Slidell, La.
- Jimmy De Moss — Photography Studio.
- Hans Neilsen — Retired.

USMC:
- Dave Anderson — 1st Lieutenant USMC, Platoon Commander 2nd Platoon, Bravo Company 1st Battalion 1st Marine Regiment, Purple Heart, Combat Action Medal.
- Pete Barber — Captain USMC, Pilot F-4, VMFA 232, 134 Combat Missions, Air Medal.

Ron Boehm

- Steve Benckenstein — Captain USMC, Pilot CH-46, HMM 265. 600 Combat Missions, 30 Air Medals, USS Tripoli.
- Fred Bonati — Captain USMC, Pilot F-4, VMFA 314. 200 Combat Missions, Air Metals, Meritorious Unit Citation, Forward Air Controller 1st Mar. Div.
- Tom Broderick — Major USMC (Ret.), Pilot UH-IE, HML 167. 225 Combat Missions, 17 Air Medals.
- Dave Clary — Captain USMC, Pilot A6A, VMA (AW) 242.
- Dave Cummings — Lieutenant Colonel (Deceased.) USMC, Two tours in Vietnam, Platoon Commander, Pilot AH-IG Cobra, HMA 367, Distinguished Flying Cross, 4 Single Mission Air medals, Bronze Star w Combat V, Purple Heart.
- Dave Noyes — Captain USMC, Platoon Commander Mike Company 3/7, XO Lima Company 3/7. Silver Star, Combat Action Medal, President's Unit Citation, Meritorious Unit Commendation, Vietnamese Gallantry Cross.
- Les Palm — Major. General. USMC, Artillery Officer 1st Battalion 13 Marines. Legion of Merit w/Valor Device, Meritorious Service Medal, Navy & Marine Corps Commendation Medal w/2 award stars and Valor Device, Combat Action Ribbon, Navy Presidential Unit citation, Navy Unit Commendation Medal, Navy Meritorious Unit Commendation Medal.
- Jack Rippy — Colonel USMC, Pilot A6A, VMA (AW) 242. 212 Combat Missions, Navy Commendation w Combat V, 14 Air Medals, Joint Meritorious Service Medal, Legion of Merit for Chief of Staff, XO, CO VMA (AW) 121. Attorney.
- Ray Smith — Major General USMC, Infantry Officer Alpha Co. 1/1. Advisor to The Vietnamese Marines. Navy Cross, (2) Silver Stars, Bronze Star, Defense Dis-

tinguished Service Medal, Navy Distinguished Service Medal, the Legion of Merit, Defense Meritorious Service Medal, Navy and Marine Corps Commendation Medal, Combat Action Ribbon, (3) Purple Hearts.

- Rick Spitz — Captain USMC, Pilot A6A, VMA (AW) 242. 144 Combat Missions, Distinguished Flying Cross, 8 Air Medals, Navy & Marine Corps Commendation Medal.
- Marty Steele — Lieutenant General USMC, Corporal 1st Tank Battalion 1966. Defense Distinguished Service Medal, Navy Distinguished Service Medal, Defense Superior Service Medal, Legion of Merit.
- Mike Sommers — Captain USMC, Platoon Commander, Company Commander Echo Company 2nd Battalion 26th Marines, Inspector Instructor, Staff Officer, AWS, Navy Commendation Medal w Combat V, Combat Action Ribbon.
- Phil Vannoy — Captain USMC, CO Golf & Hotel Companies 2nd Battalion 7th Marines. Bronze Star, Vietnamese Cross of Gallantry.
- Ron Boehm (The Author) Captain USMC, Pilot A6A, VMA (AW) 242, Forward Air Controller 1st Battalion 7th Marine Regiment. 124 Combat Missions, 7 Air Medals, 1 Single Mission Air Medal w/Bronze Star, Combat Action Ribbon, Navy Commendation w Combat V.

From Ron

So that's the story as I remember it. I hope you enjoyed it. And to all those guys listed above and all those guys that served in Vietnam that are not listed above and all those who gave the ultimate sacrifice for their country thank you for your service and God bless you. To all those that contributed to make my life so rich in memories thank you from the bottom of my heart.

> Ron Boehm
> Aliases: Little Man,
>   Boomer,
>   Low Beam,
>   Daddy Ronnie,
>   Uron,
>   Walking on Hands,
>   Capt. Ron

THE END

www.BoysOnCherryStreet.com

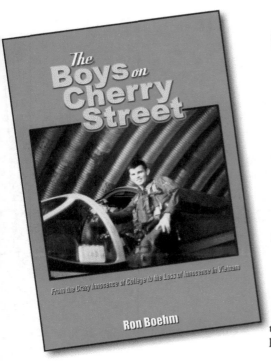